SEXUAL HARASSMENT

SEXUAL HARASSMENT
Contemporary feminist perspectives

Edited by
ALISON M. THOMAS
and CELIA KITZINGER

OPEN UNIVERSITY PRESS
Buckingham · Philadelphia

Open University Press
Celtic Court
22 Ballmoor
Buckingham
MK18 1XW

and
1900 Frost Road, Suite 101
Bristol, PA 19007, USA

First published 1997

A catalogue record of this book is available from the British Library

ISBN   0 335 19580 6 (pb)   0 335 19581 4 (hb)

Library of Congress Cataloging-in-Publication Data

Thomas, Alison M., 1956–
    Sexual harassment : contemporary feminist perspectives / Alison M.
  Thomas and Celia Kitzinger.
      p. cm
    Includes bibliographical references and index.
    ISBN 0-335-19581-4 (hb). — ISBN 0-335-19580-6 (pb)
    1. Sexual harassment of women.   2. Sex role in the work environment.
  3. Sexism.   4. Heterosexism.   5. Feminist theory.   I. Kitzinger, Celia
  II. Title.
  HQ1237.T56   1997
  305.42—dc21   97-567
                                                                                CIP

Typeset by Type Study, Scarborough
Printed in Great Britain by Biddles Ltd, Guildford and King's Lynn

Contents

Notes on contributors

BARBARA BAGILHOLE is Senior Lecturer in Social Policy at Loughborough University, UK. Her interests include equal opportunities in the fields of gender, race and disability and her research includes a survey of equal opportunities for women, ethnic minority and disabled academics; the recruitment, selection and career development of black women in the British national health service; a study of the achievement of women workers in the civil service; and the role of women in the construction industry. She is the author of *Women, Work and Equal Opportunity* (1994) and *Equal Opportunities and Social Policy* (forthcoming).

KATHLEEN V. CAIRNS is a Professor of Counselling Psychology at the University of Calgary, Canada. Her research interests are primarily focused on the psychology of gender relations, with an emphasis on identity development processes. She also maintains an active private practice in feminist counselling and is a chartered psychologist and member of the Canadian Register of Health Service Providers in Psychology.

SUSAN CONDOR teaches social psychology, women's studies, and culture and communication at Lancaster University, UK. Her research interests include feminist epistemology and cultural constructions of gender.

DEBBIE EPSTEIN is Senior Lecturer in Women's Studies and Education at the University of London Institute of Education. She researches sexuality, race and gender in the contexts of schooling and the popular media. Recent publications include *Challenging Lesbian and Gay Inequalities in Education, Border Patrols: Policing the Boundaries of Heterosexuality* (with

Deborah Lynn Steinberg and Richard Johnson) and *A Question of Discipline: Pedagogy, Power and Praxis in Cultural Studies* (with Joyce E. Canaan). She is currently working with Richard Johnson on *Schooling Sexualities*, to be published by Open University Press.

CARRIE HERBERT trained as a teacher in the UK before emigrating to Australia, where she worked for 13 years in the South Australian Department of Education as teacher/adviser, lecturer and child protection officer. After returning to England and completing a PhD at the University of Cambridge, she set up her own consultancy business, specializing in issues of equal opportunity including sexual harassment at work and school, personal and professional development, child protection and bullying. Her publications include: *Talking of Silence: The Sexual Harassment of School Girls* (1989) and *Countering Sexual Harassment: A Training Pack* (1993).

CELIA KITZINGER is Director of Women's Studies at Loughborough University, UK. She is the author of nearly 100 articles or chapters on issues relating to feminism, and has published seven books including *The Social Construction of Lesbianism* (1987); *Changing Our Minds: Lesbian Feminism and Psychology* (with Rachel Perkins, 1993); *Heterosexuality* (with Sue Wilkinson, 1993); and *Representing the Other* (with Sue Wilkinson, 1996). She is currently writing about the role of 'experience' in feminist theory and practice.

JUNE LARKIN is an Assistant Professor in the Women's Studies Programme at the University of Toronto, Canada. She is also a coordinator of the Women's Sexual Harassment Caucus at the Ontario Institute for Studies in Education (OISE) and author of *Sexual Harassment: High School Girls Speak Out* (1994).

BARBARA LITTLEWOOD is a lecturer in the Department of Sociology at Glasgow University, where she teaches on gender. She is also co-convenor of the Centre for Women's Studies there. She has edited a volume entitled *Uncharted Lives: Extracts from Scottish Women's Experiences 1850–1982* and has published articles in *Cultural Studies, Critical Social Policy* and *Gender and History*.

LINDA MAHOOD is an Assistant Professor in the Department of History at the University of Guelph, Canada. She is the author of *The Magdalenes: Prostitution in the Nineteenth Century* (1989), *Policing Gender, Class and Family, 1850–1940* (1995), and co-editor with Bernard Schissel of *Social Control in Canada: Issues in the Social Construction of Deviance* (1996).

HELEN MOTT is a research assistant in the Psychology Department at the University of Bristol, UK. She is currently working on a doctorate, supervised by Susan Condor, on the social psychology of sexual harassment and secretaries. Her research interests also include the psychology of gender and language.

PAULA NICOLSON is Senior Lecturer in Health Psychology with the Health Policy and Management Unit of the School for Health and Related Research at the University of Sheffield, UK. She is doing research on sexual harassment and gender discrimination in medical education in the UK and Spain with a colleague, Chris Welsh. She is also working in the areas of women's reproductive health, particularly postnatal depression and sexuality. Her book, *Gender, Power and Organisation: A Psychological Perspective* was published in 1996.

ALISON M. THOMAS is a Senior Lecturer in Psychosocial Studies at the University of East London, UK. She is currently studying the impact of the introduction of sexual harassment policies in universities in Canada and the UK; her other ongoing research interests are in gender relations and the social construction of gendered identities. In addition to her publications in these areas, she collaborated with Robyn Rowland on a special feature on feminists mothering sons, which was published in *Feminism & Psychology: An International Journal* (February 1996).

Acknowledgements

We would both like to thank our contributors for their hard work on their chapters, and for their passionate concern about sexual harassment as a key feminist issue. We have both been encouraged and heartened by the powerful feminist writing submitted for this book. Our grateful thanks go also to Jacinta Evans and Joan Malherbe at Open University Press for their patience with our delays, and for their help with the various ups and downs of putting this book together.

Additionally, Alison would like to thank Nigel Wells for keeping house and home together at the crucial stages (and for not complaining about the state of the study over the last year or more!) and Catherine and Gareth for reminding her that there are other important things in life apart from writing books. Celia would like to thank Sue Wilkinson for giving her a home during the major building work on her own house while this book was being compiled. *And* for putting up with the lengthy phone calls, piles of paper, and preoccupation with the topic!

Finally, thank you to the British Sociological Association for permission to reprint Debbie Epstein's chapter from *Sex, Sensibility and the Gendered Body*, edited by Janet Holland and Lisa Adkins, published by Macmillan Press Ltd., 1996.

1

Sexual harassment: reviewing the field

ALISON M. THOMAS and CELIA KITZINGER

Sexual harassment is a crucial issue for feminists. Men's use of sexuality in exerting control or exercising power over women – at home, in the workplace and in other arenas – has been at the centre of feminist struggle for at least the last century. Sexual violence in the form of prostitution, rape and child sexual abuse were key targets of first wave feminism at the turn of the century (Jeffreys 1987); with the rise of second wave feminism in the 1970s, date rape and sexual harassment grew out of and extended these concepts. Today, sexual harassment is identified by feminists as one manifestation of the larger patriarchal system in which men dominate women (Farley 1978; MacKinnon 1979).

In this introductory chapter, we first chart the historical development of the concept of sexual harassment and assess its current standing at a time of anti-feminist backlash. We then highlight the particular contribution made by the chapters of this book to the development of feminist theory and practice in this area, both in relation to people's implicit definitions and understandings of the concept sexual harassment – their willingness to label particular behaviours in this way; and in relation to the function of sexual harassment as a form of power over women and as a backlash against feminism.

Developing the concept

The term 'sexual harassment' is of relatively recent origin. While the behaviours it describes are, of course, centuries old, the term itself is

usually said to have emerged in the mid-1970s in North America, and subsequently to have been adopted in the UK in the early 1980s. Media use of
the term (one index of its general acceptability) seems to have begun in
1975 when the *New York Times* published an article with the headline
'Women begin to speak out against sexual harassment at work' (Nemy
1975, cited in Bacchi and Jose 1994: 268, f1), and by 1977 even the *Ladies
Home Journal* had published an article on the topic (cited in Alliance
Against Sexual Coercion 1981). It was four or five years later before the
term reached the UK. According to feminist sociologists Sue Wise and Liz
Stanley (1987: 30)

> There seems to have been no mention of any such animal as 'sexual
> harassment' in the English press, certainly none that we could find,
> before the reporting of American sexual harassment cases and the
> review of feminist and feminist-influenced books on the subject at the
> end of 1979.

According to several sources (Alliance Against Sexual Coercion 1981;
Kramarae and Treichler 1985; Weeks *et al.* 1986; Wise and Stanley 1987) the
term sexual harassment was initially coined in the mid-1970s in Ithaca,
New York, by a group called Working Women United, formed under the
leadership of the Human Affairs Program at Cornell University. Media
coverage of two unsuccessful attempts to seek legal redress for what we
would now call sexual harassment had appeared between 1972 and 1974,
and helped to set the stage for naming the problem. The immediate concern of Working Women United, however, was the case of Carmita Wood,
an administrator at the university who left her position because of sexual
harassment from a well-known faculty member, and who was subsequently denied unemployment benefits. This group conducted a preliminary survey of women workers, held the first reported 'speak-out' on
sexual harassment, and helped with Carmita Wood's appeal. They also
commissioned a research branch which generated publicity and research,
and which eventually became a national information, counselling and
referral service for victims of sexual harassment in the greater New York
area. The first recorded use of the term sexual harassment was in a survey
developed by this group in May 1975 (Benson and Thomson 1982: 236).

Between 1975 and 1979, a series of North American publications and
groups addressed issues of 'sexual coercion', 'unwanted sexual attention'
and (increasingly) 'sexual harassment', marking a broadening of attention
from the more extreme forms of sexual violence (in particular, rape), with
which early second wave feminist writing had been particularly concerned (Griffin 1971; Brownmiller 1975) to include the full continuum of
male abuses of power against women. The second key group involved in
campaigning on sexual harassment, the Alliance Against Sexual Coercion,
was formed in Boston in June 1976, by three women who had previously

been involved in rape crisis centre work (Alliance Against Sexual Coercion 1981). Although not published until 1979, the draft manuscript of Catharine MacKinnon's book, *Sexual Harassment of Working Women*, was circulated around women's groups and feminist organizations from the beginning of 1975 and was tremendously influential (cf. Weeks *et al.* 1986; Minson 1991, cited in Bacchi and Jose 1994: 268, f1). This book, too, used the term sexual harassment in making the legal argument which later became the basis for finding sexual harassment a form of sex discrimination (MacKinnon 1979).

It was the eventual publication of MacKinnon's (1979) book which, along with the publication of Lin Farley's (1978) *Sexual Shakedown*, is generally credited with bringing the problem to public attention, and giving the term a wide currency. (A third book, published at the same time, Constance Backhouse and Leah Cohen's 1979 *The Secret Oppression: Sexual Harassment of Working Women* is cited as influential in the early, but not in the later literature.) The effect of the term was to transform what had been a private trouble into a public issue. According to Lin Farley (who became involved with the topic while teaching a course on 'Women and Work' at Cornell), she had identified in her research a form of male behaviour in the workplace which, she said, 'required a name and sexual harassment seemed to come about as close to symbolizing the problem as the language would permit'. In Catharine MacKinnon's (1979: 1) words, 'lacking a term to express it, sexual harassment was literally unspeakable, which made a generalized, shared, and social definition of it inaccessible'. Commentators concur that 'women were "naming" an experience they had endured in silence for many years . . . once the problem was named, women could at last speak out and mobilise politically to tackle it' (Bacchi and Jose 1994: 263).

The power of the label was in enabling women to single out a piece of (previously undifferentiated) everyday experience, and to identify it as a problem shared by many women – a problem which demanded changes in male behaviour. This is clear in, for example, British feminist Sandra McNeill's description of a 1980 workshop on 'Women and Work' at which the topic of sexual harassment was raised:

> We discovered we had all suffered from this, plumbers or University lecturers. As woman after woman cited incidents we breathed out a sigh of relief. We had (almost all) been so isolated. Felt nutty almost in complaining, blamed ourselves for reactions we 'had provoked', or suffered in confused silence. Now we knew it was a common problem . . . We must begin to collectively fight back.
>
> (McNeill 1985: 85)

Since the 1970s, there has been a wide range of surveys documenting the incidence of sexual harassment and testifying to its frequency and pervasiveness. One of the earliest North American surveys (carried out in

1976 and reported in Sanford 1979) was conducted by *Redbook* magazine, and it found that 88 per cent of the 9,000 respondents said that they had received unwanted sexual attention at work. The first comprehensive national survey of sexual harassment was conducted by the US Merit Systems Protection Board in 1981 and found that of over 20,000 people (all federal government employees) around 42 per cent of female and 15 per cent of male respondents reported experiencing 'unwanted sexual attention' in the workplace during the previous 24 months. In Britain, in the same year, there were two surveys of sexual harassment in local government (carried out by Camden and Liverpool branches of the National Association of Local Government Officers), which showed that 52 per cent of women had experienced sexual harassment at work, as had 20 per cent of men (reported in Wise and Stanley 1987: 30). A survey conducted in 1981 by the Canadian Human Rights Commission found that 49 per cent of women respondents and 33 per cent of men had experienced 'unwanted sexual attention' (CHRC 1983). Research also demonstrated that those who experienced sexual harassment were liable to suffer from a variety of symptoms of emotional or physical distress as a result – most commonly nervousness, irritability and uncontrolled anger.

Remarkably quickly, public bodies and institutions in both Britain and North America began to see sexual harassment as a serious cause for concern, and to formulate specific codes of practice and grievance procedures to deal with it. Within a decade of the feminist 'invention' of 'sexual harassment', it had been defined as a trade union issue (National Association of Local Government Officers 1981; Trade Union Congress 1983), a civil liberties issue (Sedley and Benn 1982), as an equal opportunities issue (Equal Employment Opportunities Commission 1980) and, in Canada, as a human rights issue (Canadian Human Rights Act 1980). The problem of sexual harassment was formally recognized in both educational (Brandenberg 1982; Crocker 1983) and occupational settings (e.g. Alfred Marks Bureau 1982).

In the USA, courts established sexual harassment as sex discrimination in employment (and hence as a violation under Title VII of the Civil Rights Act of 1964) and in education (making it actionable under Title IX, the Education Amendments of 1972). The first successful case was Williams *v.* Saxbe in 1976, which involved a supervisor's retaliation with annoying comments, unfavourable reviews, and unwarranted reprimands against a female employee's refusal of his sexual advances (cited in McKinney and Maroules 1991: 30). Sexual harassment such as the above in which submission to sexual demands is made a requirement of employment, promotion or other employment benefits (or, in educational settings, of grades), is known as quid pro quo sexual harassment. US law also recognizes a category of environmental harassment, defined as behaviour which interferes with an individual's work performance or which creates

an 'intimidating, hostile or offensive working environment' (cited in Mc-
Kinney and Maroules 1991). Since 1985, the Canadian Human Rights Act
has treated sexual harassment as a violation of a person's human rights in
so far as it constitutes discrimination on the basis of sex, and provincial
human rights codes have followed the same principle.

In British law, too, sexual harassment is illegal in so far as it can be construed as an act of sex discrimination under the provisions of the 1975 Sex
Discrimination Act (or, when it results in unfair dismissal, under the
Employment Protection Act). The first case in which it was successfully
argued that sexual harassment was a form of sex discrimination (Porcelli
v. Strathclyde Regional Council) reached the Employment Appeal Tribunal in 1986 when Jean Porcelli, a laboratory technician in a Scottish
school, described how two male laboratory technicians had harassed her
in ways they would not have harassed a man – by commenting on her
physical appearance, brushing up against her, and making sexually suggestive remarks. In 1991, following a report by Rubenstein (1987), the
European Economic Community issued a Recommendation and Code of
Conduct on Sexual Harassment. This echoes the US legislation in identifying both 'quid pro quo' and 'environmental' harassment, and stresses
the unacceptability of sexual harassment of any kind on the grounds that
it is detrimental to 'the dignity of women and men at work' (European
Commission Recommendation 92/131 EEC, reproduced in Rubenstein
and De Vries 1993).

In many ways, then, the story of sexual harassment is a feminist success
story. Before the 1970s the label didn't exist and the behaviour it identified
was just part of everyday life – a problem without a name. The term sexual
harassment was invented as part of women's renaming of the world,
reflecting and constructing women's experience and labelling a form of
behaviour newly recognized as something which women need not pas-
sively endure, but can actively protest and resist. Over the last two
decades, organizations, institutions, and national and international legal
systems have been forced to take on board and to incorporate concerns
initially raised by feminists. The personal experience of women has been
recognized in a political context.

Backlash

However, the 1990s saw the development of a clear anti-feminist backlash,
with feminist gains attacked as coercive and dictatorial instances of 'political correctness'. In 1993, a *Sunday Times* journalist wrote: 'One doesn't
want to make ludicrous comparisons' and went on to make one: 'It seems
fair to say that America today vis-à-vis feminist thought is at the point
Germany reached before the Nazis took over' (cited in Moore 1993: 11). At

such a time, it is hardly surprising that the concept of 'sexual harassment' (constituting, as it does, one of feminism's notable successes) should have become a particular target. According to Suzanne Moore (1993), 'the discrediting of Anita Hill goes far beyond what happened in an office 10 years ago. It is about the discrediting of a whole movement.'

At a time of anti-feminist backlash – especially, though not exclusively, in North America – codes of conduct designed to protect women from sexual harassment have been attacked as inspired by 'feminazis' who are enemies of free speech. Universities and their sexual harassment policies have been at the centre of this furore, with anti-feminist critics condemning them for putting in jeopardy the principles of academic freedom. Students at the Massachusetts Institute of Technology burned copies of the 68 page booklet *Dealing with Harassment at MIT* which they described as 'a total abrogation of free expression' (Davies 1994). In Canada, in the early 1990s, there were a number of campaigns against sexual harassment and sexism in universities across the country – including, notably, the 'chilly climate' work which originated in the faculty of law at the University of Western Ontario and subsequently extended to include the Universities of Victoria, British Columbia and Manitoba (Brodribb *et al*. 1995; 1996). Findings relating to the 'chilly climate' for women in Canadian universities were widely reported in the media, and became the subject matter for a book which aggressively attacks feminism, especially feminist campaigns against sexual harassment, as part of 'a rising tide of puritanism and authoritarianism masquerading behind benevolent slogans' (Fekete 1994). North American writers frequently describe sexual harassment codes as 'censorship' or as violations of the right to freedom of speech (in the USA, First Amendment rights). Allusions to the McCarthy era of the 1950s are commonplace, ranging from references to 'MacKinnonites' (supporters of sexual harassment codes, mockingly labelled to imply unswerving allegiance to the feminist Catharine MacKinnon), to explicit parallels such as that drawn by University of Toronto professor John Furedy, who heads the Society for Academic Freedom and Scholarship:

> In the McCarthy era, the attack on freedom of speech was found outside the academic community. Here it is coming from inside the university itself. This is more Salem-like. The community is conducting its own witch-hunt.
>
> (cited in Trevena 1995)

Another leading anti-feminist author comments that 'a government that can label sexual language it considers incorrect as sexual harassment has more potential for abuse than a government that can label political language it considers incorrect as a threat to national security' (Farrell 1993: 221).

The authors of these attacks are often men, but the media's preference is (of course) for female spokespersons – especially if they also claim to be speaking as 'feminists': Camille Paglia, Katie Roiphe and Helen Garner all attack the concept of sexual harassment as part and parcel of the victim feminism they decry. Although they choose to label themselves as feminists, or as sympathetic to feminism, they seek to redefine most of women's experiences of sexual harassment as 'personal' and as 'just part of everyday life' – in other words, to reverse the feminist campaigns which succeeded in rendering these experiences both public and political.

Backlash spokespersons generally accept the need for sexual harassment legislation to prevent the worst abuses of power – usually identified with the most overt and most explicit cases of sexual violence, the quid pro quo sexual harassment cases. Katie Roiphe, for example, supports legal sanctions against quid pro quo harassment ('Any professor who trades grades for sex . . . deserves to face charges'; Roiphe 1993: 104). Yet these constitute only a small minority of the significant number of sexual harassment complaints that are made: for example, out of the 11,983 cases recorded by the US Equal Employment Opportunities Commission in 1993, just 5 per cent fell into this category. What Roiphe and others oppose is the extension of sexual harassment legislation, policies and codes of conduct to cover what they see as 'trivial' cases relating to the 'ordinary', 'everyday', 'natural' interactions between men and women. Roiphe singles out the part of Princeton University's definition of sexual harassment which includes 'leering and ogling, whistling, sexual innuendo, and other suggestive or offensive or derogatory comments, humor and jokes about sex' (Roiphe 1993: 100) and claims that women should be able to handle such things at a personal level, arguing that such ordinary, mundane, and humdrum instances are not the appropriate targets of policy or legislation. In this way, sexual harassment is taken back out of the public, political domain and firmly relocated in the personal arena. Katie Roiphe makes this explicit in her claim that feminists 'translate what seem like everyday occurrences into the language of outrage and political indignation' (Roiphe 1993: 107). What she wants is 'to transform everyday experience back into everyday experience' (Roiphe 1993: 112).

Yet it is precisely these aspects of sexual harassment which feminists have identified as key to the subordination of women:

> Most sexual harassment is what we've called small, mundane and accumulating; and it permeates our lives . . . It's crucially important to name the 'dripping tap' behaviours, events, and situations as *sexual harassment*: by doing so we recognise that they're important and common, rather than trite and confined to 'just me' and my 'peculiarities', and we see them as limiting, oppressive and ethically wrong *political* behaviours because they attempt to disempower us. Out of this we come to see that 'politics' is about power, influence and

control, and can be located in the most humdrum and supposedly 'insignificant' of things.

(Wise and Stanley 1987: 114)

The evolution of the concept of sexual harassment involved, crucially, a renaming of one particular aspect of women's everyday experience; back-lash spokespersons want to turn back the clock, returning sexual harass-ment to the realm of undifferentiated, unnamed, 'ordinary life'.

Developing feminist theory and practice

As we have seen, a key achievement of second wave feminism was to single out sexual harassment as a part of women's personal everyday experience, and to give it a political definition and name. Today two things are clear: first that many women (and even more men) have never – despite all the policies, codes of conduct and legislative apparatus – accepted this feminist redefinition of women's experience; second, that (while men continue to use sexual power to intimidate and control women) the definition of this behaviour as sexual harassment (as opposed to 'just the way things are') is now under major attack as part of the anti-feminist backlash. The chapters in this book address both of these points. The Chapters in Part I focus primarily on questions related to women's definitions of sexual harassment. The chapters in Part II are directed more towards examining the ways in which sexual harassment serves to but-tress and perpetuate heteropatriarchal power relations. Inevitably, there is some overlap: questions of power and questions of definition are inextric-ably connected. Nevertheless, it seems that there are two key questions for contemporary feminism. First, how has it come about that most women refuse to define their experiences as sexual harassment? Second, how does sexual harassment continue to reinforce male dominance and female sub-ordination?

The chapters which comprise Part I of the book all begin from the obser-vation that sexual harassment continues to be part of the everyday experi-ence of many women. This is in spite of the considerable efforts made over the last decade to educate people about its unacceptability, and thereby to eradicate it. The most recent survey of federal employees by the US Merit Systems Protection Board (MSPB 1994) found sexual harassment to be reported at essentially the same level as in its two previous surveys (in 1980 and 1987). It is also still the case that people (both men *and* women) fail to recognize it when it occurs. Despite alarmist fears that women are making huge numbers of unsubstantiated claims of sexual harassment it is clear from all the research to date that many women remain uncertain as to which behaviours properly qualify as sexual harassment, and are unwilling to label male behaviour in this way: for example, whereas 49 per cent of the women interviewed in the survey carried out by the Canadian Human Rights Commission reported one or more instances of 'unwanted sexual attention', only 30 per cent of them (i.e. 15 per cent of the total number of women interviewed) identified their experience as 'sexual harassment' (CHRC 1983). Had the only question asked been 'Have you ever experienced sexual harassment?', the number of positive responses would have provided a serious underestimate of the actual number of women suffering 'unwanted sexual attention' – a phrase commonly used as a definition of sexual harassment (e.g. Herbert 1989).

The findings of large-scale surveys such as this one are corroborated by qualitative data, including our own interview research (Thomas and Kitzinger 1990; 1994; Kitzinger and Thomas 1995). From our interviews, it was apparent that women frequently would *not* label as sexual harassment incidents that they nevertheless recounted to us as examples of sexual attention that was clearly unwanted. While most women were able to describe incidents they personally experienced as sexual harassment, there were huge areas of disagreement between women about which behaviours the term legitimately covers. Yet it is also perhaps not surprising that, despite such variations among women, none the less both in our research and in many other surveys, it is clear that women as a group consistently define more experiences as sexual harassment than do men (cf. the overview by Riger 1991; see also Collins and Blodgett 1981; Adams *et al.* 1983; Kenig and Ryan 1986; Powell 1986). Further definitional problems arise because women also have ethnicities, sexual identities, (dis)abilities and are otherwise politically marked in ways which cross-cut gender as the source of harassment; the demand that a particular incident be labelled for complaint purposes as (for example) *either* sexual *or* racial harassment serves only to obfuscate rather than to clarify women's experience (cf. Brant and Too 1994; see also Giuffre and Williams 1994). In sum, then, the term 'sexual harassment' is subject to different interpretations both within and across the sexes, and is also related to harassment based on other politically marked identities.

These disagreements and uncertainties make it hardly surprising that the codes of conduct and policies designed to prevent the behaviour so labelled are less effective than had been hoped. A 1993 survey of British employers by the Industrial Society found that 40 per cent had adopted some form of sexual harassment policy, and this compares with around twice that percentage in the United States (Industrial Society 1993). None the less, many of those women who identify their experiences as sexual harassment are unwilling to take action against their employers, or to use the policies designed to ameliorate their situation. The 1994 US survey cited earlier (MSPB 1994) revealed that a mere 6 per cent of those survey respondents who reported experiencing sexual harassment had taken any formal action. Another study produced very similar findings: going to one's boss or supervisor to complain accounted for only 7.8 per cent of the total responses; compare this with the far more common decision to ask for a transfer or to quit the job, which accounted for 17 per cent of responses. Only 2 per cent sought legal help (Loy and Stewart cited in McKinney and Maroules 1991).

In general, there is a repeated finding that actual victims behave quite differently from how research participants or the general public say they would behave (Fitzgerald 1993; Gutek and Koss 1993). While students and other research respondents facing hypothetical scenarios talk of confronting the harasser and/or making formal complaints, actual victims report behaving far less assertively. The most common responses are what Gardner (1980) describes as 'internally focused': the victim pretends that the situation is not happening or has no effect (denial); she ignores the harassment and does nothing (endurance); she detaches herself psychologically from the situation; or she blames herself for the behaviour of the harasser. Among 'externally focused' responses, the most common is avoidance; the victim simply attempts to avoid situations in which she may be subject to the harassing behaviour. Another externally focused response is appeasement (the attempt to put off the harasser without direct confrontation). As Gardner notes, by far the most *infrequent* response to sexual harassment is to seek institutional or organizational relief (i.e. notifying a supervisor, bringing a formal complaint).

The first part of this book addresses, from a range of different perspectives, the problem of women's non-labelling of incidents as sexual harassment, and/or their refusal to seek institutional or legal redress. In the opening chapter of this part, Chapter 2, Carrie Herbert, a sexual harassment consultant, sees the problem as one of ignorance, confusion, and misconception on the part of both women and men, both victims and perpetrators. She gives examples from her own work of this widespread ignorance and argues that the solution is education. She says:

> We must talk to young women and girls about male oppression, patriarchy and masculine myths of sexual prowess, uncontrollable sexual urges and other such tales. We have to provide them with a political understanding of their gendered situation, to help them understand how power has been appropriated by men and masculine institutions, how the system is perpetuated and why it is so powerful in its oppression of women . . . At the same time we can no longer ignore the ignorant and cavalier attitude by some men towards this behaviour . . . We must raise their awareness of the feelings and perceptions of women and girls.

In Chapter 3, Paula Nicolson describes women's experience in a predominantly male domain – the 'toxic organizational context' of medicine.

She sets sexual harassment in the context of sexism and gendered practice in medicine more generally, and addresses in particular the question of senior medical women's relative lack of awareness of sexual harassment (compared both with more junior women and with men). Paula Nicolson sees this lack of awareness as a consequence of women's socialization into the patriarchal values of the medical school. 'As women become more senior in the hierarchy,' she says, 'they dismiss sexual harassment as easily dealt with'. This indicates that they are suffering from 'the negative influence of patriarchal culture on women's socialization and sense of "sisterhood"' and in so far as they identify as 'doctors' rather than as 'women', she describes them as having 'divorced themselves from a major part of their identity'. Where Carrie Herbert attributes ignorance about sexual harassment simply to the failure to educate, Paula Nicolson sees this ignorance or lack of concern as an 'educated' ignorance – that is, one which is learned in the process of developing an occupational identity.

Whereas Nicolson's chapter discusses the role of women in a traditionally masculinized work setting, Chapter 4 by Helen Mott and Susan Condor explores instead the position of women in a traditionally feminized job – secretarial work. Here the problem of non-recognition of sexual harassment is even more acute. Helen Mott and Susan Condor note that women employed in gender-specific jobs may be particularly likely to suffer sexualized representation and treatment at work; as the extracts they cite from secretarial manuals illustrate, the relationship between a secretary and her boss is 'profoundly intimacized, gendered and heterosexualized': she becomes his 'office-wife'. This heterosexualized construction of secretarial employment has important implications for the way in which secretaries themselves make sense of gender inequality, sexual harassment and sexual objectification in their working lives. In particular, secretaries often may not label as sexist or sexual harassment behaviours which could objectively be so defined. Helen Mott and Susan Condor explore the ways in which the secretaries who responded to their survey 'were generally unwilling to voice an objection to . . . normative, possibly mundane forms of sexualization' in the workplace. They suggest that this is in part because events which are routine, habitual or mundane ('just part of life') become functionally invisible, and that naming such everyday forms of sexualization as sexual harassment may become a cause of pain, and possible mortification, for those individual women who currently work as secretaries, and who achieve a sense of self-worth through the "good" performance of the role'. Their provocative argument is that the resistance of secretaries to labelling their experiences as sexual harassment places researchers and researched in 'a bitter hermeneutic struggle as we assert our feminist visions over versions of the world in which sexual harassment is "just a joke"'. Concepts of gender, sexism and sexual harassment are 'mediated images' or 'macro-formations of social life' which are not necessarily available in common-sense, everyday life, but which can be accessed from 'the academic power-house', from which it might be possible to 'formulate a feminist account of sexual harassment which does not rely on everyday consciousness'.

In Chapter 5, Kathleen Cairns continues this exploration of women's apparent unwillingness to apply the label of sexual harassment to their experiences, or to act formally against the harasser.

> If, after all our attempts to educate women about harassment and to establish accessible, non-punitive procedures to deal with it when it occurs, women continue to have trouble applying the term harassment to their own experiences, and if, even when they do label their experience correctly, they do not use the means available to them to combat harassment, then we must consider the probability that we still have not fully understood the nature of harassment and of women's responses to it.

In exploring the problem of women's self-blame and silence in relation to sexual harassment, Kathleen Cairns draws on feminist psychological theories of women's development and suggests three mechanisms which work to perpetuate women's silence. First, women are psychologically disempowered by the fragmentation of their Selves due to the patriarchal socialization of women as Other to a male norm. Second, women have 'accommodated' to male-defined norms of femininity and have consequently developed a very circumscribed sense of personal agency (in contrast to the psychology of entitlement in men). As a result of these two processes, women may believe that their experiences are not 'real' or that it is they who are in the wrong. Third, silence is also used as a form of resistance – as a way of holding back and refusing to participate. According to Kathleen Cairns, 'Patriarchy, as a system of power relations, mounts a constant and unremitting assault on girls' and women's sense of self, producing confusion, demoralization, *and ultimately complicity in their own subjugation*' (our emphasis).

Arising directly out of concern with these problems of non-recognition and inaction, feminists are developing increasingly sophisticated analyses of the power dynamics involved in sexual harassment. Patriarchal power, as manifested in and through sexual harassment, is the dominant theme of the second part of the book, in which the authors address sexual harassment specifically as a way of men 'doing power' over women and sustaining (hetero)patriarchal relations. As our analysis of the backlash illustrates, sexual harassment (along with date rape) has been singled out as a particular target for those seeking to undermine feminist gains. In so far as sexual harassment policies *do* now begin to present a threat to men's freedom to act as they please *vis-à-vis* the women they work with, some men are now fighting back with a vengeance to preserve their assumed 'rights'. Over the years, an interesting transformation has occurred, such that something which started out as an explicitly feminist campaign to protect women's rights (and which subsequently came to be formally recognized as being of more general public concern) has now been reinterpreted by a growing and highly vocal section of society as 'a female assault upon the rights of men' (Ramazanoglu 1987: 66). The backlash has resulted in a renewed identification of the concept of sexual harassment with feminist politics, but in the context of a climate of strong anti-feminism. Now that many broadly 'liberal feminist' views are widely accepted (at least in principle) in western societies, and have become the modern orthodoxy (for example, the basic principle of women's equal rights), they are no longer identified as 'feminist'. In this so-called 'postfeminist' era, the term is reserved for those ideas associated with more radical feminist politics, and hence remains a marker of unacceptability. This conspicuous emphasis on sexual harassment as a *feminist* concept has the effect of providing a further deterrent to potential complainants. Many women are now aware of the term sexual harassment and their refusal to identify their experiences in this way cannot simply be interpreted as the result of ignorance; rather, they prefer *not* to identify their experience as sexual harassment because they are reluctant to identify themselves with a feminist issue – if for no other reason, because to do so could make them targets for further abuse by anti-feminists.

In sum, although the majority of women and men now recognize as unacceptable the more obvious forms of sexual harassment (what Wise and Stanley 1987 label 'sledgehammer' harassment), there remains widespread resistance to the idea that personal remarks, off-colour jokes and ogling (all examples of the kind of mundane, everyday occurrences that Wise and Stanley likened to a dripping tap) might constitute harassment too. We would argue that education cannot (on its own) bring about an end to sexual harassment, so long as sexual harassment is one mechanism through which men exert power over women and through which heteropatriarchal power is sustained and reinforced. The chapters in Part II, then, address in different ways this question of power in relation to sexual harassment.

As June Larkin illustrates in Chapter 6, sexual harassment continues to restrain and restrict women, and to mould young women into conformity with heteropatriarchal norms. She describes street harassment as 'part of a system of sexual terrorism that reminds young women of their vulnerability to more extreme forms of abuse'. Young women 'learn to adapt, restrict and regulate their behaviour to minimize the likelihood of a violent encounter with men', and it is sexual harassment on the street which accounts, in part, for the contracting world of the adolescent girl. In June Larkin's words:

When a young woman is continually reminded of the risks that accompany her developing body, when she is constantly under the scrutiny and surveillance of males, and when she lives in a state of constant vigilance, it's unlikely that she'll ever develop a sense of herself as a powerful and autonomous person. Unlikely, too, that she'll ever develop the strength to work against the process of her subordination.

In Chapter 7, Alison Thomas turns the spotlight away from women as victims of sexual harassment and focuses instead on the vexed question of why men harass women. She contends that both psychological and sociological approaches to this question have tended to lead to oversimplistic analyses, and instead proposes a psychosocial approach, which focuses on how men themselves construct harassing behaviour. Drawing on data from her own research, she argues that, for many men, the development of a masculine gendered identity ('doing masculinity') is inextricably linked with the conspicuous display of attitudes and behaviours which objectify women. Men's failure to identify this as sexual harassment can be attributed to their primary concern with constructing themselves as masculine in ways that differentiate them from women, in accordance with the demands of heteropatriarchal society.

In the following chapter, Debbie Epstein underlines a similar point, regarding the power of the patriarchy to enforce compliance with its rules. In a provocative and wide-ranging chapter, she focuses in particular on the ways in which the harassment of gay men functions to enforce compulsory heterosexuality through the punishment of deviance from heterosexual norms of masculinity. Relating this form of harassment to that experienced by lesbians and by heterosexual women, she argues that 'the harassment both of women and of gay and/or "effeminate" men, then, seems to be related to the enforcement of heterosexuality.'

The final two chapters address the issue of sexual harassment in relation to the backlash against feminist gains in Canada (Chapter 9) and in India (Chapter 10). In Chapter 9, Linda Mahood and Barbara Littlewood analyse the media's narrative of sexual harassment, relating its form to that of the Victorian melodrama, and point to the 'highly conservative anti-feminist ends' to which such narratives are put. Whether the issue is framed in terms of sexual danger or campus witch hunt, the message of these narratives serves to keep women 'in our place'. In particular, as Linda Mahood and Barbara Littlewood show, 'The new victims of the "campus witch hunt" are the smooth cheeked sons, who after all are only engaging in pranks, and the professors, those jolly old rogues, whose friendly pats and hugs are misinterpreted'. They conclude that, 'The new melodramatic plot, as told by contemporary narrative, works as a "reactionary" critique of feminist politics'. As they indicate, this is often an explicit critique, laced with references to 'feminazis' who are limiting freedom of speech and spoiling everyone's fun.

Finally, Barbara Bagilhole relates Indian feminists' cogent analysis of the increase in violence against women in India as 'a backlash in response to women assuming new roles'. As she points out, while it is internationally the case that sexual harassment is used as a means of controlling women, the problem in India is 'exacerbated by the fact that the present legislation preventing sexual harassment is so inadequate, rarely enforced, and – in terms of the workplace – non-existent.' She quotes the All India Democratic Women's Association (AIDWA) who comment that violence (including 'Eve-teasing') is perpetuated in order 'to silence [women] and prevent them from fuller participation in social development'. According to the Indian Centre for Women's Development Studies, sexual violence is 'being used as a weapon of political intimidation'.

In this introductory chapter, then, we have outlined the historical development of the concept of sexual harassment from its first use in the mid-1970s to the present day. We have indicated the importance of the term in enabling women to name a particular experience, to render it problematic, and so to begin to resist it. We have looked at some of these forms of resistance, including the conduct of surveys in order to chart the incidence and prevalence of sexual harassment, and the development of workplace codes of practice and grievance procedures in order to deal with it. In the sense that considerable progress has been made in these areas, we have argued the fight against sexual harassment can be seen as a notable success story for feminism. However, we have also examined the contemporary backlash against these gains. We have highlighted the fact that many women who identify their experiences as sexual harassment are unwilling to utilize the policies designed to combat it, and that such unwillingness is exacerbated both by the disagreements and uncertainties about the 'proper' definition of sexual harassment, and by the negative connotations now taken on by any issue associated with feminism.

The chapters collected here make two specific contributions to contemporary feminist theory and practice in relation to sexual harassment. In Part I, they identify and address in some analytic detail the problem of women's failure to label specific behaviours as sexual harassment (or to seek appropriate redress). They examine how and why the non-recognition or non-labelling of sexual harassment occurs, with particular attention to specificities of context and circumstance, and they consider what may be done to ameliorate this situation. In Part II, they address sexual harassment specifically as a way of 'doing power' and reinforcing heteropatriarchy in the context of the anti-feminist backlash. These chapters begin to develop more sophisticated analyses of the power dynamics involved in sexual harassment, particularly in understanding its role in maintaining a heteropatriarchal power base in the face of feminist gains.

Men's use of sexuality to exercise power over women has been a central arena for feminist analysis and political action throughout this century.

Sexual harassment, a key strategy in this exercise of power, has been named and resisted by feminists for more than two decades. While considerable gains have been made, the contemporary backlash also poses a considerable threat – in the face of which the development of more sophisticated theory and more effective practice regarding sexual harassment is essential. Collectively, the chapters in this book offer a range of new insights and strategies for advancing the feminist struggle against sexual harassment in the late 1990s.

References

Adams, J., Kottke, J. and Padgitt, J. (1983) Sexual harassment of university students. *Journal of College Student Personnel*, 23: 484–90.

Alfred Marks Bureau (1982) *Sex in the Office*. Borehamwood, Herts: Statistical Services Division.

Alliance Against Sexual Coercion (1981) *Fighting Sexual Harassment: An Advocacy Handbook*. Boston, MA: Alyson Publications.

Bacchi, C. and Jose, J. (1994) Historicising Sexual Harassment. *Women's History Review*, 3(2): 263–70.

Backhouse, C. and Cohen, L. (1979) *The Secret Oppression: Sexual Harassment of Working Women*. Toronto: Macmillan.

Benson, D.J. and Thomson, G.E. (1982) Sexual harassment on a university campus: The confluence of authority relations, sexual interest, and gender stratification. *Social Problems*, 29: 236–51.

Brandenberg, J.B. (1982) Sexual harassment in the university: Guidelines for establishing a grievance procedure. *Signs: Journal of Women in Culture and Society*, 8: 320–36.

Brant, C. and Too, Y.L. (eds) (1994) *Rethinking Sexual Harassment*. London: Pluto Press.

Brodribb, S., Bardon, S., Newhouse, T. and Spencer, J. (1995) Appeasement won't warm chilly climes in poli sci. *Times Colonist*, 15 July: A5.

Brodribb, S., with Bardon, S., Newhouse, T. and Spencer, J. and with the assistance of Kyba, N. (1996) The equity franchise. *Women's Education*, 12(1): 12–20.

Brownmiller, S. (1975) *Against Our Will: Men, Women and Rape*. New York: Simon and Schuster.

Canadian Human Rights Commission (CHRC) (1983) *Unwanted Sexual Attention and Sexual Harassment: Results of a Survey of Canadians*. Ottawa: CHRC/Research and Special Studies Branch.

Collins, E. and Blodgett, T. (1981) Some see it . . . Some won't. *Harvard Business Review*, 59: 76–95.

Crocker, P. (1983) An analysis of university definitions of sexual harassment. *Signs: Journal of Women in Culture and Society*, 8: 696–707.

Davies, J. (1994) Codes of Mr and Miss Conduct. *Times Higher Education Supplement*, 14 January: 14.

Equal Employment Opportunities Commission (1980) *Guidelines on Discrimination because of Sex*. Washington, DC: EEOC.

Farley, L. (1978) *Sexual Shakedown: The Sexual Harassment of Women on the Job*. New York: Warner Books.

Farrell, W. (1993) *The Myth of Male Power*. London: Fourth Estate.

Fekete, J. (1994) *Moral Panic: Biopolitics Rising*. Montreal: Robert Davies Publishing.

Fitzgerald, L.F. (1993) Sexual harassment: Violence against women in the workplace. *American Psychologist*, 48: 1070–6.

Gardner, C.B. (1980) Passing by: Street remarks, address rights and the urban female. *Sociological Quarterly*, 50(3/4): 328–56.

Garner, H. (1990) *True Stories: Selected Non-Fiction*. Melbourne: Text Publishing.

Giuffre, P.A. and Williams, C.L. (1994) Boundary lines: Labeling sexual harassment in restaurants. *Gender and Society*, 8(3): 378–401.

Griffin, S. (1971) Rape: The all-American crime. *Ramparts*, September: 26–35.

Gutek, B.A. and Koss, M.P. (1993) Changed women and changed organizations: Consequences of and coping with sexual harassment. *Journal of Vocational Behavior*, 42: 28–48.

Herbert, C. (1989) *Speaking of Silence: The Sexual Harassment of Schoolgirls*. London: Falmer.

Industrial Society (1993) *No Offence? Sexual Harassment, How It Happens and How to Beat It*. London: Industrial Society.

Jeffreys, S. (1987) *The Spinster and Her Enemies*. London: Pandora.

Kenig, S. and Ryan, J. (1986) Sex differences in levels of tolerance and attribution of blame for sexual harassment on a university campus. *Sex Roles*, 15: 535–49.

Kitzinger, C. and Thomas, A. (1995) Sexual harassment: A discursive approach. In S. Wilkinson and C. Kitzinger (eds) *Feminism and Discourse: Psychological Perspectives*. London: Sage.

Kramarae, C. and Treichler, P.A. (1985) *A Feminist Dictionary*. London: Pandora Press.

McKinney, K. and Maroules, N. (1991) Sexual harassment. In E. Grauerholz and M.A. Koraleski (eds) *Sexual Coercion: A Sourcebook on Its Nature, Cause and Prevention*. Toronto: Lexington Books.

MacKinnon, C. (1979) *Sexual Harassment of Working Women: A Case of Sex Discrimination*. New Haven, CT: Yale University Press.

McNeill, Sandra (1985) Sexual harassment at work. In d. rhodes and S. McNeill *Women against Violence against Women*. London: Onlywomen Press.

Merit Systems Protection Board (MSPB) (1981) *Sexual Harassment in the Federal Workplace: Is It a Problem?* Washington DC: US Government Printing Office.

Merit Systems Protection Board (MSPB) (1994) *Sexual Harassment in the Federal Workplace: Trends, Progress and Continuing Challenges*. Washington DC: US Government Printing Office.

Moore, S. (1993) Who's afraid of Anita Hill? *The Guardian*, 21 May: 11.

National Association of Local Government Officers (1981) *Sexual Harassment is a Trade Union Issue*. London: NALGO.

Powell, G.N. (1986) Effects of Sex Role Identity and Sex on Definitions of Sexual Harassment, *Sex Roles*, 14: 9–19.

Ramazanoglu, C. (1987) Sex and violence in academic life: Or, you can keep a good woman down. In J. Hanmer and M. Maynard (eds) *Women, Violence and Social Control*. London: Macmillan.

Riger, S. (1991) Gender dilemmas in sexual harassment policies and procedures. *American Psychologist*, 46(5): 497–505.

Roiphe, K. (1993) *The Morning After: Sex, Fear and Feminism*. London: Hamish Hamilton.

Rubenstein, M. (1987) *The Dignity of Women at Work: Report on the Problem of Sexual Harassment in the Member States of the EC*. Luxembourg: Equal Opportunities Unit, DVG, European Community.

Rubenstein, M. and De Vries, I. (1993) *How to Combat Sexual Harassment at Work: A Guide to Implementing the European Commission Codes*. Luxembourg: Commission of the European Community.

Sanford, W. (1979) *Fighting Sexual Harassment: An Advocacy Handbook*. Boston, MA: Alyson Publications.

Sedley, A. and Benn, M. (1982) *Sexual Harassment at Work*. London: National Council for Civil Liberties.

Thomas, A. and Kitzinger, C. (1990) Sexual harassment: When it isn't seen that way. *British Psychological Society Psychology of Women Section Newsletter*, 5: 4–7.

Thomas, A. and Kitzinger, C. (1994) 'It's just something that happens': The invisibility of sexual harassment in the workplace. *Gender, Work and Organisation*, 1(3): 151–61.

Trade Union Congress (1983) *Sexual Harassment at Work*. London: TUC.

Trevena, C. (1995) Sexual politics. *The Guardian*, 15 August: 14.

Weeks, E.I., Boles, J.M., Garbin, A.P. and Blount, J. (1986) The transformation of sexual harassment from a private trouble into a public issue. *Sociological Inquiry*, 56: 432–55.

Wise, S. and Stanley, L. (1987) *Georgie Porgie: Sexual Harassment in Everyday Life*. London: Pandora.

PART I

Refusing the label, declining to protest

2

Off with the velvet gloves

CARRIE HERBERT

Over the last few years, my job as a sexual harassment educator and consultant has taken me to a variety of educational institutions: schools, universities and colleges where I have met with people who want to do something about sexual harassment. There are those who want me to help them write and implement a policy on sexual harassment, those who want to assess the frequency of the phenomenon, those who want to train a variety of people to deal with people who are victims of it in an effective and sensitive way, those who want me to train managers to intercept, intervene and to bring incidents to a rapid but effective conclusion, those who want me to raise people's awareness to the issue of sexual harassment generally, those who want to have people trained as investigators to be able to conduct an investigation efficiently and competently, those who want me to teach some of their pupils about the topic, and latterly those who want me to conduct an investigation into a particular case of sexual harassment which has gone horribly wrong or to deal with a perpetrator who they don't know what to do with. Alongside this institutional demand there are a series of phone calls from individuals, all women or girls, so far, who want to discuss with me their own case or experience of sexual harassment.

What all these groups and individuals have in common is their individual and collective ignorance as to what sexual harassment is, how it is manifested, the range of ways it can occur, their legal responsibility under the law, or their legal right to protection under the law and many other issues to do with intent, liability and victimization. There is far too much confusion around the issue. There is a high level of misconception, the main problem turning on the different perceptions that men and women have of sexual harassment. There is also a rationalization on the part of some that sexual harassment is a feminist complaint.

All those positions lead me ultimately to the same conclusion; there is much ignorance, misconception and misplaced anxiety about sexual harassment and in order to be able to deal with it effectively and efficiently we must use education as the tool for behavioural and attitudinal change about this issue.

Education is better than punitive treatment for a number of reasons. It gives people the chance to look at and review their own behaviour, or behaviour they have received, in a more constructive and proactive way than suddenly finding oneself in the middle of a case, and having to respond reactively either as the victim or the perpetrator. It allows for changes in attitudes and values which can only come about if the person themself decides that change is due.

There are other reasons for change. The first is the moral well-being of all the people in the institution. Whether it is a school, a college, an institution or a company every member of that community has the right to work and study in a safe environment. A safe environment means that the culture in that organization is free from sexual harassment. If the climate is one where people are frightened, humiliated, demeaned and subjected to unwanted sexual behaviour or behaviour meted out to them because they are a particular sex, they cannot work or study effectively. Their morale and confidence is eroded and their job performance is reduced. Their stress levels are increased and they may begin to have physical symptoms as a result. Headaches, vomiting, uncontrollable crying and stomach ulcers are some of the ways stress caused by sexual harassment is manifested.

The second reason for change is that of the financial consequences. If sexual harassment is not dealt with appropriately there may be loss of productivity, increase of staff absenteeism and turnover, truanting, failure of exams, poor morale, expensive mistakes and injuries caused by lack of concentration. Clearly cases brought to an industrial tribunal are time consuming and expensive, not only from the compensation claims awarded, but for the personnel tied up in the investigation, preparation and execution of the case.

For the victim too there are serious financial consequences. She (and most cases of sexual harassment are women or girls being sexually harassed by men or boys) may decide to leave the job or ask for a transfer. If she is a schoolgirl she may begin to play truant (and thus miss out on valuable teaching and learning), drop out of school, decide not to take exams or be unable to pass the exams due to her lack of attendance in class, anxiety or stress levels. She may drop out of university or other educational institution which could have led to a better paid job due to her higher qualifications. The following case study shows the consequences of sexual harassment for one individual.

Sophia's story

Sophia arrived from New Zealand as a student wishing to study for a Master's degree at an English university. She already had a first degree from a South African university and another Master's degree from a New Zealand university. She had hopes of studying for a PhD and thought that she would ease herself into the British education system for a year before she decided whether she wanted to study here for a longer period. She was also concerned to know whether her academic ability was high enough for a higher degree in the UK.

Behind her in New Zealand she left a husband and three children; the oldest was 10, the second one was six and the youngest just two and a half. Sophia was South African by birth, was the daughter of a highly qualified veterinary surgeon and had attended a variety of church boarding schools based on the English private school tradition. She was a devout Catholic and attended the city Roman Catholic cathedral on a regular basis. She was clever, she was warm, she was anxious, she was a woman, she was Black, and she was vulnerable.

For Sophia the sexual harassment began as soon as she started her course at the university. The perpetrator of the harassment was her lecturer and personal tutor. Sophia had been assigned a woman tutor but at the last moment the academic responsible for the course changed her tutelage from his female colleague to himself. Sophia had no say in this changeover.

At the first tutorial Dr David Frank asked her searching and intimate questions about her personal life: her husband, her children, how she would manage without her husband, where she was living and what she liked doing. Sophia had been surprised and shocked at the nature of the conversation; this was not what she had expected. This was not how she had been taught to behave and she was dismayed at the kind of conversation in which she found herself. However, because she was in a new and different country she persuaded herself that perhaps this was the way in which male tutors at English universities operated. She didn't like it but she had no power in this relationship with him to prevent what was happening. She felt she had no right to ask him to stop; she had no friends, colleagues or fellow students she knew well enough to turn to and ask for help and no one to ask whether this was normal behaviour. She was not in a position to question his method of working; she had no strategies to handle his intrusion, like asking him to stop, or changing the focus or fogging the issue by answering neutrally or blandly, and she had no other experience with which to make a comparison.

The personal and intimate questions continued until the day when she went for a pre-arranged tutorial with him to discuss her project. During the course of the meeting he unzipped his flies and began to masturbate. Sophia was horrified, humiliated and petrified. She fled from the room. However, this performance was to be repeated over a three-month period, punctuated with requests for dates, incessant sexual innuendoes and invitations for sexual encounters at weekends. Finally Sophia summoned up the courage to ask another lecturer who specialized in her area if he would supervise her dissertation. This was reluctantly agreed to by Dr Frank, who shouted at her for changing tutors.

Sophia said and did nothing about this treatment, hoping that she would be able to finish her year and go back to New Zealand and her family. All thoughts of staying on to do a PhD were forgotten. She just had to finish her dissertation, pass her exam and get away.

Sophia failed her dissertation and the course. Twelve months after the letter which had informed her that she had failed she met a person who listened to her story, believed her and took her to the university to resolve the case. The university's first official comment was that the case was out of date. Their second response was to hire some of the most powerful solicitors in London to fight their corner. The last part of the official drama for the university unfolded in a room of the London solicitors, with Sophia telling her story yet again, providing evidence and witnesses to her distress at the time, as well as displaying clear veracity and professionalism. Her voice was true, her story was accurate, her memory was honest. However, the bottom line was that it was her word against that of Dr Frank. The acts of sexual harassment had happened in private with no eyewitnesses. She was a woman, a student, Black, a wife, with no power, no money, no influence and no friends. He was a man, a lecturer, white, single, with power, money, influence and colleagues and friends to support him. A week later Sophia threatened to take her own life. Friends called a GP who talked her through the crisis.

Since these occurrences in 1990/1 Sophia has lived off the kindness and charity of a variety of friends and acquaintances who provide her with accommodation, food, clothes and money. She has never returned to New Zealand, her husband or her children.

So what went wrong? First, Sophia – in common with many other women – did not understand the concept of sexual harassment enough to be able to deal with it effectively. Although there was a sexual harassment policy at the university, no effort had been made to train people who might be affected by such behaviour. Some training had been offered to managers, tutors, heads of faculty and other senior personnel, but no one had thought to train those most likely to be affected, students, women and part-time workers.

Second, we know that there are people in the workplace who are particularly vulnerable to harassment. Research shows these to be Black women, single female parents, separated, divorced or recently widowed women, women who work in non-traditional worksites, part-time workers, lesbians and disabled women, as well as women who have recently been promoted, who have started work for the first time, or women who are new to an organization. Sophia had four of these attributes. She was Black, separated from her husband (not formally, but by 15,000 miles), working in a non-traditional worksite (women in higher education account for less than 20 per cent of the students) and had just joined an organization where she was new to the culture, the climate and the customs. No effort had been made by her university to help people specially at risk by giving them advice, warning or information which might have helped them.

The third factor was the lack of expertise at the top in dealing with the case when it finally came to light. Support and sympathy were forthcoming from the bottom, but the closing of ranks around the alleged perpetrator by those at the top of the institution was extraordinary in its silent power, protecting its own with a head-in-the-sand position.

The fourth significant factor was the way in which people, and by that I mean fellow students, friends, colleagues and staff, were much happier believing the line that the woman student must have got it wrong somehow, because the man couldn't possibly have done it – he was such a nice chap. This could only mean, by implication, that there was something wrong with the woman. The fact that Sophia was Black, studying away from her home, devoutly religious and from another culture provided an explanation for what happened to her. 'Perhaps she had misread the signs'. 'Perhaps she imagined that he was doing that'. 'She was a bit old-fashioned and very religious'. 'How come she had left her two and a half-year-old son to do a degree in England?' 'Was it normal for a woman to leave her husband?' or 'Why didn't she tell him where to get off if he was really doing that?' Most people also believed that the man concerned hadn't done it, was in the right or at least unaware that what he had done was wrong. There were comments such as: 'I can't believe Dr Frank would have done that; he is such a nice man *and* he's written a book on equal opportunities'.

Sexual harassment had a profound effect on Sophia's life and on her family, her career, her future, and her self-esteem. She attempted to take her life because she was in despair about what was going on. She was subjected to humiliation, degradation and to literally unspeakable and unbelievable events. She had no one to turn to. While she had tried to approach certain people, she had essentially not been believed or not taken seriously. This happened within a university – a place where it is often considered there is a heightened social awareness and access to equal opportunities and social justice. An ordinary male lecturer somehow had the personal power, institutional backing and society's condonement to get away with it. What can be done?

Briefly, systematic sexual harassment training awareness must begin in all schools beginning at the age of 5 and continuing until students leave. The education must be comprehensive and both explicit and implicit. Had Sophia known for sure what sexual harassment was, if she had some strategies to deal with it, and had other people at the university known what it was and been able to deal with it effectively, this chapter would not have needed to be written.

This case is by no means unique, and if we look at what some of the women and girls who I have come across in my training work have said about sexual harassment, or about unwanted and unwelcome behaviour that they have received, we can begin to see how widespread is the ignorance of women and girls about what constitutes sexual harassment.

When I first got to the sixth form college I really liked it, but then I started getting funny letters. I never found out who they were from, but they were sick, really sick. They were sexual fantasy letters, with me always being the girl that men were doing things to. It was disgusting. I was so ashamed and embarrassed that I didn't tell anyone. I mean how can you show a teacher or your dad a letter like that, they might think you were funny. Anyway, they finally stopped. But I still don't know who wrote them. I think he was a pervert but I don't think it was sexual harassment.

(Year 12 female student in sixth form college)

Well, it wasn't serious enough. She had been married and was divorced, she had medical problems, you know, women's problems, not that she was explicit about what operation she had had, and as soon as she came into the college, I knew. You know how you get a feeling that some people won't be able to cope properly. And then this happened. To be honest, I think, well I don't want to say she asked for it, but, I mean she is a pretty girl and he is only a young man. But then when I heard she had taken an overdose, two bottles of wine and a handful of Prozac. Well, I think she is a bit unbalanced really and I'm not sure she will ever be able to complete the course.

(A senior woman lecturer in a college of further education at an investigation into the sexual harassment of this woman student)

I remember one thing that happened when I was there, but I don't think it was sexual harassment, and anyway it didn't happen to me. We were having some tee shirts made for the company. The acronym for the company had about seven largish letters across the front. Well, the manager was talking about this and looked across at Marge, who, you know, is quite big, and said that she would have no difficulties showing off all the letters whereas I would probably only be able to show one letter properly. Well, I didn't mind, but Marge went bright red and looked really embarrassed. I told her that he didn't mean anything by it, but she was quite upset.

I've got a manager who used to make remarks about what I wore and he made comments about the fact that I got married. I got married about seven months ago now. Anyway, he used to say that if Rob, that's my husband, couldn't keep up he would oblige. I finally told the union rep what was going on and together we went to see him. He was so angry about me telling the rep. He yelled and screamed. He didn't once apologize. He just told the rep to 'get that bitch out of my office'. Yeah, the remarks and comments have stopped but now he won't even look at me, let alone talk to me. The other day he asked generally if someone could do something and I said I could, and he just ignored me and walked off. I don't consider what he did was right but I don't think it's sexual harassment.

However, it is not only the women and girls who are unsure of what constitutes sexual harassment, what unwanted attention looks like, or what to do about it. Men and boys too it seems are equally unclear and ignorant of the facts surrounding sexual harassment.

We don't really have sexual harassment in our school. You see it's a predominantly boys' school; 700 boys and just 25 girls in the sixth form. I mean the girls all stick together and stand up for themselves. We did have one incident at the end of last term, but I don't know what I would call it. I mean, it wasn't sexual harassment, but I would like your opinion of it. The school were all waiting in the hall for the headmaster. It was the final assembly before Christmas. We had the orchestra on the stage all ready. One of the sixth form girls from the orchestra arrived late. She had to walk up the centre aisle and across the stage in front of the whole school to her place. She was wolf-whistled, catcalled and cheered. I mean I was sort of embarrassed, on her behalf, but I couldn't have done anything. It would have made the situation worse. Anyway I wasn't sure whether she liked it or not.
(Senior male teacher at a well-respected public school)

But, I'm a rugby player. It's not directed at anyone in particular, it's just how we are. I mean, are you saying that I can't do that anymore? That's an infringement of my rights. I have always behaved like that and I have the right to continue.
(Response made by a 19-year-old male student at a college of further education, when confronted with a formal complaint of sexual harassment against him)

So what can be done to break down the ignorance around the subject of sexual harassment? Isn't it time we took the gloves off and told the truth? Let us look at some of the strategies that can be used.

First, as teachers and managers in schools we have a responsibility to educate those within the school or college community to what sexual harassment is and what to do about it. We must talk to young women and girls about male oppression, patriarchy and masculine myths of sexual prowess, uncontrollable sexual urges and other such tales. We have to provide them with a political understanding of their gendered situation, to help them understand how power has been appropriated by men and masculine institutions, how the system is perpetuated and why it is so powerful in its oppression of women. We also need to provide these girls with some skills in order to challenge and confront sexist incidents or situations, or at the very least, offer a listening and supportive ear. Providing them with a political understanding will have the facility to take the behaviour away from the personal and make it a part of the social world which we inhabit.

At the same time we can no longer ignore the ignorant and cavalier attitude by some men towards this behaviour. Sexual harassment is not just an issue for women. While it remains a concern for women alone little will be done to ensure men are made aware of their unwanted and unsolicited attentions. We must raise their awareness of the feelings and perceptions of women and girls in particular, although we can be reassured that some men are now finding the sexual harassment of women by some men an embarrassment, and as such creating an offensive and hostile working environment.

We also need to change the working environment, the ethos and the atmosphere in which we provide students, both girls and boys, with education, in order that they can tell us, teachers, without delay when something of this nature happens. We have to break the silence about sexual harassment, about sexual exploitation, about sexual abuse and about unwanted sexual attention. We have to give male students clear indications of when certain behaviour is inappropriate and/or offensive, and this must be done consistently, frequently and as a matter of course, not as extraordinarys or as a knee-jerk response to an incident. One of the ways of doing this clearly is to make sure that sexual harassment is put on the curriculum, both implicity and explicitly.

If students see male teachers behaving in a macho aggressive fashion, if some teachers talk in a derogatory way to girls, if girls are touched or patted or flirted with by male teachers, if the subject of discrimination is seen as a bandwagon topic and laughed at or sighed at, then younger males will copy and use these tactics too. Sexual harassment is a common and frequent problem which is often then seen as that; as something unremarkable. Rather than each student seeing it as an individual attack, a personal slur or a private put-down, it must be discussed and put into perspective. Most women and girls at some time in their lives experience unwanted and unwelcomed sexual attention from someone in a position of power or authority over them. Sexual harassment of women and girls is not a private enterprise on the part of one man, rather it is part of the systematic social control of women which elsewhere I have called female-controlling-practices (Herbert 1989). Further, it is not an isolated rare occurrence, rather it is a daily routine for some girls, comprising sexist put-downs, sexual intrusions, sexual assault, sexualized comments, gestures and innuendoes.

The third aspect is similar to the second; what we need for young men and boys is an equally tough and rigorous method of telling them that their behaviour is no longer acceptable, that it creates a hostile and intimidating work environment, that it is offensive and humiliating to some of the listeners, both male and female. One way of doing all this is to address within schools, education programmes and the curriculum, the issue of sexual harassment. We must begin to tell the truth about sexual harassment by bringing the topic into the education system. How can this be done? First, those at the top must begin the process by recognizing how detrimental and discriminatory sexual harassment is to the potential of girls' education.

A range of facilities within each institution must be created: each school must have at least one member of staff who is trained in this topic so that they understand the issues; this teacher has the role of educating and raising the awareness of staff and students in their organization to the issues; there must be a policy in each school; each school must have an informal way of resolving problems; each school must decide how best to put this issue on the agenda for the pupils through personal and social education, across the curriculum generally and in other specific curriculum areas such as English and drama and finally each school must have a sexual harassment contact officer or 'listener', to whom staff or students may go directly to discuss a concern they might have. Within each school there must be a user friendly grievance procedure and a policy for dealing with cases. The aim is for the grievance procedure to be swift, efficient and fair.

However, it must also be remembered that a school or college is a workplace for a great many people. Besides the students, there are teachers or lecturers, cleaners, administrative officers, clerks, telephonists and grounds people, to name just a few. These people too have a right to be protected from discrimination on the ground of sex (or race for that matter).

Often those working in British schools, especially teachers, do not regard it as an employing body, like other institutions, but a place where the main emphasis is on the educational development of those at the school, the students. However, with the freedom of grant maintained schools and others seeking to opt out of the local education authority system, so too come employment responsibilities. The European Commission (1991) defines sexual harassment as 'unwanted conduct of a sexual nature, or other conduct based on sex affecting the dignity of women and men at work'. It continues and describes this behaviour as including 'a range of unwelcome physical, verbal or non-verbal conduct'. The code emphasizes that it is the unwelcome or unwanted nature of the conduct which distinguishes sexual harassment from friendly behaviour or sexual attention that is welcome and mutual. It goes on to say that:

> It is unacceptable if such conduct is unwanted, unreasonable and offensive to the recipient; a person's rejection of or submission to such conduct on the part of the employers or workers (including superiors or colleagues) is used explicitly or implicitly as a basis for a decision which affects that person's access to vocational training or to employment, continued employment, promotion, salary or any other employment decisions; and/or such conduct creates an intimidating, hostile or humiliating working environment for the recipient.
>
> (European Commission 1991)

What has also changed in schools with the freeing up of LEA control is the responsibility of the schools and colleges themselves. Staff have a right, as I have already said, to be protected from acts of discrimination on the grounds of sex. But with whom does this responsibility lie? It lies with the employer; that is, the person within the school who hires, fires and pays the wages. In most cases this will be one of the following: a headteacher, a chair of the board of governors, the board of governors, a church leader or a church authority. Section .41(2) 6.10 of the Sex Discrimination Act (1975) says that the person liable for any act of sexual discrimination done with his or her authority (whether express or implied, and whether given before or after the act) by his or her agent is the employer or principal. This means that it is not the perpetrator of the harassment who is regarded as liable or responsible, and it will not be the harasser who will be sued in court or taken to an industrial tribunal. It is the employer or principal. It goes on to say that an employer is liable for the discriminatory acts of his or her employees done in the course of their employment, whether or not they are done with his or her knowledge or approval. Lawyers call this 'vicarious liability'. The Act provides a defence to an employer who would otherwise be liable for an unlawful act by one of his or her employees, if he or she can prove that such steps were taken as were reasonably practicable to prevent the employee from committing the unlawful act in question or unlawful act of that kind.

So in brief, systematic sexual harassment training in schools and universities must begin with these three aims. First to raise the teachers' and lecturers' awareness of sexual harassment; second to give them practical ways of dealing with this concern in their own classrooms and lecture theatres, and in the educational environment generally; and third to begin the process of educating the boys and men not to do it in the first place and how to empower the girls and women to deal with it if it does occur.

If we do not take off the velvet gloves and tell the truth I think we will have let our students down, for we will not have given them the information that they, like Sophia, need to know.

References

European Commission (1991) *Council Declaration and Code of Practice. Protecting the Dignity of Women and Men at Work*. Luxembourg: Commission of the European Community.

Herbert, C. (1989) *Talking of Silence: The Sexual Harassment of School Girls*. London: Falmer.

3

Gender inequality, sexual harassment and the toxic organization: The case of medical women

PAULA NICOLSON

Introduction

Medicine has traditionally been a patriarchal profession, and despite two decades of increased female entry to medical school and equal opportunities legislation, there is still evidence that women doctors and medical students are experiencing sexual harassment and gender discrimination which has resulted in limitations to women's medical careers (Nicolson and Welsh 1992). Women's presence in senior tiers of the medical profession has on the whole increased since the 1970s. However, it has not resulted in effective or visible support for women in junior clinical positions or medical school. In the analysis presented here, I will argue that the socialization of women and men in medical school and in junior clinical posts subtly but firmly reproduces male dominated patterns of interaction and power arrangements.

This chapter is based upon my research on sexual harassment and gender inequality in medical education.[1] I began the study during my first year as an academic psychologist in a medical school as a response to the shock of entering a patriarchal culture that appeared to far outstrip any environment, in its privileging of the masculine, that I had experienced before. At my appointment board it had been announced that more than 40 per cent of the student population was female. As I became more visible among the student body, the more I was approached by these women for support, and the more I realized that many of my experiences were duplicated for these young women. However, I had the benefit of insights from the outside world, support from friends, and was also able to employ a feminist analysis of the organizational processes. Many of the students experienced the sexism as their own inadequacies which prevented them from examining the problems any further. In this chapter I outline the relationship between personal and structural processes which are precipitated by overt and covert sexism in an insular, patriarchal culture such as medical school and the wider medical profession. I use examples from the research and personal experience to illustrate my arguments.[2]

Experiences of inequality

> We are not talking about prejudice or sexism as a particular bias against women or as a negative stereotype of women. We are talking about the consequences of women's exclusion from a full share in the making of what becomes treated as *our* culture. We are talking about the consequences of a silence, an absence, a non-presence.
>
> (Smith 1978)

Women, as a group, have almost no influence on the structure and culture of medical practice. However, medicine continues to be a popular option for women who have entered medical training in increasing numbers since the mid-1970s, and many schools in the UK are now admitting around 50 per cent women (Nicolson and Welsh 1992). Around 38 per cent of students entering US medical schools overall are women, with six medical schools having more female than male entrants (Eisenberg 1989, quoted in Silver 1990).

Despite this amount of women entering medical studies, women do not reach senior positions in the profession in any numbers, even though technically there has been enough time for the proportion of women in senior positions to increase in response to increased medical school entry (Nicolson and Welsh 1992). For example even in adult psychiatry where relatively high numbers of women gain senior posts, only around 25 per cent of consultants are female (Department of Health 1991/2). In general hospital medicine the figure is 6.4 per cent, and only 12.9 per cent in obstetrics and gynaecology (Department of Health 1991/2). This latter figure is disturbing given that 100 per cent of that particular patient population is female. Indeed, since the 1970s the proportion of women in senior posts in obstetrics and gynaecology has declined (Lefford 1987). Further, in subspecialties of medicine, there are clear variations between patterns of gender distribution and status in the profession overall (Elston 1993), so that in surgery (where financial rewards are high as well as professional accolade) there are only 3 per cent women consultants (Department of Health 1991/2), and in general practice and public health (relatively low status occupations) women are prevalent, although the bulk of the more senior posts remain occupied by men (Department of Health 1991/2; BMA 1993).

Why should this imbalance occur? The official rhetoric at the levels of the medical school, the employer and the Royal Colleges has focused upon issues of motherhood, childcare and the lack of availability of part-time training as the major barriers to women's careers (e.g. Royal College of Obstetricians and Gynaecologists 1991; Royal College of Surgeons through the WIST [Women in Surgical Training] scheme, see Department of Health 1991/2). But while it is true that women retain responsibility for domestic and childcare arrangements, it is not appropriate to pin the entire burden of gender imbalance in medicine upon these issues. There is no evidence that women enter or graduate with qualifications significantly different from those of their male colleagues, but it is certainly the case that by the end of their undergraduate training women have self-selected into particular branches of the profession, leaving the more 'desirable' special-ties to their male colleagues (Nicolson and Welsh 1992). Indeed it is clear that women are being diverted or excluded from the professional hier-archy, and this is a consistent trend (Department of Health 1991/2). What is missing from the usual framework of analysis is a psychological dimen-sion, not only to explain the way that medical students and doctors of both sexes come to see female doctors' roles and career paths, but to account for the processes whereby gender discrimination and sexual harassment per-sist.

Gender discrimination and sexual harassment

Sexual harassment, most broadly defined, refers to the unwanted imposition of sexual requirements in the context of a relationship of unequal power.

(MacKinnon 1979: 1)

Sexual harassment is the 'unsolicited non-reciprocal male behaviour that asserts a woman's sex role over her function as a worker'.
(Benokraitis and Feagin 1995: 31, with reference to Singleton 1990)

Sexual harassment is any unsolicited and unwelcome sexual advance, request for sexual favours, comment or physical contact when such a contact has the purpose or effect of unreasonably interfering with an individual's work or academic performance or of creating an intimi-datory, hostile or offensive working or academic environment.

(Nicolson and Welsh 1992)[3]

Sexual harassment is the blatant sexualizing of women by men and exploi-tation of unequal power relationships; it is part of the process of covert discrimination against women. The notion of sexualizing the workplace appears so inappropriate to the perceived overt function of work organizations such as hospitals or universities, that it has been difficult for many to name and politicize the notion (Hearn and Parkin 1987; see for example, Carroll in Morris 1994). Recent years, however, have witnessed an increase in legislation, policy and case law through which sexual harassment at work has been defined and thus identified and challenged.

The possibility that relationships between female and male doctors and medical students (and doctors and their patients), with special access to other people's bodies, may involve sexual harassment is both abhorrent and even unbelievable to some people. This includes people in the profession itself. However, our study clearly showed that sexual harassment exists: around 25 per cent of students and staff reported an awareness of sexual harassment, a percentage equivalent to that found in a wider student survey (Sheffield University Students' Union 1992). Further, it is likely that this is an underestimate, because descriptions of gender inequality/discrimination provided by respondents who did not record incidents of sexual harassment, nevertheless frequently corresponded to the definition of sexual harassment presented above.

Gender discrimination and sexual harassment are along the same continuum. Overt and covert discrimination which results in medical women with ambition and talent failing to fulfil their potential while men of equivalent ability do so, is the consequence of a *toxic organizational context* where sexual harassment and discrimination are supported and accepted. They are taken for granted as part of the culture of medical school and the professional clinical experience. Such a context has an effect beyond that of wasting women's career potential. There is a visible process whereby women who stay the course shift their allegiances from a naive identification with other women medical students and a sense of personal inability to an identification with maleness and competence, which is unobtainable and thus destructive.

Echoes of the past

The discrimination against women as potential doctors and as patients is not new. Women were excluded from clinical training and practice until the late nineteenth century (Ehrenreich and English 1979; Elston 1993), and medical attitudes towards women patients have typically reflected an inherent misogyny apparent in many of the early surgical and medical practices and debates surrounding women's ill health (Dally 1991; Moscucci 1993). So why have women persisted in the pursuit of a medical career?

Jean Donnison identified three main arguments used in favour of a female medical presence and a female oriented medical service in the nineteenth century, and it does not require too much effort to see their relevance today. First of all, 'a large number of women ... *had* to work, and their exclusion from this occupation ran contrary to the prevailing economic doctrine of Free Trade' (Donnison 1988: 79). The medical profession, as demonstrated above, continues to be popular with young women who comprise between 40 and 60 per cent of medical school intake, and enter the profession proportionately (Department of Health 1991/2). It seems though that within the profession neither women nor men take women's careers and employment opportunities as seriously as men's. Women doctors are marginalized, with a disproportionate number of men in senior posts, even in general practice which is where the majority of women doctors work (Department of Health 1991/2; Nicolson and Welsh 1992).

Second, the potential benefit of having women doctors is still not taken seriously, and this again has resonance with a nineteenth-century appeal that there were:

> Many women in urgent need of medical attention who refused to consult a man or, if they did, could not bring themselves to give him a full account of their more intimate symptoms, or to permit him to make a thorough examination. For these reasons it was imperative that there should be fully qualified female practitioners for women desiring attendance by their own sex.
>
> (Donnison 1988: 79)

While there are qualified female practitioners, most consultant obstetricians and gynaecologists, specialists in women's reproductive and sexual health, are men, and many women patients are uncomfortable with this state of affairs. The Royal College of Obstetrics and Gynaecology has supported the expansion of part-time training opportunities designed to enable women to combine motherhood and a career, but sustained improvement in the numbers of women entering and remaining in the specialty is problematic. There was in fact a decrease in the number of female consultants in obstetrics and gynaecology during the early 1960s (Lefford 1987). This necessarily raises questions about the *culture* of the profession and that specialty in particular, because it appears that when women do begin to achieve senior status, organizational factors emerge, which limit their numbers.

Third, Donnison (1988: 79) said, 'it was hoped that medical women would take more interest in the diseases of women and children, a department of medicine thought by many not to receive proper attention from the profession'. While women are not reaching senior levels or influential positions in gynaecology in large numbers, the child oriented clinical specialties such as paediatrics and child psychiatry do have relatively high numbers of female consultants. Even so the senior posts are still disproportionately occupied by men (Department of Health 1991/2).

Socialization and the toxic culture

I feel that selection for a place at medical school starts with bias against males – by taking equal ratios of males and females. Many more males apply for medical school than females, and so the chance of a male being offered a place is less than a female.

> (Anonymous male hospital consultant and honorary lecturer attached to a medical school)

Sensible women will want to have a family and this is more compatible with some specialties than others.

> (Anonymous male hospital consultant and honorary lecturer attached to a medical school)

These are two of several quotations revealing thinly veiled misogyny from those entrusted with the training of medical students and junior doctors, of whom half or more are women. The culture of the profession, paradoxically, is both clearly visible and hidden during the five year socialization process at medical school, but it does operate effectively in a number of ways to transmit the inherited value system to medical students of both sexes. The medical school represents a toxic context for women. It reinforces negative gender stereotypes and poor self-image. For example 20.5 per cent of the students surveyed perceived an overall disadvantage for women on the course. This included that 'females are seen to want to give up hospital medicine to have families and end up as GPs' (fifth year woman), and more directly that women were 'treated badly by certain male consultants, being told repeatedly that women shouldn't be in medicine; or made to feel foolish by male medical students; (fifth year woman), or that 'menial tasks are more readily deferred to the female medical students, while "men" talk! Maybe it is pride and arrogance, but after five years of training, I hate being called "nurse"' (sixth year woman). These transmitted values represent the first barriers to women's achievement, but because they are masked, and taken for granted as part of the 'normal' organization of any university department and mirror the arrangement of the profession, there is little awareness of their complex and insidious nature (Nicolson and Welsh 1992).

Organizational structures and gendered practice

Doctors are trained as undergraduates and postgraduates through a mainly 'apprenticeship' model and models and mentors are vital to those who wish to achieve excellence. There is a distinct absence of female role models for young women and men entering medicine, not only because of the scarcity of senior women in the medical profession overall, but also because universities compound this situation. In universities in the UK only 3 per cent of professors are women, 6 per cent of senior lecturers, 14 per cent of lecturers and 32 per cent of contract research staff (AUT 1990). This ratio is exaggerated in science-based subjects such as medicine, which suggests that from their first moments in medical school women and men are unlikely to experience the presence or influence of many women. In our survey of the medical school lecturers, of 67 respondents only 13 (18.8 per cent) were women (Nicolson and Welsh 1992).

Further, the system of informal patronage in the medical profession acts as a barrier to equal opportunities, and this extends down through the profession to medical students (BMA 1993). Senior staff act as mentors to promising students and junior doctors, and women (and ethnic minority groups) are doubly disadvantaged as research on mentoring indicates the effectiveness of same-sex mentor relationships (Richey *et al.* 1988), and because:

> patrons will relate best to those who follow their own image . . . this means that already disadvantaged groups such as women, overseas doctors and doctors of ethnic minority origin, are least likely to benefit from the system, even though they are in most need of support.
>
> (BMA 1993: 1)

There is also evidence from our study that a significant number of senior women do not support other women whole-heartedly, which compounds the problem of scarcity in relation to mentoring and patronage (Nicolson and Welsh 1992).

While there may be no deliberate intent on behalf of medical educators in general to undermine the confidence of female medical students, there is a disregard of the quality of experience for women in particular, so that as in all other traditionally male professions, young women are having to encounter the patriarchal traditions and values through which they judge themselves, are being judged, and will eventually come to judge their patients. This contributes to the phenomenon through which women deny gender as an issue in their careers or their professional judgements (Marshall 1984; Mackenzie-Davey 1993; Nicolson and Welsh 1993).

Examples of how this might happen are common in medical education. Many young women find that in anatomy classes, it is considered acceptable to cut off a female breast and throw it in the waste bin, while penises and testicles are routinely treated with great reverence. Many who have made this observation are ridiculed by anatomy demonstrators (typically recently qualified junior doctors). This practice *per se* debases the female body, while the treatment of students' protests ensures that young women's public acknowledgement of this debasement is curtailed and may lead them to the recognition that they should be quiet about matters relating to the female body.

Another germane example which led to a female student making a successful complaint resulting in a minor disciplinary action, arose when a lecturer discussing obesity, used the final 10 minutes of the lecture to show slides of an extremely fat woman in a bikini, exhibiting a number of 'provocative' poses. When a female student complained that this was both gratuitous in that it contributed nothing to the lecture content and sexist in that it devalued women, the male lecturer publicly humiliated her in front of more than 100 students by accusing her of being humourless. This resulted in anonymous hate letters from other students. This case was dealt with sympathetically by senior people in the medical school through a genuine desire to improve the overall teaching environment for students, and because the student had, unusually, regular contact with an overtly sympathetic female lecturer (the author) which enabled her to set the complaint in motion. Many others who feel uncomfortable or upset by sexist practices do not know what to do or who they are able to trust among the staff and so choose to keep quiet for fear of damaging their future career chances.

This incident was however, merely an exaggeration of the way that female bodies and women are typically viewed in medical school, and while most men, who are in positions of authority, often do not predict what will support or what will offend women, women are similarly unaware of what behaviours are subject to male approval. Male culture contains various forms of etiquette which are commonplace for men and alien to most women, emerging directly from gender role socialization (Archer 1989), and instilled in the normative practices in medical organizations from general practice, hospitals, medical schools, professional organizations and Royal Colleges. These include joining sports clubs, especially rugby, and for professional career purposes, associating with senior colleagues at lunch and after work. As one fifth year female student said,

> there is a lot of chumminess amongst certain male consultants and male students, especially with regard to being members of certain sports clubs. For instance, a male student can afford to miss teaching sessions etc. if he has a quiet word with his consultant who is sympathetic to that sport.

Many women (and some men) are unaware that such activities are construed as 'duty' rather than pleasure, so that many young women would say that they wanted to go to the library and work rather than become involved in these activities, unaware of the formality of the informal associations. Women inclined to enter male domains, such as the consultant's dining room, are likely to be embarrassed by stares, comments and the consequence of eating alone, none of which beset her male contemporaries.

Sexuality and the toxic context

In medical school, as in other larger organizations, the rarely explicit issue of sexuality is always present (Hearn and Parkin 1987). This exists on a number of levels. For example many senior men seem unaware of the ethical, emotional and legal taboos against blatant public comments about women's bodies. Medical students have reported a range of these, from comments to a woman in a seminar about the delightful nature of her legs, to remarks to an overweight woman designed to embarrass. One woman in the sixth year said, 'when I didn't know something, I was told to "stick it up in front of my make-up mirror". It is the casual/unconscious sexism that is so infuriating' (Nicolson and Welsh 1992). These remarks are implicitly endorsed by the establishment, as witnessed in an issue of a university medical school magazine which included regular contributions from lecturers and doctors. The featured 'page 3 style' photograph of a young woman co-existed with conventional news and views from the ranks of the medical school. The picture was titled '. . . fancy that?' with the subtitle 'How we would like Christine to look' (Medsoc Editorial 1991: 5).

The dangers to a woman's career of senior men's perceptions of junior women doctors' and medical students' level of attractiveness often goes unnoticed. Women are socialized into seeing their attractiveness as an important asset (Wolf 1990), and therefore may be pleased when it appears to ensure they have the pick of junior clinical posts. Indeed many young male medical students have complained that middle-aged male consultants are influenced by female beauty which disadvantages the men. 'Some consultants seem to treat attractive female students more favourably than the rest by offering them house jobs when they qualify, not to mention that nearly all of them do well in their clinical exams and attachments when not all of them are good students' (fourth year man) (Nicolson and Welsh 1992). This remark does more to bring the misogyny of male students into focus than detract from the skills and abilities of 'attractive' female students, but it does clarify the way in which women are identified and distinguished in this culture by their appearance. Initially the misogyny in this practice may be masked when the junior woman experiences herself as 'popular'. However, this apparent preference by a senior man for a woman junior colleague does not display itself when women apply for and fail to achieve senior posts. This initial preference undermines many young women's ability to judge the extent and power of patriarchal values in medicine.

Conversely, women who in various ways are not deemed attractive to senior men, may be seen as 'too aggressive' and lose career opportunities because they are not seen as sexually desirable (Hollway and Mukarai 1990) which indicates the extent of the double bind for women in all organizations. This treatment of women by senior men apparently on the basis of their appearance exaggerates the problematic relationships between women in the profession. If appearance has an economic value, then older women who are routinely deemed less attractive by definition are not going to be encouraged to support potential 'rivals'. There are also issues about unethical intimacies and even consensual sexual relationships between lecturers or clinical teachers and students (British Psychological Society 1990) and the problems these may cause for the (usually) female student herself and her colleagues. Sexual contact between a female student or junior doctor and a senior male doctor almost invariably will lead to her being disadvantaged, even though when the relationship is going well she may feel she has access to certain information and knowledge that will benefit her career. As Hearn and Parkin (1987) have observed, it is the woman who will have to resign at the end of an affair.

From larva to queen bee: acknowledging responsibility

In our study 27.3 per cent of the student group and 22.4 per cent of the lecturers reported an awareness of sexual harassment at the medical school which was mainly directed towards women by men and many (52 per cent of the students and 13.8 per cent of the lecturers reporting it) observed it on more than one occasion (Nicolson and Welsh 1992).[4] This is a reflection of wider employment data, in which 42 per cent of women and 14 per cent of men reported some form of uninvited and unwanted sexual attention at work (Forster 1992) and in the broader study of university students in which 25 per cent reported sexual harassment (Sheffield University Students' Union 1992).

The absence of senior women does not only mean the absence of mentors, role models and a generalized female influence, but it also ensures that the gender-power relations characteristic of patriarchy prevail. These favour the young men entering and being socialized into the medical profession, and act to give them psychological and practical priority over the young women in subtle and not so subtle ways (Hansard Society Commission 1990; Hollway and Mukarai 1990; Nicolson and Welsh 1992; BMA 1993). The relative absence of women in mentoring roles in relation to students however represents a paradox. Senior women do not necessarily support junior ones. In the case of sexual harassment in our study it was the *male* staff who were most likely to be aware of and concerned about the sexual harassment of female students and junior doctors. For example:

On several occasions a member of staff has made improper advances at female secretaries.

(man in 30s)

A member of academic staff has made unwelcome advances towards others – firstly a junior doctor, secondly one of the clerical staff.

(man in his 40s; Nicolson and Welsh 1993)

While female *students* were more aware than their male colleagues of sexual harassment both to themselves and to other women, this changed dramatically among the senior staff. Within the senior staff, men were either concerned and aware of sexual harassment or trivialized it. Women were less aware, and only appeared to notice if it happened to them. Concern for the experiences of *other* women appeared to be sadly lacking.

It is this disturbance of what should be natural alliances between women, something that is difficult to disrupt among men, that is of crucial importance to understanding women's experiences in organizations. It reflects the negative influence of patriarchal culture on women's socialization and sense of 'sisterhood'. As women become more senior in the hierarchy, they dismiss sexual harassment as easily dealt with. Thus one woman academic said

a professor of [a particular specialty] department made a stupid (but nasty) remark in an otherwise serious meeting, designed to put me down and prevent me arguing for a particular option in a meeting on departmental policy. Pointless, silly, off-putting, no sexual approach intended, but simply to put me off my stride. It didn't.

(female in her 40s)

A female senior clinician said her experience had been an 'unwanted advance from [a] male colleague – rejected firmly' (woman in her 30s). This change represents a complex socialization process into *coping* which positions women as competent and affirms their distinction from other women who do not cope and are thus not competent. Although it is tempting to dismiss such women as proverbial 'queen bees', what has happened to them is far from advantageous. In the course of managing toxic organizations and coping with overt and covert sexism, they have divorced themselves from a major part of their identity, and although they may not recognize the importance of being a woman through choosing to see themselves as 'a doctor first and foremost' (woman in her 50s), they ignore the fact that the medical establishment still views them as 'other'. There is no way women on their own can counteract the forces of patriarchy.

Women and the boys' club

Women making complaints of sexual harassment and discrimination are routinely humiliated and their working environment is often hostile. While it seems impossible for effective complaints to be made against senior men, complaints against senior women are numerous and well publicized. Wendy Savage, a senior lecturer and honorary consultant in obstetrics and gynaecology was suspended during the mid-1980s for professional misconduct (Savage 1986).[5] Her subsequent analysis of events leading up to and following this affair made explicit the role of gender-power relations in the clinical establishment. Savage attributed her suspension and criticism made of her clinical practice directly to the patriarchal structure of medicine and its operation within her specialty of obstetrics and gynaecology in particular, as well as inherent misogyny operating on a personal level in her health authority. Her account detailed discriminatory processes at several levels – the interpersonal, the organizational and the cultural. There seemed no individual, or structure within the hospital, health authority or Royal College that was not inherently biased in favour of the male dominated status quo. Thus her defence was supported largely by friends, lawyers and patients rather than from within the obstetrics and gynaecology hierarchy. This is not surprising when in the Royal College of Obstetricians and Gynaecologists, male members are invited to join clubs for which membership is limited to selected men alone and women seem unable or unwilling to contest this either by seeking membership or forming parallel associations.

> Excluded from the cosy male get-togethers where, it is rumoured, all the consultant posts are 'fixed', women have formed their own club but it does not seem to be an effective pressure group for women, either as obstetricians or as patients. The incongruity of a specialty devoted to women being almost totally controlled by men has always struck me forcefully.
>
> (Savage 1986: 59)

The level at which policy and practice are organized and the specialty is regulated has an effect that penetrates postgraduate medical education and cannot be eradicated by the introduction of part-time training posts and the acceptance of career breaks. Savage is well aware of the issues of patronage and reproduction of values through recruitment. She cites examples from decision making processes about appointments and pro-motions panels. In one case, a male professor

> weighed in with a vote for 'the chap we know'. It was then that one of the panel mounted an amazing attack on the Australian woman, repeating gossip that she was a difficult woman to work with, con-tinuing innuendo about her personal life which it would be wrong to repeat. I was disgusted by this behaviour and so angry that I could hardly express my disapproval. I left the room abruptly.
>
> (Savage 1986: 24)

Women it seems are evaluated on criteria other than those used to evaluate men. There are recent examples where this is blatantly clear. For example Helena Daly was sacked from a consultant post in 1993 for 'personal misconduct' when it was alleged she had been rude to secretaries and nurses. A letter in the *British Medical Journal* on behalf of the Medical Women's Federation in support of her, made it clear that she had been judged as a *woman* rather than a doctor and that this was a relatively common occurrence.

> The bad behaviour of some doctors is accepted as the norm in a stressful environment. It may even be rewarded with respect and sometimes affection. How different the response if that doctor is a woman.
>
> (Markham 1993: 686)

Women have to cope with this dual assessment – as professionals in competition with men, and as female professionals where they have to be both better than men professionally and feminine socially and professionally. It is a crucial dilemma. It can be no coincidence that apart from Savage and Daly, well publicized professional and personal misconduct cases appear to have women, such as Marietta Higgs or Carole Starkey, at their centre and part of the case against them is that colleagues were afraid to tell them that their practices appeared to be inadequate (see Nicolson 1993). Does this mean that women really are difficult to work with and will not respond to criticism, or are there organizational factors which expose the mistakes of women rather than those of men?

Medical practice is stressful, and consultants have much personal power in the decisions they make, but their decisions and clinical procedure that lead to those decisions are acted out in public through the clinical team. While there is anecdotal evidence to indicate that men are regulated invisibly through a quiet word in the ear, it is equally the case that women are permitted to proceed even though their practices might be, or appear to be dubious – or at least until there is such a potential problem that drastic action such as suspension is required. Women are left vulnerable through exposure which may lead to their downfall at worst or their disillusionment at best.

Constructing experiences of sexual harassment

Sexual harassment will not go away *especially* if it is ignored. Women and men need to acknowledge its existence and recognize its varied manifestations, as well as realize that it is neither harmless nor as easily dismissed as some of the men and women in our study suggested. The behaviours that constitute sexual harassment may be masked or appear less serious than those experienced by women in lower status occupations because they may not appear to be as aggressive or blatant. Professional organizations (e.g. hospitals, universities, legal practices, professional associations, schools) tend to have norms of behaviour which prohibit overt and violent actions as have been reported in relation to the police, fire service and so on. Here sexual harassment is likely to be verbal and low key. Thus the victim's plight is likely to be invisible, and the overall ethos of not rocking the boat will be applied against anyone who complains about harassing behaviour that on the surface is not impinging on the environment. For example, in the case of Anita Hill, the lawyer who brought a case of sexual harassment against Judge Clarence Thomas, there was a public demonstration of ambivalence towards the female victim (Morris 1994).

Frances Conley, a neurosurgeon at Stanford University medical school, who resigned in protest against a persistent sexual harasser being appointed to head her department, is quoted as saying,

> What women put up with in the medical field is more subtle. But it can be just as devastating because it happens far more frequently, it's pervasive, and it's a cultural thing. It's like a ton of feathers. We all get hit daily by a feather of verbal abuse dropping on us.
>
> (Conley in Morris 1994: 111)

Women in medicine believe (often correctly) their careers will suffer if they complain, and thus despite being privileged over the part-time semiskilled workers in material ways, they have potentially more to lose and so keep quiet or at least take anonymous action.

An account in the *British Medical Journal* in October 1992 (Anonymous 1992) was indicative of this. She recalled examples of an older senior male colleague who grabbed her bottom, another similar man who would brush against junior women, enter colleagues' rooms at night, and offer to swap duties for sex. As was the case in our study, this writer also recalled having her complaints that some lecturers' slides or comments were sexist and gratuitous, dismissed, which made it clear to her that the medical establishment was saturated with sexism and sexual harassment, but that there was little support to enable anyone to complain overtly.

Anita Hill suffered sexual harassment and her reputation suffered subsequently, during and after the case she brought. Thomas's staff declared her to be a ' "very hard, arrogant, opinionated" woman who "looked after herself" ' (see Morris 1994: 22). Hill herself became extremely stressed by the court hearing, which she lost.

Women in the professions, by virtue of their relatively low numbers and the dominant organizational/professional ethos are unlikely to get support from a peer group. It is therefore important to acknowledge both that personal assertiveness and organizational mechanisms for dealing with sexual harassment are not adequate for combating the problem; indeed they may result in a culture that dismisses its existence – 'because if it happened we would know about it wouldn't we?'

Conclusions

Women's entry to the medical profession has not proven to be a serious challenge to male power, and the consequent gender imbalance at senior levels and in certain specialties has upheld the traditional culture, obscuring all but the most severe and dramatic discrimination against women as doctors. The current arrangement of the profession where men are dominant in numbers and seniority reinforces patriarchal values which dictate the way that medical culture and knowledge continues to evolve, through what is considered priority. Sexual harassment and discrimination are common and exist on both overt and covert levels, because the relevance of sexual harassment and discrimination to women's experiences of the medical context as toxic remains unacknowledged within the culture. The organization of medicine along these lines ensures that the women who do have successful careers in medicine do not support other women, as they fail to identify gender as an issue in their careers (Marshall 1984; MacKenzie-Davey 1993) or relevant to patient care. The cost of their survival to themselves and others remains as yet unmeasured.

Notes

1 This research was undertaken with my colleague Christopher Welsh to whom I am grateful for both academic and personal support.
2 This was a pilot study with a sample drawn from three groups:
   • female and male students from a medical school which has an equal opportunities admission policy. The student group at the time of this study comprised around 50 per cent women. Eighty-four returned the questionnaire (42 women and 42 men), a response rate of 45 per cent. Mean age of the respondents was 22.4 years ranging from 19 years to 32 (SD 3.163).
   • academic staff in the same university. Questionnaires were sent to 100 people. Sixty-nine (69 per cent) responded. Fifty-six (81.2 per cent) responses were from men, and 13 (18.8 per cent) were from women. The mean age (same for men and women) was in the 41–50 age group.
   • hospital consultants and principals in general practice involved in the clinical teaching of medical students. Four hundred and twelve questionnaires were originally sent out. Responses were achieved from 139 (38.5 per cent) of the sample, of which 111 (79.9 per cent) were from men, and 25 (18 per cent) were from women with 3 (2.2 per cent) not declaring their sex. The mean age of the sample for men was 44 (SD 7.56) and for women 42.7 (SD 6.69).

3 This is the operational definition used in our survey adapted from the University of Sheffield guidelines.
4 This includes the context of the clinical team as well as the lecturing environment.
5 She was cleared of all charges by the inquiry.

References

Anonymous (1992) Personal view: Unprofessional behaviour. *British Medical Journal*, 305: 962.

Archer, J. (1989) Childhood gender roles: Structure and development. *The Psychologist*, 9: 367–70.

Association of University Teachers (AUT) (1990) *Goodwill Under Stress: Morale in UK Universities*. London: AUT.

Benokraitis, N.V. and Feagin, J.R. (1995) *Modern Sexism: Blatant, Subtle and Covert Discrimination*. Englewood Cliffs, NJ: Prentice Hall.

British Medical Association (BMA) (1993) *Patronage in the Medical Profession*. London: BMA.

British Psychological Society (1990) Sexual harassment and unethical intimacy between teachers and trainees: Discussion and Policy. Unpublished document, Division of Criminological and Legal Psychology Training Committee, Leicester.

Dally, A. (1991) *Women Under the Knife: A History of Surgery*. London: Hutchinson Radius.

Department of Health (1991/2) Medical and dental staffing prospects in the NHS in England and Wales 1990. *Health Trends*, 23(4): 132–41.

Donnison, J. (1988) *Midwives and Medical Men: A History of the Struggle for the Control of Childbirth*. London: Historical Publications.

Ehrenreich, B. and English, D. (1979) *For Her Own Good: 150 Years of the Experts' Advice to Women*. London: Pluto.

Eisenberg, C. (1989) Medicine is no longer a man's profession. *New England Journal of Medicine*, 321: 1542–44.

Elston, M. (1993) Women doctors in a changing profession: The case of Britain. In E. Riska and K. Wegar (eds) *Gender, Work and Medicine*. London: Sage.

Forster, P. (1992) Sexual harassment at work. *British Medical Journal*, 305: 944–6.

Hansard Society Commission (1990) *Women at the Top*. London: Hansard Society for Parliamentary Government.

Hearn, J. and Parkin, W. (1987) *'Sex' at 'Work': The Power and Paradox of Organisation Sexuality*. Brighton: Wheatsheaf Books.

Hollway, W. and Mukarai, L. (1990) *The Position of Women Managers in the Tanzanian Civil Service*, Report of the Civil Service Department Government of Tanzania. Bradford: University of Bradford.

Lefford, F. (1987) Women in medicine. Women doctors: A quarter century track record. *The Lancet*, 30 May: 1254–6.

Mackenzie-Davey, K. (1993) Women balancing power and care in early careers: Am I feminine or just one of the lads? Paper presented at the British Psychological

Society's Psychology of Women Section Annual Conference, University of Sussex, July.

MacKinnon, C.A. (1979) *Sexual Harassment of Working Women*. London: Yale University Press.

Markham, G. (1993) When women doctors behave as men. Letter. *British Medical Journal*, 307, 11 September: 686.

Marshall, J. (1984) *Women Managers: Travellers in a Male World*. New York: Wiley.

Medsoc Editorial (1991) *Northwing*. Sheffield: Sheffield University Students' Union.

Morris, C. (1994) *Bearing Witness: Sexual Harassment and Beyond*. New York: Little, Brown and Co.

Moscucci, O. (1993) *The Science of Woman: Gynaecology and Gender in England 1800–1929*. Cambridge: Cambridge University Press.

Nicolson, P. and Welsh, C.L. (1992) *Gender Inequality in Medical Education*, Preliminary Report to Trent Regional Health Authority. Sheffield: Trent Health.

Nicolson, P. and Welsh, C.L. (1993) From larva to queen bee. Paper presented at the British Psychological Society's Psychology of Women Section Annual Conference, Sussex University, 1 July.

Nicolson, P. (1993) Doctoring the records. *Guardian*, 6 September: 11.

Richey, C.A., Gambrill, E.D. and Blythe, B.J. (1988) Mentor relationships among women in academe. *Affilia: Journal of Women and Social Work*, 3(1): 34–47.

Royal College of Obstetricians and Gynaecologists (RCOG) (1991) *A Career in Obstetrics and Gynaecology*, training brochure. London: Royal College of Obstetricians and Gynaecologists.

Savage, W. (1986) *A Savage Enquiry: Who Controls Childbirth?* London: Virago.

Sheffield University Students' Union (1992) *Report on Sexual Harassment*. Sheffield: University of Sheffield.

Smith, D.E. (1978) A peculiar eclipsing: Women's from men's culture. *Women's Studies International Quarterly*, 1: 281–95.

Wolf, N. (1990) *The Beauty Myth*. London: Vintage.

4

Sexual harassment and the working lives of secretaries

HELEN MOTT and SUSAN CONDOR

Cultural constructions of the secretary: femininity, heterosexuality and organizational culture

In the UK more than 10 per cent of all women who work outside the home are currently employed in secretarial or clerical occupations (Office of Population Censuses and Surveys 1994). Most social psychological studies of sexual harassment however, have paid little specific attention to the working lives of secretaries. In fact, social psychologists have rarely theorized or researched sexual harassment in the context of those very domains in which women are most typically employed (including, for example, nursing and primary school teaching). Rather, social psychological studies have been largely confined to analysing the prevalence and the subjective understanding of sexual harassment in one specific context: North American university life. Of the articles on sexual harassment published prior to 1994 listed on the PSYClit database, 88 per cent report research conducted in the USA, and more than 70 per cent report studies using either academic staff or students as respondents. The authors of these reports typically do not reflect on the specific context in which the data were gathered, and often simply present their work as an analysis of sexual harassment *per se*. While there is clearly some utility in treating the sexual harassment and sexual objectification of women as generic cultural (and possibly cross-cultural) practices (Wise and Stanley 1987), it is also important to recognize how these practices may be subject to various forms of local realization. In this chapter we shall consider some of the ways in which sexualization and sexual harassment may be understood in

the specific context of secretarial employment. We shall start by considering general cultural representations of the secretary in the light of theories
about organizational cultures in late modernity. We shall then go on to
describe a study of the way in which a sample of British secretaries
described and accounted for gender inequality, sexual harassment and
sexualization in their own working lives.

Secretarial employment as 'women's work'

There are, on the face of it at least, good reasons for suggesting that an
analysis of the sexual objectification and harassment of secretaries should
be dealt with, if not as a special case, at least with some sensitivity to the
particularities of the working conditions and dominant cultural representations of secretarial employment (see Pringle 1989a; 1989b). The first
thing to note is that although secretarial employment was originally a
male preserve, by the mid-twentieth century the role had come to be occupied almost exclusively by female employees (Anderson 1988; Crompton
1988). UK figures suggest that 99 per cent of people currently working in
secretarial roles are women (Office of Population Censuses and Surveys
1994). In this respect, secretarial work is quite typical of female employment; most women still work in occupations which are designated as
'women's jobs' (Cockburn 1988). It is not simply the case that most of the
people who apply for, or who are appointed to, secretarial work just
happen to be women; it is probably true to say that the female gender of
the employee has become a defining feature of secretarial employment.
The actual work performed by 'secretaries' varies enormously, and can
include typing, clerical assistance, telephone duties, and a wide range of
administrative tasks. There is, however, no single task or responsibility
that identifies a job as being secretarial. The definition of secretarial
employment often seems to rely not so much on what an employee actually *does* within an organization, as the fact that the role incumbent is a
woman. Male employees doing equivalent work are generally accorded
some title other than 'secretary' (Pringle 1989a).

It is well known that 'women's jobs' tend to be both vertically and hier-
archically segregated from work roles typically performed by men (Hakim
1977). In the case of secretarial work, the gender-specificity of employment
is so pronounced that men do not even occupy the higher level positions
within the occupation itself (as is the case in other occupations numerically
dominated by women, such as nursing or primary school teaching; Cockburn 1988).[1] Secretarial work is generally less well-paid and affords fewer
possibilities for promotion than service, clerical or technical roles occupied
by men within the same organizations, and people occupying higher-level
managerial positions still tend to be preponderantly male. However, it
should also be noted that the official status of a secretary within an

organization is often curiously ambiguous. Secretarial work is regarded as a white collar occupation, and secretaries are expected (and often coached) to adopt middle-class demeanour and values which may appear to set them above men working in blue collar roles within the same organization. Moreover, women who work in secretarial roles – particularly those designated as a private secretary or personal assistant – are often constructed as part of a managerial team (Pringle 1989a).

Many academic accounts have suggested that women employed in gender-specific jobs may be particularly likely to suffer sexualized representation and treatment at work. In what has become the classic work on the subject, Catherine MacKinnon (1979: 18) suggested that women who are employed in 'feminized' jobs may be particularly vulnerable to sexual harassment.

> In such jobs a woman is employed as a woman. She is also . . . treated like a woman, with one aspect of this being the explicitly sexual. Specifically, if part of the reason the woman is hired is to be pleasing to a male boss, whose notion of a qualified worker merges with a sexist notion of the proper role of women, it is hardly surprising that sexual intimacy . . . would be considered part of her duties and his privileges.

Even after a decade of feminist activism the situation appeared little changed. Writing in 1988, Stanko similarly commented that, 'being female, in women's work, may in fact be a "set up" for harassment' (p. 95).

The question of the gender composition of occupational roles has been accorded considerable importance in Barbara Gutek's sex-role spillover theory of sexual harassment (see Nieva and Gutek 1981; Gutek and Morasch 1982; Gutek 1985, 1989). Gutek defines sex-role spillover as, 'the carryover into the workplace of gender-based expectations for behavior that are irrelevant or inappropriate to work' (Gutek and Morasch 1982: 55). This, she argues, can result in situations in which women are expected to demonstrate stereotypically feminine qualities which are not strictly relevant to requirements of the job, including situations in which women workers are treated as sex objects: 'When women are propositioned by men at work, touched sexually, or made the object of sexual comments or gestures, that is an indication of a spillover of sex-role expectations and behavior into the work-role' (Gutek and Morasch 1982: 58–9).

Sex-role spillover, Gutek argued, is most likely to occur in two types of work setting with rather different consequences. First, when a woman is employed in a role which is normally held by a man her gender becomes extremely perceptually salient; she is seen first and foremost as a woman, and only secondly in terms of her work-role. The second type of situation in which sex-role spillover is likely to occur is when a woman is working in a traditionally-defined 'woman's job'. In this case, according to Gutek, *the job itself* comes to be seen as essentially feminine. Gutek noted that women who work in these 'women's jobs' may have difficulty perceiving the existence of sex-role typecasting, since the other people doing the same job (who would normally constitute an individual's comparison group) will be treated in much the same way (see also Di Tomaso 1989). Similarly, when a workplace becomes routinely sexualized, this may 'depress the number of behaviors labelled as sexual harassment because workers may become habituated to sexual behavior at work due to constant exposure' (Konrad and Gutek 1986: 424).

Although the sex-role spillover thesis has enjoyed considerable popularity within the social psychological literature there are a number of features of this account which appear somewhat problematic. Perhaps the most obvious problem from a feminist perspective is that the construct of sex-role spillover, as outlined by Gutek and adopted by other researchers since, does not appear to problematize the notion of sex role more generally. In particular, it implies that stereotypes of femininity and heterosexuality may be legitimate ('relevant' or 'appropriate') in other (non-work) contexts. More generally, the sex-role spillover thesis may be seen to rest on a naive Weberian construction of the workplace as a separate public sphere in which human action is (or ought to be) shaped only by formal procedures uncontaminated by personal characteristics, emotions, desires, and informal relationships, all of which properly belong to the domain of private life. The assumption that it may be possible and desirable to maintain a hard and fast distinction between activity that is appropriate to the domain of private life as opposed to the sphere of paid employment tends to distract attention from the multiple and often subtle ways in which the workplace may be routinely and profoundly personalized, gendered and sexualized (cf. Wise and Stanley 1987; Hearn *et al.* 1989; Pringle 1989a; Minson 1991; Adkins 1995). Naturally, it is possible to identify some settings in which the formal requirements of a job are apparently opposed to current norms and habits of gendered and sexualized forms of interaction. A good example is provided in Susan Martin's (1978/1987: 305) interesting account of female police officers in Washington DC, in which she notes how:

> Policewomen face interactional dilemmas because they are both police officers, expected to behave according to norms governing relations among peers, and women who are expected to adhere to the norms governing male–female interaction. The former call for symmetrical interaction among status equals, the latter for asymmetrical relations between superordinate (males) and subordinate (females) with the additional complications posed by sexuality.

In other cases it may be much harder to distinguish the norms governing male–female interaction in private life from those governing the performance of a particular work-role or professional relationship. We shall argue that, in the case of secretarial employment, it may be especially difficult to conceive of the work-role as essentially separable from cultural notions of femininity and heterosexuality (see also Pringle, 1989a, 1989b). In the following pages we shall consider two ways in which the secretarial role may currently be understood. Both of these have implications for the way in which sexual harassment may be viewed in relation to the workplace identities of secretaries.

The secretary as team member

The Weberian (1968) ideal type of bureaucratic life, in which the workplace is occupied by 'cooperative strangers' (Moore 1962: 87) and behaviour is regulated according to impersonal roles and rules, has been superseded by new constructions of corporate life which conceive of the workplace as an arena within which the personal and social needs of the individual should be met (Rose 1990). Since the end of the Second World War increasing emphasis has been placed on informality at work, and on cooperation between employees. A new ethics of management has emerged: one which stresses communication and consultation rather than overt authority and discipline. In the new democratic corporation, work is undertaken by teams of colleagues. Increasingly, workers have come to be treated less as physical bodies or anonymous role occupants from whom labour can be exacted, and more as individuals with feelings and social needs to be met within the workplace. During the 1980s particular stress came to be placed on self-actualization through work, leading to a situation in which paid employment is increasingly 'construed as an activity through which we produce, discover and experience ourselves' (Rose 1990: 103). Whereas previously formal bureaucratic norms may have been antipathetic to friendship and informality among workers and, as a consequence, were inclined to view sexual fraternization as incompatible with productivity (Horn and Horn 1982; Burrell 1984), in the new companionate workplace the pleasure of the worker is viewed as a necessary precondition for productive labour. As du Gay (1993: 14) noted, in contemporary 'post-entrepreneurial' corporations, 'the relations between work life and non-work life and identity – between what is properly inside and what is properly outside the orbit of the organization – are progressively blurred'.

Within the democratic, companionate workplace there is a general commitment to the idea that secretaries should not be treated as interchangeable role-occupants, much less as private servants, that they should be accorded respect and should be able to find their work personally satisfying and rewarding. The secretary may be positioned as part of a cooperative enterprise; we have already noted the way in which secretaries may be constructed as part of a management team. That secretaries themselves may subscribe to this ideology of workplace equality has been discussed by Pringle (1989a) who noted how secretaries – in her terminology – 'misrecognize' hierarchical relations in the workplace. According to Pringle, secretaries often believe themselves to enjoy a reciprocal relationship with other members of the management team which is not, in fact, borne out by a study of actual working practice. We shall be arguing in this chapter that the (potential) construction of the secretary as a colleague may colour her relations not only with management, but with other members of the workforce more generally.

This ideology of the democratic companionate workplace has provided the enabling conditions for the emergence of feminist demands for equal opportunities and opposition to practices which may cause offence to, or impede the self-actualization of, female employees. However, as Minson (1991) has argued, these demands also rely on a Weberian view of corporate life as regulated through a set of formal (possibly legally enforced) regulations in which the personal characteristics (including the gender) of the employee have no rightful place. Minson suggests that the construction of the workplace as an arena within which informality is encouraged and personal needs are met may result in a situation in which it is harder to argue specifically that sexual attentions 'do not belong at work'.

At this stage it is worth noting how many feminist authors seem to find themselves caught between two political stools when they consider the issue of sexual harassment at work. On the one hand, as we have seen, feminist activists may be committed to the idea that sexual activity does not belong in the workplace. On the other hand, feminists have also challenged the idea that there should be no room in the rationalized bureaucracy for emotion or private life. As a consequence, many formal definitions of sexual harassment try to skirt this issue, and end up obscuring the very distinction which they intend to clarify. For example, MacKinnon (1979) whose work did much to promote public recognition of sexual harassment as a legal issue, was keen to emphasize that it was not her aim to repress the free expression of sexuality within the companionate workplace: 'Objection to sexual harassment at work is not a neopuritanical moral protest against signs of attraction, displays of affection, compliments, flirtation, or touching on the job' (p. 25).

A common strategy used to distinguish between legitimate 'compliments, flirtation, or touching' and illegitimate 'sexual harassment' relies on a judgement of whether a particular form of sexual behaviour impedes (or contributes to) any particular woman's self-actualization and pleasure-at-work. A pamphlet by Women Against Sexual Harassment (quoted in Beckett 1994) defines sexual harassment as: 'Unwanted and unreciprocated behaviour of a sexual nature. It is NOT about fun and friendship, but is unwelcome behaviour at work leading to unacceptable employment practice'. One author has gone so far as to suggest that, to the extent that sexual harassment reflects the dominance of masculinity in the workplace, a solution might be to work towards a situation in which women have equal 'rights' to sexual expression at work (Pringle 1989a).

The problem with such formulations is that they essentially bracket the question of the authenticity of female desire, and instead use this as a touchstone against which the legitimacy of a particular social practice may be determined. Moreover, in focusing on the subjective experience of individual women, such accounts fail to engage with those wider political questions concerning the larger-scale social functions of sexual objectification which have informed the work of feminist theorists (e.g. Wise and Stanley 1987). We shall return to this question at the end of this chapter.

The secretary–boss dyad

The second type of account constructs the secretary as working for a single 'boss'. Although this formulation might appear somewhat anachronistic, it is in fact a dominant trope in the discourse of training courses and secretarial skills manuals. For example, in their 1988 text, *Secretarial Skills*, Cornish *et al.* explain to the reader that:

> The word 'girl' is used advisedly – not that we think men incapable of being good secretaries, but secretarial work still tends, in this anti-sexist world, to be primarily a female preserve – and so, for ease of reading and perhaps also for elegance of expression, we shall refer to the secretary as female and the employer, generally, as male.
>
> (pp. 11–12)

Notwithstanding the authors' disclaimer, we can see how in this account (and many others like it) the secretary is positioned as one element in an essentially gendered binary pair: the female-secretary and the male-boss. This construction of a secretary working for a male boss is sometimes used by male managers to enhance their status, but its most overt manifestation is in the discourse of secretarial training schemes and manuals (Pringle 1989a). In the absence of any concrete evidence we can only speculate on the functions that this construction may serve for women who work as secretaries. Rather paradoxically, perhaps, it may raise the status of the individual secretary or typist in her eyes and those of others (the highest status secretarial jobs tend to be those of 'personal assistant'). In addition, the position of working for a single boss affords the possibility of intimacy, patronage, and some level of independence and personal recognition which women working as secretaries often experience as the most pleasurable aspects of their working lives (Pringle 1989a). This individualized representation of both management (*the* boss) and workforce (*a* secretary) may prevent identification between, and collective action on the part of, women working in secretarial roles (MacKinnon 1979). On the other hand, this construction does apparently render explicit those dynamics of power which are often occluded by constructions of the workforce as a team of colleagues. The term 'boss' (who the secretary works 'for' rather than 'with') signals the essentially supportive nature of secretarial work. The identification of the boss with a male figure also potentially renders visible the gendered dimensions of power which, while omnipresent in many workplace settings, are often paradoxically obscured by equal-opportunities rhetoric (Hearn and Parkin 1987).

The positioning of the secretary in an individualized, essentially gendered, relationship with the organization (represented in a form of synecdoche by the figure of the male 'boss') infuses popular understanding of the work performed by, and the character required of, the woman who undertakes secretarial employment. It is well known that the tasks undertaken by the secretary necessitate such feminine attributes as loyalty, modesty, concern for detail, social sensitivity, tact and amicability. Of course, the role of secretary is not unique in this regard. As many commentators have noted, 'women's work' typically requires supposedly feminine characteristics such as 'caring' or 'nimble fingers' (e.g. Cockburn 1988), and women have often been excluded from 'men's work' (including work in science, politics, management and industry) on the grounds that they do not possess the necessary 'masculine' rationality, objectivity or physical strength (Kanter 1975; Eastlea 1981; Mills 1989). In the particular case of secretarial employment, however, this may be given a particular gloss by virtue of the fact that these feminine qualities and activities are understood to be exercised in the context of a specific *interpersonal* relationship between the (female) secretary and her (male) boss. To quote again from *Secretarial Skills*:

> she is a sifter of information, an arranger, a correspondent, a confidante, friend, organizer, stand-in, bulwark against any slings or arrows that come his way. If all this sounds unbearably steadfast, there is another aspect which should be seriously considered: as a secretary there is nothing, absolutely *nothing* which is 'not your job'. If his shoes need cleaning, you must be the shoe-shine boy; if he needs a stitch in time, you must be the needlewoman; if his office is a tip, you must be the charlady. (We have already mentioned that you should probably keep supplies of polishes for furniture, shoes and possibly even silver, needles and thread and a good hangover cure.) Before you are put off forever by visions of scrubbing and cleaning in between letters, let us say that these chores should not be your everyday lot. A secretary is expected to look well-groomed, and you should not be expected to wreck your nails and good clothes by constant requests to do the housework.
>
> (Cornish *et al.* 1988: 99; emphasis in the original)

The topic of physical appearance is mentioned somewhat in passing in this particular quotation. However many academic accounts have emphasized the importance of heterosexual attractiveness in the working lives of secretaries (McNally 1979; Hearn and Parkin 1987; Anderson 1988). Although a formal emphasis on 'grooming' has declined over the past 20 years, it is still common for sections of secretarial courses and training manuals to be devoted to issues of bodily management and attractive self-presentation (Pringle 1989a). Of course, it is not only secretaries who are expected to conform to certain standards of dress and deportment at work. It is common for both male and female workers to be given quite specific direction concerning dress and self-presentation. However, as Adkins (1995) points out, the requirement that employees be 'attractive' (rather than simply 'smart') seems to be peculiarly directed at women. It is worth noting, too, that advice directed to *secretaries* may present the requirement for attractive self-presentation not so much in terms of the need to impress a company's clients or the public as for the private delectation of their boss (cf. Adkins 1995).

The sexualization of the secretary may extend beyond mere injunctions to maintain an attractive appearance. Several commentators have suggested – to borrow Foucault's (1978) terminology – that the body of the secretary is saturated with heterosexuality. Benet (1972: 2) suggested that, 'The first thing that comes to many a man's mind when he thinks about secretaries is sex', and more recently Pringle (1989a: 12) argued that in Australia, the word 'secretary' functions culturally as 'a metaphor or euphemism for sex'. Hearn and Parkin (1987), among others, have pointed to the prevalence of the figure of the secretary in male heterosexual pornography. Once again, the secretary may not exist as a (sexual) figure in her own right so much as constitute one part of a sexual pairing. Pringle commenting on the secretary–boss relationship, claims that 'outside of the sex industry itself it is the most sexualized of all workplace relationships' (1989b: 158).

This profoundly intimacized, gendered and heterosexualized image of the relationship between a secretary and her boss is not confined to male heterosexual fantasy; the secretary–boss couple also figure strongly in women's romantic fiction (e.g. Lindsay 1976). The fantasy of a pleasureable intimacy between secretary and boss may also be presented to secretaries as one of the perks of the job. For example, in their recent manual, *The Professional Secretary*, Spencer and Pruss (1995: 118) inform their readers that:

It is still the case that many male bosses marry their female secretaries, and many bosses leave their partners for their secretaries. If you are spending eight hours or more each day with one person then a bond arises that can lead to friendship, and sometimes to attraction.

Depending on the personal circumstances of you both, this can be positive and healthy, and lead to a 'fairy-tale ending'.

The construction of secretarial employment in terms of a gendered, sexualized personal relationship between a secretary and her boss has implications for the way in which sexual harassment can be understood. In this version of the workplace, the position of secretary is constructed in such close dialogue with contemporary notions of femininity that it becomes virtually impossible to identify sex-role spillover or sexual harassment to the extent that these are constructed as invasions of gendered expectations into an otherwise essentially gender and sex-free zone (see also Pringle 1989a; Minson 1991).

Secretaries and bosses in the democratic workplace: the companionate marriage

Up to this point we have noted the existence of two dominant constructs of the identity of the secretary within the organization. The first places the secretary as one member of a team of colleagues, a worker who attains fulfilment through satisfying labour in an atmosphere of fun and friendship. The second places the secretary in a supportive role, working for a single male boss. Each of these discourses has implications for the way in which the sexualization of working women is manifested. In the 'team member' construction sexual intimacy may be regarded as legitimate in so far as it represents fun between equal-status colleagues. In the 'boss's intimate' construction, the definition of (essentially feminine) secretarial work may be so thoroughly saturated with cultural notions of femininity and (hetero)sex that it becomes hard to sustain any meaningful distinction between sex role and work role.[2] These two, apparently contradictory, constructions of secretarial work are not mutually exclusive points of view; they appear to coexist in many contemporary cultural products and practices. However, it might be oversimplistic to treat these simply as different (competing) linguistic repertoires (cf. Potter and Wetherell 1987). Rather, it is possible to identify at least one way in which these two apparently contradictory versions of the role of the secretary may be reconciled. This involves the deployment of that most prevalent of cultural metaphors through which male–female relations may be understood: the marital partnership.

The 'office-wife' metaphor is a familiar one. It is widely used in social scientific accounts of the role of the secretary within the organization (e.g. Kanter 1977; Pringle 1989a), and its use is also well-established in a range of popular texts including secretarial skills manuals (e.g. *Almost a Marriage*, Sugg 1966) and romantic fiction (Lindsay 1976). It is important to note, however, that the construction of the secretary-wife related through marriage to her boss-organization accomplishes very different symbolic work within these two domains. In the social sciences in general, and the feminist literature in particular, the marriage metaphor is commonly used in conjunction with a Weberian notion of the pure public sphere to draw attention to the abuse of female workers in so far as they are expected to perform emotional, personal or domestic services for their employers. In contrast, in secretarial skills manuals and women's romantic fiction, the secretary-wife metaphor is deployed to rather different ends. Here, it is used to *obscure* the distinction between the world of work and the world of personal life. The secretary-wife metaphor does this work by buying into contemporary ideologies of the companionate marriage – a voluntary union of equals in which the partners are bound together by affective bonds (Mowrer 1930; see Giddens 1990). Viewed through the metaphorical lens of the companionate marriage, support work and personal services to another individual (and, by extension the organization which he symbolically represents) is not necessarily or unambiguously servile. It is ideally (if not always in actuality) one contribution to a mutually fulfilling reciprocal relationship. The companionate marriage provides a face-saving metaphor for the secretary who might otherwise have to embrace a shameful recognition of her subordinate status (cf. Goffman 1963). In the democratic workplace in which employees recognize themselves through 'their' work, to be essentially supporting the work of another is to relinquish any claim to be a person of equal value in one's own right – to enjoy the status of a colleague. The metaphor of the companionate marriage, in which secretary and boss are involved in mutually supportive, satisfying work paradoxically enables the secretary to claim an identity as a person in her own right.

The way in which the secretary-wife metaphor may be used to grant the female secretary a legitimate identity as a productive person (rather than merely a support worker) is manifested most clearly when it draws upon a 'power behind the throne' notion of the role of the wife. The secretary-wife can be presented as the driving force behind the work ostensibly done by her husband-boss. This is nicely illustrated in the words of Pamela Lumb, secretary to the 1995 *Daily Mail* 'Boss of the Year' (reported in *The Guardian*, 15 May 1996): 'Our relationship was similar to a marriage – only without the sex. As long as I let Mr Smith believe he had made the decision over something, I could get him to do whatever I wanted'.

The secretary-wife trope also accomplishes a more general ideological task. It buys into the ultimate romantic fantasy: the dream of achieving personal wholeness through a reconciliation of those aspects of the self fragmented by social relations in modernity. We are all aware of pervasive cultural discourses which present working women as inhabiting fractured, dissonant, identity-spheres. Agony aunts bombard us with advice on how to manage the stress caused by the supposedly incompatible demands of our double identity; advertisements present us as precariously juggling our work roles and personal (or domestic) lives (Condor 1993). Irrespective of whether any secretaries would ever want to marry any of the men they work with, the secretary-wife figure satisfies a general human fantasy of identity completion: the vision of a virtual world in which one may one day come to live happily ever after. The romantic vision offered to women (who may not themselves work as secretaries) is one in which the worlds of work and of personal life are no longer distinguishable. It offers the vision of a fantastic life in which a woman no longer has to struggle to demarcate those aspects of herself and her activities which belong in the office from those that belong at home, and in which she is no longer required to constantly monitor, manage or juggle her appearance and actions accordingly.

Secretaries' accounts of their working lives: discrimination, sexual harassment, and fun at work

Up to this point we have been considering contemporary cultural constructions of the identity of the secretary in the organization. Analyses of cultural products (including romantic fiction, training manuals and feminist writings) do not necessarily inform us directly about popular common sense (see Condor 1997a). In this section of the chapter we shall turn to consider a rather different question – how do secretaries themselves make sense of gender inequality, sexual harassment and sexual objectification in the context of their own working lives?

In the following pages we describe a study in which accounts of these issues were collected from a sample of British secretaries using a self-report questionnaire. This study was originally conceived as part of a multistage investigation in which the issue of the sexual objectification of secretaries would be analysed both through self-reports and through ethnographic observation of interactions in the workplace.

The study

The questionnaire was presented as a survey of secretaries' experiences and relationships in the workplace. It comprised 35 questions (most of which were open-ended) covering a range of topics. Initial questions asked for general information concerning respondents' perceptions of the role of the secretary, their feelings about their present job, their images of the ideal working environment and so forth. Later questions asked specifically about sexual harassment and gender discrimination in the workplace. The final section included questions on the characteristics of their present workplace (number of employees etc.) and personal details of the respondent (age, marital status, political beliefs etc.).

The target population for this study was defined broadly as women who identified themselves as 'secretaries' or as 'typists'.[3] Potential respondents were approached through the companies in which they worked. Care was taken to recruit from a range of organizations and to ensure that no more than two of the organizations were drawn from the same domain of business (e.g. advertising, food retail etc.). Some of the target companies were approached informally, but in most cases initial contact was made by telephone to the personnel officer, public relations manager or director, who was asked whether it would be possible for the 'secretaries and typists' in their organization to participate. In most cases, questionnaires were delivered to the contact-person, and distribution was arranged by them. In order to satisfy respondents that their replies would be treated confidentially, each respondent was provided with a pre-paid envelope, and was asked to post their questionnaire directly to the researchers.

Seventy-one completed questionnaires were returned. One of the respondents was male, but for the purposes of analysis we shall focus only on the accounts of the 70 female secretaries who returned the questionnaire. These respondents' ages ranged from 19–54 years with an average age of 33.4 years. Twenty-four of the respondents described themselves as single, 13 as cohabiting and 33 as married. Of the 46 women who were married or cohabiting, two had partners who were unemployed, 21 had partners employed in white collar occupations and 21 in blue collar occupations. Only seven of the respondents reported having children.

From the women's reports, it seemed that our respondents were currently working under a wide variety of different conditions. Of the 47 respondents who answered the question, 15 worked in an office on their own, 17 shared an office with between one and nine others, eight shared with between 10 and 49 others and seven respondents reported sharing office space with over 50 other people. Of the 56 respondents who gave information concerning the gender composition of the workplace, the 40 women working in white-collar organizations reported working with roughly equal proportions of male and female employees, while the 16 women employed in blue-collar organizations reported a four to one ratio of male to female employees. These data do not, of course, give us information concerning the roles of men and women in these organizations, nor of the actual amount of contact (or quality of contact) that the secretaries had with other male and female employees.[4]

The responses

Gender at work?
Let us start by considering the question of to what extent, and in what ways, the respondents spontaneously alluded to gender as an organizing

principle in their workplaces. When answering the initial open-ended questions about their working lives, the secretaries generally evidenced little appreciation of, or concern for, gendered aspects of their working environment. No respondent spontaneously raised issues concerning sexism or sexual harassment in response to questions such as 'What (if anything) do you like about your job? or 'What (if anything) do you dislike about your job?'. Nor did they raise such issues when describing the types of people they got along with best or worst at work, the characteristics of their ideal boss or colleague or their ideal working environment. No respondent mentioned issues relating to sexual discrimination, sexist treatment or sexual harassment in response to the question, 'What are the best and worst experiences that have ever happened to you at work?'. No respondent at any stage expressed concerns about the dominance of *hetero*sexuality in their workplace (cf. Pringle 1989a, 1989b).

One should, of course, be wary about reading too much into this absence. It could well be that the respondents took the gendered division of the workplace for granted. They may have assumed that the researcher would already know that, as secretaries, they would be in a gender-distinctive work-role. Research has shown that respondents tend not to report things that they assume that the researcher already knows. This is often interpreted in terms of Grice's (1975) 'maxim of quantity' which dictates that an interlocutor should not provide redundant information (see Schwarz *et al.* 1991). On the other hand, it is interesting to note that respondents did tend to mention other 'obvious' aspects of their work-role such as filing, keyboarding, repetitive work and low pay.

It is also worth remembering that the respondents probably read through the questionnaire before starting to answer (and possibly did not answer the questions in the order in which they appeared in the questionnaire). When the respondents answered the initial questions they were probably aware, then, that subsequent questions would ask specifically for details concerning sexual harassment, sexual objectification and gender-typing at work. Hence the respondents may have tacitly assumed that the researcher did not anticipate receiving this information to responses to other questions. Again, this issue – which is sometimes discussed in terms of the 'given-new contract' (Clark 1985) which dictates that, when multiple questions are asked, the questioner requires substantially different information from the answers to subsequent questions – is one which has been discussed at some length in studies of questionnaire and interview design (Schwarz and Strack 1991; Strack and Schwarz 1992).[5]

Sexism at work

The questionnaire contained three items which asked explicitly about sexual discrimination, sexual harassment and sexualization. These were introduced towards the end of the questionnaire for two reasons. First, we hoped that by ordering the questions in this way we might avoid contaminating answers to the more general questions by inadvertently priming the subject of sexual harassment (cf. Strack and Schwarz 1992). As we have just noted, in the event this may have paradoxically contributed to an *underreporting* of gender-related issues in response to the general questions. The second rationale behind the ordering of the questions was that we did not want the study to appear threatening either to the organizations through which the questionnaire was distributed or to the secretary-respondents as members of these organizations. We felt that if questions pertaining to issues of sexism and sexual harassment were nested within a set of more neutral items this might encourage responses, especially from those women who might have been put off by a questionnaire which was apparently solely concerned to elicit reports of sexist practices in the workplace. With hindsight it seems that we were only partly successful in achieving this aim. At the end of the questionnaire the respondents were asked if they had any further comments. The answers given by three respondents indicated that they had interpreted the questionnaire as being primarily concerned with eliciting accounts of sexism. Two of these respondents expressed some concern over this: one commented on a 'bias towards sexual harassment that is not immediately obvious', and one commented that, 'Women do not get a raw deal in the workplace. We can play on our feminism [*sic*] and defend it at our convenience. Being female is good'.

We shall start by considering the answers obtained in response to the most general of these three questions. This question (question 21a) read: 'Do you think that your sex or age affects the way that other people treat you in your job?'. Forty-three respondents answered in the affirmative. However, responses to question 21b ('If yes, in what kinds of ways and why?') indicated that only 25 of these answers pertained to gender rather than to age.[6]

How are we to interpret the finding that only 25 of our respondents reported that the treatment they received at work was in any way influenced by their gender? Leaving aside the unlikely possibility that 65 per cent of our respondents did indeed work with other people who were entirely gender aschematic (Bem 1981; cf. Adkins 1995), there are a number of plausible interpretations of this finding. It is quite likely that some of the respondents might have been simply unwilling to provide an account to the researcher. They may have been fatigued (the questionnaire was, after all, pretty long); they may have thought the answer too obvious to warrant personal testimony, or thought the space provided for an answer too small to begin to give a reasonable account. In particular, it is likely that at least some of the respondents would have been suspicious of the researcher's motives in asking this rather sensitive question. Responses to the open-ended question at the end of the questionnaire indicated that the respondents were – not surprisingly – sometimes confused about the aims of the research and the interests of the researcher. Whereas some respondents appeared to accept our presentation of the study as an attempt to elicit secretaries' views: 'Secretaries rarely get a "voice" – so it made a refreshing change!! Thank you'; others appeared more sceptical: 'Where is the question about the *Littlewoods* catalogue?' asked one respondent (one assumes ironically!). Given that the questionnaires were distributed through the organizations in which the secretaries worked, it would be understandable were they to be cautious about answering a question which might be interpreted as an invitation to voice complaints about their companies. On the other hand, it is worth noting that their responses to the question, 'Can you describe the person or people that you get along worst with at work?' suggested that they were not always disinclined to criticize their colleagues.

A second possibility is that the majority of respondents *were* generally unaware of ways in which their treatment as individuals was dependent upon their gender, or that they lacked the language to translate their tacit awareness into 'discursive consciousness' (cf. Giddens 1986). Feminist politics, epistemology and methodology is often based on the assumption that women's lives afford the ideal standpoint for the analysis of systems of gender inequality (e.g. Harding 1993). This position is summarized in Nancy Hartsock's (1983: 284) much-quoted claim that:

> women's lives make available a particular and privileged vantage point on male supremacy, a vantage point which can ground a powerful critique of phallocentric institutions and ideology which constitute the capitalist form of patriarchy.

However, it is often remarkably difficult for women to see general systems of gender inequality from the perspective granted by their own everyday lives (Kelly *et al.* 1994). Social facts – including facts about gender inequality – often exist at a level of statistical abstraction to which the individual subject may have no direct access. For example, Crosby and her associates have found that people are able to perceive the existence of gender discrimination when data are presented to them in aggregate form, but are unable to see it when the same data are presented case by case (Crosby *et al.* 1989). We shall return to this issue at the end of the chapter. For the time being we should note that, even armed with aggregatory statistics concerning gender-typing, it is still impossible to know how or if any *particular* women's everyday life would necessarily have been different had she been a man. The problem of recognizing which aspects of one's own workplace encounters are coloured by gender may be, as Gutek argued (see pp. 51–2), particularly difficult when the variables of gender and occupation are perfectly correlated. It is reasonable to suppose that individual secretaries might experience difficulty in factoring out the effect of their *gender* from the effect of their being a secretary. As we shall see, even the women who did answer 'yes' to this question tended to present accounts in which the labels 'woman' and 'secretary' were treated as coterminous.

Of the 25 women who did say that they thought that their sex affected the way in which people treated them at work, only one mentioned how this had influenced the work opportunities available to her:

> My sex affects me in that I'm finding it difficult to leave the category of 'secretary' and move to Managerial.
>
> (Angie)[7]

Six respondents referred to working in a 'male dominated' environment, although it was not always clear exactly what they meant by this. In some cases it seemed that this was a reference to gendered relations of power within the organization: 'In a man-dominated environment, women are increasingly "put upon"' (Jackie). However, in other cases it may have been intended simply to convey information about the gender composition of the workforce and the salience of their own sex within it.

Apart from the references to 'male domination', the women who reported that their sex influenced the way in which people treated them at work tended to voice two general complaints. Both of these demonstrate a commitment to the ideal of the democratic workplace in which employees are accorded respect, and are treated in terms of their individual characteristics and abilities rather than as anonymous, interchangeable role occupants (cf. Rose 1990). The first type of complaint drew attention to the way in which the respondent as female-secretary was positioned as inferior:

> A secretary wears a certain 'hat' therefore people react to the position – i.e. a visitor would expect a secretary to provide tea at a meeting – but would not look for it at a meeting of colleagues on the same level.
>
> (Sandra)

> Being a woman, in a predominantly male, technical environment can sometimes be a problem. Some men feel the secretary isn't good enough, they must speak to the boss.
>
> (Nicky)

A common version of this complaint drew attention to the way in which the female-secretary was treated by men as an irrational 'object':

> Being treated as of little intelligence; talked at not with. (They have no idea that I am a qualified teacher with a BEd!)
>
> (Celia)

> A secretary is still expected to be a bit stupid and female so people look at me and treat me accordingly. They soon find out I'm not stupid.
>
> (Alana)

Females are generally thought of as not having a brain – 'blond [*sic*] bimbo'. Women are still thought of as being subservient.

(Sarah)

A lot of the men are chauvanists [*sic*] and think of us as dolly birds who haven't got a brain between us and that we are only at work for them to look at.

(Bev)

Men most often think females are stupid, incapable of stressful work or pressurised work. And are only there to be looked at!

(Liz)

Most of these quotations make some reference to sexual objectification and might be read as an objection to sexualization at work *tout court*. For reasons which will become apparent later, we would resist this simple reading, and would instead suggest that what these quotations illustrate is a resistance to sexualization *in so far* as it takes the form of identity-stripping or 'mortification' (Goffman 1961). It is notable that in all of these instances of (objectionable) workplace sexualization the woman is being spoken (or thought) *about* rather than *to*. As Gruber (1992: 457) suggests, these forms of behaviour 'objectify a woman in a double sense: she is treated as a nonperson, who . . . is not formally acknowledged as a co-participant in social interactions; and her *sexuality*, as opposed to personal or professional characteristics, is the topic of discourse'. Referring back to the last section of this chapter, we would argue that these quotations illustrate a commitment on the part of the women to the ideal of the workplace as a team of colleagues – what our respondents are objecting to is not the experience of being treated in terms of their sexuality *per se*, but the experience of being denied their rights to be recognized as an equal, rational citizen in the democratic workplace.

The second general type of complaint centred on the responsibility for domestic duties ascribed to respondent as female-secretary:

I'm sure I wouldn't be expected to make all the drinks if I was male.

(Ellen)

Being expected to fulfill [*sic*] 'Womanly, wifely' duties. Tea-making, general dogsbody.

(Celia)

Being a woman, I think that men expect you to get coffees (i.e. if a manager comes out of a meeting and asks someone to get coffee for his meeting he is more likely to ask a woman than a man sitting in the office).

(Carla)

These objections are interesting since they suggest that these women have been incompletely ideologically incorporated into the world of secretarial domestic work which, as we have already seen, may be presented to them in training courses and secretarial skills manuals. This is not to say, however, that these women necessarily totally reject the 'office wife' discourse. After all, 'modern' marriages are often seen to involve a 'fair' distribution of domestic chores; in the companionate marriage wives should not be treated as dogsbodies:

> I think it probably still is a male dominated work environment, and a lot of men still like a female secretary to be a substitute for their wives, answering to their whims. However, there are some very nice men nowadays, who treat women as equals.
>
> (Edwina)

Sexual harassment at work
As we have already noted, no respondent spontaneously mentioned sexual harassment when answering general questions about their working environment. This issue was raised explicitly in the third section of the questionnaire, which was entitled, 'Sexual Relations in the Workplace'. The first question in this section reads as follows: 'Do you know of anybody (including yourself) who has experienced sexual harassment at work?', and, 'If yes, can you describe the details?' The question did not specify what was meant by 'sexual harassment' in order that we might see how the secretaries themselves understood the term.

Seventeen of the 70 respondents (24.3 per cent) answered 'yes' to this question. One woman replied 'no', but nevertheless answered the second part of the question ('If yes, can you describe the details?'). In her answer she referred to consensual sexual activity and to gender discrimination in general, and stated explicitly that she was hesitant about applying the label 'sexual harassment':

> Not exactly 'harassment' but in a large company such as this things do happen, but by mutual agreement. Have never experienced harassment personally, but do feel that as a woman you are expected to make the coffee/wash up. Do resent this at times.
>
> (Rosemary)

A few women mentioned instances in which they had been on the receiving end of sexual innuendos and 'personal comments':

> Mine was not of a serious nature. Certain people (men) were making suggestive comments, it took me a long time to pluck up courage to say something because I didn't want to cause too much of an atmosphere in my work place. But basically, I told him in a firm manner that I wasn't happy with what he was doing. On another instance,

someone made a comment about the cloths [*sic*] I was wearing. A union member photocopied an article about harassment at work which identified what circumstances could be classed as sexual harassment, and comments on clothing was mentioned. So I highlighted this part, stuck it on the wall by my fax machine where I knew this person would see it. I work with mostly men and I can have a laugh and a joke and I'm certainly not a feminist. But if a situation ocurrs [*sic*] that you are not happy with then you should say something.

(Claudia)

Once again, although this woman answers the sexual harassment question with reference to an occasion on which she was the subject of 'suggestive comments', she tacitly acknowledges that it might be contentious to frame this as sexual *harassment*. The representation of these instances as sexual harassment is warranted (both in the incident she describes and, by extension, in her account to us) with reference to an 'objective' definition of the term provided in the article given to her by the union member. This little vignette provides suggestive evidence concerning the practical utility of feminist attempts to delegitimate particular forms of activity by defining them as sexual harassment. However, it is also interesting to note that the article to which Claudia refers appears to reify particular *acts* as sexual harassment. It does not appear, in Claudia's rendition at least, to define sexual harassment ultimately in terms of the response of the recipient.

Most of the cases of sexual harassment reported to us involved instances of unwanted physical contact:

Being handled at 18 upon my breasts in a safe, by my manager, and told to keep quiet about it.

(Catherine)

Touching another secretary's bottom. Slapping of female's thighs and bottom. Placing arm around female under their arm with the intent of touching side of breasts.

(Sarah)

Trying to kiss me at parties. Stopping me on the stairs and not letting me pass. Generally touching me and standing real close.

(Liz)

In some accounts the inappropriate nature of the physical advance was signalled by reference to the marital status of one of the people involved:

Escorted back to car. Pushed against wall in car park. Wedding ring thrown on floor.

(Sue)

I do not know if this counts as sexual harassment but about 2 years ago I had a manager who kept on having dreams about me. On the day I left before I got married he found me in a quiet corner and gave me a kiss on the lips and said this was what happened in the dream.

(Jill)

One man in particular (who is married) decided to start making comments on the clothes that I was wearing, whether it be long dresses or short skirts. It got to the point that he said to a colleague of mine that he would like to see me with no clothes on.

(Lynn)

There are three things that we should like to highlight about these responses. First they demonstrate a limited interpretation of the term sexual harassment. The term seems to be applied in the main to instances of sexual assault or to inappropriate sexual advances. We did not receive any accounts of *quid pro quo* harassment (MacKinnon 1979) in which, for example, work advancement is offered in exchange for sexual 'favours'. It also seemed that the women were confining their use of the term sexual harassment to refer to purely sexual approaches, rather than to requests for a relationship (cf. Gruber 1992). Neither did we receive many accounts of the forms of behaviour which are often collectively termed, 'environmental harassment' (such as flirtation, sexual comments, or leering). This is partly explicable by the fact that the following question went on to ask specifically about such matters, and respondents might have assumed that these issues need not be raised in response to the sexual harassment prompt. It is worth noting, however, that neither did we receive any responses which alluded to those aspects of environmental harassment which were not covered by the subsequent question (e.g. the display of pornographic images).

Second, it is worth noting that in several of the vignettes the sexually-harassing act is marked as falling outside established norms of proper social conduct. Sometimes the counter-normative status of the acts was marked with reference to the marital status of one of the parties. In several cases the scene of the action is set in a backstage region (Goffman 1967) away from public view: a deserted car park, a safe, a quiet corner. This is interesting in view of the fact that many ethnographic analyses provide accounts of sexual harassment or 'worker flirting' as a form of public display, occurring in frontstage regions (e.g. Collinson 1988; Konecki 1990).

This leads to our third point: that these accounts focus on discrete, atypical events or incidents. There is little evidence that these women were using the term sexual harassment to mark a personal objection to behaviours which are nevertheless common occurrences in the workplace. The term sexual harassment is typically used by these respondents to signal the fact that a particular act represented an extraordinary disruption to the routine of everyday life. In this respect our data confirm Pringle's (1989a) observation that secretaries tend to see sexual harassment as an exceptional act. Other authors have also noted that there may generally be a low level of workplace tolerance for unwelcomed sexual advances resulting in the situation in which a single instance of a sexual advance may be categorized as harassment, while behaviours which are understood to be relationship advances need to be repeated before they are to be seen as harassment (Collins and Blodgett 1981; Schneider 1982; Gruber 1992). Again, this representation (of sexual harassment as a discrete event) may have been, in part at least, a product of the way in which the question was worded. However, when we consider these three observations together, it does seem that the women who answered this question generally took the term sexual harassment to refer to forms of sexual behaviour which lie outside the realm of normal conduct (cf. Wise and Stanley 1987).

Suggestive remarks at work
The second set of questions in the 'Sexual Relations in the Workplace' section of the questionnaire read as follows: 'Sometimes secretaries and typists talk of things like people at work making sexual comments or suggestive remarks to them, or leering or even touching their bodies. Do any of these things happen to you at work?'; 'If yes, what kinds of things – can you give examples?'; 'How often do you experience this kind of thing?' and 'What do you think about it and how do you deal with or respond to it?'

Nineteen of the women (27.1 per cent of the sample) replied 'yes' to the first part of this question. Responses to the question, 'How often do you experience this kind of thing?' generally gave the impression that suggestive remarks were experienced relatively infrequently. Six respondents answered 'not often', and two respondents suggested they had had a unique experience. In addition, a further six respondents suggested that this was something that they had only experienced in the past: 'Presently – Not at all. In the past – too often'; 'Not often in my new position'; 'Not now (different company)'; 'Every day (used to at other company)'. Only six respondents suggested that they currently received suggestive remarks routinely. Of these, one reported that such things occurred 'regularly', one that they occurred 'weekly' and one reported such things happening '2 or 3 times a week'. Only two respondents said that they experienced suggestive remarks daily, and one woman reported that such things happened 'Every 10 minutes (joke)'.

Were we to accept these reports as direct testimony concerning the extent of environmental harassment we might have some grounds for optimism. Taken together, these responses suggest that environmental harassment occurs fairly infrequently, and it seems that secretaries may change their jobs when they find themselves in an environment in which it does occur (cf. Pringle 1989a). Does this reflect the fact that sexual harassment policies are now having an effect? Although it does seem likely that, by the mid-1990s, the ethics of workplace conduct may have undergone some change, we remain somewhat sceptical that the sexualization of women workers in general, and secretaries in particular, has declined to this extent. Certainly these reports do not square with the findings of some preliminary ethnographic research, which suggests that secretaries are still routinely sexualized in their dealings with the male members of the organizations in which they work (Mott 1993).

So why did so few secretaries report 'sexual comments or suggestive remarks' as a routine occurrence in their working lives? In addition to the factors already mentioned when discussing the underreporting of gender discrimination, it is worth noting that questions which ask for estimates of the frequency of mundane behaviours are notoriously difficult to answer accurately (Schwarz 1990; Burton and Blair 1991). This is partly due to problems of accessing the necessary information (human memory does not normally encode frequency data), and partly due to the fact that routine occurrences are liable to be taken for granted. It is common knowledge in some areas of sociology and social anthropology that events which are habitual or mundane may become functionally invisible (see MacKinnon 1979; Wise and Stanley 1987; Condor 1997b).

Another reason why so few of our respondents reported much experience of suggestive remarks may have been that they were disinclined to be drawn into a discourse which had already been set up as being about (illegitimate) harassment. As we shall see, most of the respondents who *did* say that they had experienced suggestive remarks resisted interpreting them as harassment.[8]

A few women did indicate that they found suggestive remarks at work to be unacceptable or upsetting. For example:

Q: If yes, what kinds of things – can you give examples?
A: Very suggestive comments: I wouldn't mind giving them one. Look at the size of those. If that skirt got any shorter etc.
Q: What do you think about it and how do you deal with or respond to it?
A: Offended, disgusted. Ignore or snap back with a term of rebuff.

(Sarah)

However, most of the respondents who said that they had experienced this sort of behaviour seemed keen to emphasize that they did not regard it as particularly important. Such events might be treated as unexceptional:

I think it is what you expect from some male colleagues. I tend not to react to any comments.

(Denise)

This statement, in which suggestive remarks are dismissed as being 'just what you expect', contrasts vividly with the way in which sexual harassment was commonly presented as an extraordinary act (just what you wouldn't expect).

Sexual comments were often dismissed as 'just silly talk':

> When I worked in a firm of Engineers the majority of staff were male. They would make comments on the length of my skirt or did I have tights or stockings on – that was all – just silly comments – quite harmless – and I just laughed them off.
>
> (Carol)

> Hi gorgeous, spank me, if you say something innocent they will turn it around into a smutty conversation, but they don't mean it. I know for a fact if you said, how about it then, they would run a mile.
>
> (Judith)

Again, this is interesting in the light of the fact that the respondents generally seemed to interpret the term sexual harassment in terms of *actual physical advances*. Even Claudia who (as we noted above on pp. 67–8) did allude to having been the object of suggestive comments in answer to the sexual harassment prompt, suggested that this should not be seen as a serious example of sexual harassment.

It was commonly commented that suggestive remarks should be understood as 'a joke'. Of the 23 respondents who said that they had experienced suggestive remarks, 14 at some stage made some reference to joking or humour. Responses to this question were generally quite terse, and in the absence of context it is rather difficult to interpret exactly what these references to joking were intending to convey. What seemed clear, however, was that whatever other work the joke repertoire might be doing, it almost always signalled to researchers that they should not interpret these events as serious examples of misconduct on the part of men:

> I used to quite often have remarks made, but generally made in a joking manner!
>
> (Rosemary)

> I've only ever experienced any of the above in jest. Nothing serious.
>
> (Paula)

The claim that these jokes are acceptable – nothing serious – was often warranted with reference to the supposed intentions of the men. The jokes were acceptable because they were not *meant* to insult or humiliate the woman:[9]

> It is mostly in fun and not meant to be offensive so you can laugh about it.
>
> (Alison)

This statement – in which remarks which are 'not meant to be offensive' are treated as fun – is quite different to the way in which the respondents described instances of sexualization in which their feelings were not apparently considered (see pp. 67–9).

More generally, it seemed that our respondents were inclined to present sexual remarks as acceptable jokes in so far as they could be read ironically – that is, they did not indicate any propensity towards physical action (which was, as we have already seen, a prominent feature in their accounts of harassment, see also Popovich *et al.* 1992):

> It is only done in a joking way. We get blokes leering and making remarks but they don't mean anything by it. We don't have any touching or anything like that. I think that would be going a bit too far.
>
> (Bev)

> The men make smutty comments, but you know it is only a joke, really they are very protective towards us.
>
> (Sarah)

The presentation of 'leering' and 'smutty comments' as jokes serves two functions in these accounts. First, it renders the acts themselves benign and offers 'moral amnesty' (Zillman and Cantor 1976) to the men whose actions they describe. Research indicates that sexual remarks and behaviours are less likely to be perceived as harassment if they are regarded as complimentary and / or humorous (Gutek 1985; Terpstra and Baker 1987; Bill and Naus 1992). Second, this discursive device serves to justify the fact that the respondents did not describe themselves as challenging this behaviour. In so far as 'leering', 'smutty comments' and the like are recognized as part of a joking exchange, then to treat it in any other way is to risk breaching an important interaction ritual (Goffman 1967):

> Remarks said in jest by male colleagues would not mean to hurt / intimidate and I believe would feel embarrassed if they were taken other than a joke.
>
> (Mary)

It is significant that Mary uses the term 'colleague' in her account, for it would seem that the notion of colleague may be central to the women's acceptance of instances of sexual joking. Taking our data as a whole, there appears to be a general rule whereby cases in which the woman sees herself as the butt of male humour or the passive object of male fantasy are not generally treated as anything to laugh about. However, in so far as the woman is able to situate herself as an active, equal, participant in the interaction – as a colleague among colleagues – the behaviour is dismissed as 'harmless':

It depends on the circumstances. If you're having a bit of fun and joking around with someone you know quite well it seems harmless.

(Edwina)

Jokes are essentially *communicative acts*, and a secretary's apparent acceptance of a joking remark is contingent upon the perception that the remark is directed *to* her, and that she, as a participant, has rights of response. In such cases the joke may be treated as an interactional 'gift' to be paid back in kind (cf. Turner 1971):

I tend to take this as a joke and always criticize something about them.

(Penny)

Usually respond with a fitting humourous [*sic*] remark as I beleive [*sic*] most of it is just fun.

(Jenny)

Only one respondent suggested that women are not always recognized as having full rights of response in these sorts of joking exchanges:

They don't mean anything by it and we give it back anyway. My opinion is, if the men can dish our remarks etc! Then they can take it from us too. Some of the men do get offended as they seem to think that women should be seen and not heard.

(Bev)

However, when we look at the actual details of these accounts it is not always easy to sustain the image that the women were, in fact, participating on equal terms with their male colleagues. None of the respondents gave accounts of situations in which they (or other women) actually *initiated* a joking episode. The episodes they describe all fit with the general observation about power and joking behaviour: that the powerful joke and the less powerful respond; that men joke and women laugh (Coser 1960). In the absence of further evidence it is difficult to know whether these women's accounts do reflect the fact that sexual jocularity is, in fact, seldom initiated by secretaries in the workplace, or whether this is merely a product of the method used to elicit accounts in the present study; the answers which focus on men's action and women's response might simply reflect the way in which the question was worded ('Sometimes secretaries . . . talk of things like people at work making sexual comments or suggestive remarks to them').

Irrespective of whether or not the women actually do engage in sexual joking on equal terms with their male co-workers, there may be good reasons why they should construct the situation as one of mutual banter. A good deal of research has demonstrated the importance of sexual banter in marking and sustaining symmetrical relations between (male) work colleagues (e.g. Collinson 1988), and to the extent that a secretary wishes to be recognized as a full member of a collegial team, she cannot afford to be excluded from this important interaction ritual.

Other evidence derived from the secretaries' answers to the questions about their actual and ideal working environment certainly suggests that the respondents had a general investment in the idea that an acceptable workplace environment might depend upon a culture of compulsory jocularity (cf. Pringle 1989a). Respondents demonstrated a general concern for harmony in the workplace, for 'friendship' and 'fun at work' achieved by a 'sense of humour' and 'having a laugh'. When describing their favoured or ideal boss or colleagues, respondents wrote frequently of 'easygoing' or 'laid-back' workmates:

> An easygoing type of person who is able to fit in well with everyone.
>
> (Martine)

> Easy to get along with, understandable [sic], friendly, easy to talk to.
>
> (Diane)

> Young, easy going, jovial, easy to talk to.
>
> (Nicole)

Joviality was an especially prized characteristic in a workmate. When respondents were asked, 'Can you describe the person or people that you get along best with at work? What is it about them that you especially like or appreciate?' they were more likely to refer to a sense of humour than any other quality:

> My colleague is friendly and has a sense of humour. We both dislike our jobs but are able to joke about our situation which lightens our load.
>
> (Celia)

> Anyone who makes me laugh.
>
> (Lindsey)

> Partners – have a sense of humour, quite understanding. Managers – sense of humour. Department as a whole – quite lighthearted for accountants!
>
> (Carol)

Similarly, in response to the question, 'What would your "ideal" boss (or colleague) be like as a person?' 21 (31 per cent) of the 67 respondents who answered this question specified a sense of humour:

> Easy-going, good sense of humour, committed to job.
>
> (Claudia)

> Someone with a sense of humour and would allow me to set my own guidelines.
>
> (Sandra)

It is important to note, however, that secretaries may be treading a very narrow line in their attempts to be recognized as a colleague rather than as an anonymous role-occupant through accepting and engaging in humorous exchanges. On the one hand, they need to challenge situations in which they regard themselves as being sexually objectified through humour. On the other hand, their recognition as a colleague may depend upon their ability to participate fully in humorous workplace exchanges, which are often sexualized (Mott 1993). In this context, it is worth noting the way in which Claudia (whose account of challenging sexual harassment was quoted on pp. 67–8) found it necessary to append a disclaimer which effectively retrieves her status as a cooperative participant (one of the boys) in routine workplace interaction: 'I work with mostly men and I can have a laugh and a joke and I'm certainly not a feminist'. It is also worth noting that one of the ways in which a secretary may retrieve status as a colleague is by transforming an encounter which is potentially one of sexual objectification into one of banter by asserting a right of reply (as is implied in Bev's account, above).

We might speculate on the interactional dilemmas that may be involved in this kind of facework. Sexual harassment is, as we have noted, typically understood as 'unwelcome' behaviour, and the assertion that a particular act is unwelcome is often warranted on the basis that the behaviour is unreciprocated. According to Sedley and Benn (1982: 6), for example, sexual harassment involves: 'repeated, *unreciprocated* and unwelcome comments, looks, jokes, suggestions or physical contact that might threaten a woman's job security or create a stressful or intimidating working environment' (our emphasis). To the extent that secretaries use engagement in sexual banter as a mechanism for maintaining or asserting their status as a colleague, they necessarily become implicated in this behaviour in a way which deprives them of grounds for subsequently re-presenting the behaviour as unwelcome.[10]

Creating a scene: barriers to the re-cognition of mundane sexual harassment

Up to this point we have been considering the ways in which sexual harassment and sexualization in the workplace was represented in our respondents' accounts. We have noted how (unwelcome) sexual harassment tended to be construed as an extraordinary event which transgressed established norms of appropriate conduct. We have also noted how respondents were generally unwilling to voice an objection to more normative, possibly mundane, forms of sexualization except when they constructed these as mortifying affronts to their status as a full member of the collegial workforce. In the last section we considered the investment that many respondents had in the fantasy of a democratic, companionate workplace sustained through a microculture of humour, including sexual humour.

In this final section we would like to speculate a little more on the ways in which the mundane character of sexualized behaviour in the working lives of secretaries may militate against any individual woman re-cognizing this as unwelcome harassment.

We have already drawn attention to two features of the sexualization of secretaries as *routine* behaviour: that it may often be taken for granted and functionally invisible, and that it may function (and may be understood to function) to maintain smooth, harmonious interaction between colleagues. Many extant feminist accounts suggest that naming routine, taken-for-granted forms of sexualization as 'sexual harassment' may have immediate positive consequences for female employees (e.g. MacKinnon 1979). While we have no objection to this as a political strategy (and, indeed, regard it as an essential task of feminist analysis to problematize that which otherwise might be taken for granted), it is not so clear to us that this re-cognition would have unambiguously positive consequences for individual secretaries in the context of their everyday working lives (cf. Thomas and Kitzinger 1990). We should not underestimate the extent to which it may be difficult, and indeed uncomfortable, for any particular social actor to re-cognize routine forms of social interaction as unwelcome or illegitimate. In the first place, the ability of social actors to function efficiently in complex interactional contexts often depends on an ability to effectively bracket a good deal of what goes on. Although professional ethnographers and ethnomethodologists may (in very particular, selective, contexts) choose to 'make strange' that which is normally taken for granted in everyday life, for the people who are actually engaged in the practical activity under scrutiny, this is often not an option. To 'make strange' aspects of mundane interaction rituals would be both disorienting for the social actors themselves, and (as Goffman has so clearly demonstrated) would radically disrupt the delicate choreography of social interaction. In particular, Goffman (1967: 205) has pointed to situations (significantly termed 'scenes') in which a social actor disrupts the flow of social interaction by 'acting in such a way as to destroy or seriously threaten the polite appearance of consensus, and while he [sic] may not act simply in order to create such dissonance, he acts with the knowledge that this kind of dissonance is likely to result'.

Those respondents in our study who did express an objection to sexualized treatment nevertheless often said that they did not want to 'create a disturbance'. Even Claudia, who told us of her successful attempt to challenge sexual harassment at work, nevertheless emphasized that she had not wanted to 'cause too much of an atmosphere'. In her account she constructed herself as the only potential agent of disruption; the atmosphere caused by the harassment is not mentioned. Many researchers have noted that even when women make formal complaints about forms of treatment which are *generally recognized* to be unacceptable harassment, they often find themselves labelled a 'troublemaker' (Watson 1994) and may find this a worse experience than the harassment itself (MacKinnon 1979).

The potential for causing a scene is even greater when the behaviour under consideration is not a discrete, extraordinary set of events, but is the oil which greases the machinery of 'normal' interaction. In such cases, the potential 'rewards' to a woman even of heroic triumph in challenging workplace sexualization may be even less obvious. Throughout this chapter we have argued that secretaries may have a very tenuous identity in the workplace: their status as a 'colleague' is constantly under threat, and they have a good deal to lose by any action which makes them stand out rather than fit in with normal intercourse among colleagues.

In addition to the general problems which may ensue if individuals try to re-cognize and challenge mundane forms of workplace interaction, this action may be particularly difficult to square with the identity of the secretary. The role of the secretary within the organization is often constructed as that of 'peacemaker'. Like the wifely 'angel in the house', the secretary may be understood as the 'angel in the office', working to maintain harmony in the workplace. For example, an anonymous female secretary quoted in *The Guardian* newspaper (15 May 1996) answered the question, 'How should bosses treat their secretaries?' thus: 'You should respect each other. They can be rude, but you have to put up with that; it's part of the job and it's because they're stressed – you have to unstress them'. It seems then, that it is the responsibility of the secretary to *avoid* 'stress', a role which is incompatible with disrupting routine. This view was shared by many of the respondents who returned our questionnaires. The first question of the questionnaire asked, 'What do you think makes a "good" secretary or typist?'. The good secretary, according to our respondents, possessed such qualities as an ability to get on with everyone; being patient, calm or tolerant; having a pleasant personality; being friendly; being helpful and cooperative; being polite or courteous; being cheerful; possessing tact or diplomacy and a positive attitude. And, of course, the good secretary was seen to have a 'good sense of humour'!

It has been argued that the naming of sexualized treatment at work as 'sexual harassment' may represent a 'therapeutic recognition of . . . pain' (Brant and Too 1994: 7). However, if we bear in mind the way in which the identity of the secretary is constructed and negotiated in a thoroughly sexualized workplace, we should recognize that, in some circumstances at least, the naming of routine, taken-for-granted sexualization as unwelcome harassment may become a cause of pain, and possible mortification, for those individual women who currently work as secretaries, and who achieve a sense of self-worth through the 'good' performance of the role.

Concluding comments – a funny business? Subjectivity and politics: problems for the construction of sexual harassment at work

> A sociology for women must be able to disclose *for* women how their social situation, their everyday world is organized and determined by social processes which are not knowable through the ordinary means through which we find our everyday world.
>
> (Smith 1986: 6)

The feminist project to explore political structures through personal life and subjective experience has entered the social scientific canon through an injunction to expose the mechanics of patriarchy by an attention to women's 'voice' (or, more recently, voices). We have already noted how this has achieved specific realization in political interventions in the workplace when the definition of sexual harassment rests on the question of women's desire: whether or not a behaviour is *welcomed* by the women concerned (Juliano 1992).[11] Moreover, a good deal of feminist research has been predicated on the assumption that the prevalence of, and damage done by, sexual harassment in the workplace may be revealed by asking women to report on their own experiences. Hence, for example, MacKinnon (1979: 26) suggested that women's accounts can tell us, 'what *really* happens to women, not some male vision of what happens to women' (emphasis in the original), and Stanko (1988: 92) has argued that, 'the labelling of a man's behaviour as intrusive, offensive and harassing arises from women's experience'.

In this chapter we have been somewhat more circumspect in our treatment of secretaries' accounts of sexual harassment and sexualization at work. Following the perspective adopted by Griffin (1985) we have tried to take our respondents seriously while resisting the temptation to take their words at face value. We have been wary of assuming that the accounts we collected provide us with direct evidence concerning the prevalence, process and possible psychological and social consequences of the sexualization of women workers. Rather, we have treated the words of the women as *versions* of the workplace provided for us as researchers, which possibly (but not necessarily) reflect the way in which these women do sometimes react to sexualization in the context of their own working lives. We are not assuming that, even if these accounts do say something about women's subjective experiences, this necessarily tells us all we need to know about the process of sexual harassment.

By way of conclusion we would like to discuss the need to maintain a critical distance from the accounts generated by people (either women or men) who are confronting the task of making sense of, and accounting for, their daily lives. In particular, we will question the assumption that sexual harassment can most usefully be defined and studied simply as an event which a woman perceives to be unwelcome. We shall argue that, as far as feminist social scientists are concerned, the construction of sexual harassment as unwelcome behaviour essentially brackets two important problems: the problem of pleasure and the problem of vision.

The problem of pleasure

We have seen in this chapter how the secretaries who answered our questionnaire treated instances of sexualization as unwelcome in so far as they were manifested in physical form, or in so far as they thought themselves to be treated by men purely as sexual objects. In other cases, our respondents suggested that they found aspects of workplace sexualization to be necessary for their own comfort at work. In particular, we saw how the secretaries, on occasions, represented instances of environmental harassment (sexual comments, suggestive remarks and leering) as part of a joking exchange through which they were able to gain recognition as a colleague. Were we to accept many current definitions of sexual harassment, we would be forced to the conclusion that in such cases these acts do not constitute examples of illegitimate 'harassment'. While such a position is attractive in so far as it acknowledges the democratic rights of women as equal active citizens to define their own needs and desires, it remains unsatisfactory in so far as it prevents us from exploring the ways in which wider systems of gender inequality (both within and beyond the workplace) may be sustained through interaction which is acceptable to the social actors concerned, including cultures of joviality and banter (cf. Stephenson, 1951; Emerson 1969; Ullian 1976).

With a few exceptions extant feminist perspectives on sexual harassment adopt a coercive vision of power. Hence, for example, MacKinnon discussed sexual joking at work as a means by which women are 'coerced into tolerance' (1979: 40) of sexual harassment. What this overlooks are those non-coercive forms of social regulation – the regimes of pleasure – to which Foucault (1977) has drawn our attention. To suggest that social behaviour may be regulated as much through the production of desire as through overt 'power over' is not, of course, to argue that women always enjoy their positioning as a sexual object (or even their self-positioning as a sexual subject) in the workplace. It is clear that many women suffer from the experience of sexual bullying, insults and assault. It is also clear that pervasive forms of environmental harassment (leering, teasing, compliments) *can* be experienced, to adapt Sennett and Cobb's (1972) expression, as small 'injuries of gender': potential assaults on a woman's status as a person within the workplace. It is apparent from our data that even when women presented such events as acceptable jokes, they nevertheless often resisted being fully drawn into the construction of the events as humorous. Often respondents seemed to be treating these 'jokes' as something to be tolerated for the sake of a quiet life, something which they needed to accept if they were to be recognized (and to recognize themselves) as a colleague.

Moreover, although we might follow Sacks (1974) and view the women's use of the joke repertoire as a means by which they present a bright side to an otherwise problematic aspect of their daily lives, we can also see a dark cloud behind this silver lining. It is not difficult to identify the counter-themes (cf. Billig *et al.* 1988; Condor 1997a) raised when respondents tell the researchers that environmental harassment 'is just a joke'. Every argument to the effect that 'they don't mean it' also alerts us to the possibility that (in other circumstances) they (or someone else) *might* mean it. Whenever a woman says that men do not mean to offend she tacitly alludes to those familiar situations in which men *do* use sexual comments (in the form of ridicule or abuse) to offend women (e.g. Martin 1978/1987; Mahony 1985). Whenever a woman claims that men's behaviour is 'harmless' she is tacitly acknowledging the possibility of actual sexual assault and violence (cf. Jones 1985). The status of sexual comments as a joke (rather than an insult) may always be pretty tenuous (Lees 1987). However, even when secretaries do not experience sexualization as unambiguously pleasurable (cf. Pringle 1989a) when engaged in the business of managing their everyday lives, they are nevertheless subscribing to a *fantasy* of pleasure at work. They dream of harmony, companionship, and personal recognition as a colleague of equal worth, and it is this which informs their practical, everyday struggle to get on with men.

The problem of vision

It is common for social scientists to distinguish between various sorts of functions that a social act may perform. For example, they distinguish intentions ('manifest functions') from unintended consequences ('latent functions') and distinguish proximal functions (the effects that an act may have in a particular microsocial encounter) from distal functions (wider ideological consequences realized over time and space). When feminists address the problem of 'personal life' they are often as concerned to theorize the latent as well as the manifest functions, the distal as well as the proximal effects of everyday encounters. However, very often the dictum 'the personal is the political' has led authors to assume that the widescale system of patriarchy may be discovered by a simple analysis of the motives of social actors' microsocial encounters. As a consequence, there is a tendency on the part of some feminist theory to neglect to consider the ways in which the system of patriarchy may extend above and beyond the 'lifeworlds' (cf. Habermas 1987) of any individual social actor. This, in turn, can lead to a failure to recognize any potential conflict between the immediate, everyday interests, cares and desires of individual women,

and political activity directed at recognizing, challenging and transforming the wider field of gender relations.

Furthermore, as we have already noted, feminist epistemology,
research and political practice often rely on the assumption that systems
of gender inequality may be transparent to at least some people from the
vantage point granted by their everyday lives. Exactly who it is who can
'see' this is the subject of some confusion. Many theorists assert that it is
women (or other oppressed groups) who are situated in a position from
which the social system is already known, or from which it is at least
potentially knowable. On the other hand, it often becomes apparent in
the process of research that 'women' (or rather, those who answer our
research questions) do not already know about patriarchy (i.e. they do
not perceive the world in the same way as do feminist social scientists).
Feminist theorists may, under such circumstances, suggest that it is the
'dominant social groups' who are able to perceive the way in which the
field of gender relations 'really' operates and that women's vision has
been purposely obscured by men (e.g. Spender 1980) or by a powerful
elite (e.g. Glucksmann 1994). The implication is that the social world is
already known to these others, and that the extant character of social life
attests to the manifest intentions of these all-knowing social engineers.
If this is the case, then it follows that the feminist project (and the
epistemological and political project of all social movements) is confined
to the discovery of that which is already known by those who 'have
power'.

The problem with both of these sorts of formulation is that they fail to
problematize the construct of the social body (in this case the system of
heteropatriarchy) which is the target of its theorizing. However, if we
borrow insights from the work of theorists of modernity, such as Michel
Foucault, Pierre Bourdieu and Anthony Giddens, we may begin to
appreciate how social structures towards which political strategy and
social engineering are directed are not simply 'there' to be seen and
known, or deliberately obscured from vision. Macro-formations of social
life ('gender', 'nation', 'class', 'ethnicity', 'the global market' etc.) might
better be regarded as social constructions. These (temporally and geo-
graphically dispersed) networks of social relations are rendered visible
(and imaginable) through technologies which enable us to map them
across time and over space including, for example, the collection of statistics. Visions of the social body are not available from the vantage point
afforded by everyday life. They are essentially mediated images, constructed by historians, economists, epidemiologists and social scientists.
This is not to say that visions of the social body do not permeate common
sense. There certainly exist many everyday contexts in which social actors
understand themselves as part of an 'imaginary community' (Anderson
1983), attempt to gain a political voice, to struggle over visions of the

social world, to promote fantastic visions of future possibilities, to attempt to implement changes in social life. However, our understanding of the macro-social spheres is not formulated on the basis of some pure, unmediated, 'personal experience'; it is formulated in an ongoing dialogue with expert social visionaries whose job (literally) is to produce and disseminate visions of the social body. In so far as the social world in late modernity is constructed and managed through technologies which allow the vision, and hence the government, of the social body, feminists (and social activists more generally) cannot afford to neglect this aspect of social life in favour of a focus on experientially-based 'everyday' knowledge.

This leads us to consider an ultimate irony which confronts us as feminist social scientists. For many years we have deferred to the voice of everyday experience, we have tried to understand not only sexual harassment but the myriad of pains and pleasures of gender from the point of view afforded by female lifeworlds. There is a tendency for us to value these visions precisely because they are assumed to be uncontaminated by abstract social scientific formulations. In so doing, however, we have time and again found ourselves involved not in a cosy epistemological partnership with the women whose voices we 'listen to', but a bitter hermeneutic struggle as we assert our feminist visions over versions of the world in which sexual harassment is 'just a joke', in which women are 'not oppressed', in which our respondents have 'never experienced discrimination', a world in which 'feminists are wrong' (e.g. Condor 1986; Cotterill 1992; Caplan 1994; Sangster 1994).

Before we attract the charge of autocracy, we should emphasize that we are not suggesting that feminist social scientists and social theorists should warrant their accounts of gender relations in general, and sexual harassment in particular, on the grounds that we possess a virtuous identity: an intellectual or moral superiority over other mortals. What we *do* have is access to the academic powerhouses and the skills needed for operating the machinery by which knowledge of the social body is generated and through which the social body is governed.[12] Social science departments in universities are not so much ivory towers as panopticons – privileged sites for knowing, governing (and materially constituting) the social body. If we accept that our position as social scientists may afford a legitimate – perhaps essential – site for the production of knowledge of the dispersed, dynamic network of relationships which together make up the system that we term heteropatriarchy, we may then be in a position to begin to formulate a feminist account of sexual harassment which does not rely on everyday consciousness, which accepts that desires may be the target (and the outcome) of a network of relations of power rather than a transparent medium through which the oppressive mechanics of patriarchy may be discovered.

Acknowledgements

The authors would like to thank Alan Collins, Charlie Lewis, Celia Lury, Paula Robinson and Mary Smyth for their help with the preparation of this chapter. Of course, this work could not have been completed without the cooperation of the secretaries who agreed to take part in the study and we would like to acknowledge our debt to them for providing us with their accounts of their working lives. The empirical work presented in this chapter was conducted as part of a doctoral thesis by the first author funded by the Department of Psychology, Lancaster University.

Notes

1 It is possible that this exclusion of male employees from the higher-status secretarial posts is not simply a consequence of the fact that few men are identified as 'secretaries'. As we shall see, the higher-status secretarial positions (such as that of personal assistant or PA) tend to be constituted ideologically in terms of female emotional and sexual bonding with an idealized male 'boss'. For this reason, it may be functionally difficult for male employees to inhabit the identity-space of a high level secretary.

2 It is worth noting that the construction of the boss–secretary relationship in terms of an interpersonal intimacy has not always been formulated in dialogue with notions of heterosex. As Minson (1991) reminds us, the term 'secretorie' was originally used to refer to 'a man who writes for his lord' (Day 1599/1967), and was imbued with expectations of intimacy, friendship and (etymologically) secret-keeping between men.

3 With hindsight we appreciate some problems with using this all-inclusive category. Certainly, many of the women who answered the questionnaire were keen to distinguish between 'secretaries' and 'typists'.

4 It was originally intended that this demographic information, and information concerning the working environments of the respondents, would be used to help interpret the data. In the event, responses were generally too small to allow them to be meaningfully broken down by factors such as age of respondent, gender ratio in the workplace etc.

5 To complicate matters still further, we should however recognize that respondents' motives to produce non-redundant answers tend to be tempered by (and possibly conflict with) motives to appear consistent and to maintain a reasonable narrative coherence to their answers. Throughout the questionnaire as a whole, there was evidence that individual respondents often provided markedly similar answers to separate questions (for example, referring to humour, fun, and lack of recognition for hard work, in response to a number of different questions).

6 This distinction between 'age' and 'gender' as separate social categories is somewhat problematic. It is often the case, for example, that sexism is evidenced through prejudice against mid-life and older women.

7 The convention of assigning respondents names rather than referring to them in the text by code numbers has been discussed by Bhavnani (1991). We have adopted the naming convention since we wished to identify particular speakers but found that earlier drafts of this chapter, in which code numbers were used, proved rather difficult to follow. However, cognizant of the political implications of selecting names which appear to 'fit' particular respondents, the names used here have all been borrowed from the friends of the second author, and have been assigned randomly to particular respondents.

8 This is also indicated by the observation that, of the 19 women who had said that they did have some experience of sexual comments or suggestive remarks in the workplace, 10 had (in response to the previous question) said that they had *no* experience of sexual harassment. Once again, this is partly explicable in terms of the specific context in which the questions were asked. It tends to be the case that, when a series of questions are asked, people tend to interpret each question as being linked to the one before it (cf. Grice's 1975 'maxim of relevance'). When this is the case, respondents may be motivated either to appear consistent or to emphasize how the information they are giving in response to a later question is non-redundant (i.e. different from the information they have already given).

9 It is interesting to note that in response to the section of the question which read: 'What do you think about it and how do you deal with it or respond to it?', only *four* respondents actually commented on their own *personal feelings* (e.g. Very angry; I hate it). All of these respondents explicitly constructed their experiences as sexual harassment.

10 This relates to a more general problem involved in the retrospective relabelling of sexualized behaviour as harassment. Gruber (1992) for example, notes that when a real request for sexual intimacy is veiled by humour, it may take some time for a woman to recognize this, and to subsequently recognize the exchange as one of sexual harassment.

11 The focus on the personal harm done to individuals by sexual harassment is also a consequence of the way in which workplace harassment is dealt with in the legal system.

12 This argument, of course, brackets the question of whether all inhabitants of these academic powerhouses would necessarily produce the same sort of knowledge of the social body. While, for the sake of the present argument, we are stressing the importance of particular technologies and activities for feminist visions of the social world, we do not deny that this does not fully solve the problem of the existence of different points of view.

References

Adkins, L. (1995) *Gendered Work*. Buckingham: Open University Press.

Anderson, B. (1983) *Imagined Communities*. London: Verso.

Anderson, G. (1988) The white-blouse revolution. In G. Anderson (ed.) *The White-Blouse Revolution: Female Office Workers Since 1970*. Manchester: Manchester University Press.

Beckett, J. (1994) In and out of view: Visual representation and sexual harassment. In C. Brant and Y. Too (eds) *Rethinking Sexual Harassment*. London: Pluto.

Bem, S. (1981) Gender schema theory: A cognitive account of sex-typing. *Psychological Review*, 88: 354–64.

Benet, M. (1972) *Secretary: An Enquiry into the Female Ghetto*. London: Sidgwick and Jackson.

Bhavnani, K.-K. (1991) *Talking Politics: A Psychological Framing for Views from Youth in Britain*. Cambridge: Cambridge University Press.

Bill, B. and Naus, P. (1992) The role of humor in the interpretation of sexist incidents. *Sex Roles*, 27: 645–64.

Billig, M., Condor, S., Edwards, D., Gane, M., Middleton, D. and Radley, A. (1988) *Ideological Dilemmas*. London: Sage.

Brant, C. and Too, Y. (1994) Introduction. In C. Brant and Y. Too (eds) *Rethinking Sexual Harassment*. London: Pluto.

Burrell, G. (1984) Sex and organizational analysis. *Organization Studies*, 5: 132–45.

Burton, S. and Blair, E. (1991) Task conditions, response formulation processes, and response accuracy for behavioral frequency questions in surveys. *Public Opinion Quarterly*, 55: 50–79.

Caplan, P. (1994) Distancing or identification: What difference does it make? *Critique of Anthropology*, 14: 99–115.

Clark, H. (1985) Language use and language users. In G. Lindzey and E. Aronson (eds) *Handbook of Social Psychology*, Vol 2. New York: Random House.

Cockburn, C. (1988) The gendering of jobs: Workplace relations and the reproduction of sex segregation. In S. Walby (ed.) *Gender Segregation at Work*. Milton Keynes: Open University Press.

Collins, E. and Blodgett, T. (1981) Sexual harassment: Some see it, some won't. *Harvard Business Review*, 59: 77–95.

Collinson, D. (1988) Engineering humour: Masculinity, joking and conflict in shopfloor relations. *Organization Studies*, 9: 181–99.

Condor, S. (1986) Sex role beliefs and traditional women. In S. Wilkinson (ed.) *Feminist Social Psychology*. Milton Keynes: Open University Press.

Condor, S. (1993) Denken over sekse als sociale categorie. *Tijdschrift voor Vrouwenstudies*, 14: 280–94.

Condor, S. (1997a) And so say all of us? Some thoughts on 'experiential democratisation' as an aim for critical social psychologists. In T. Ibáñez and L. Íñiguez (eds) *Critical Social Psychology*. London: Sage.

Condor, S. (1997b) 'Having history': A social psychological exploration of Anglo-British autostereotypes. In C. Barfoot (ed.) *Beyond Pug's Tour: National and Ethnic Stereotyping in Theory and Literary Practice*. Amsterdam / Atlanta: Rodopi.

Cornish, G., Coudrille, C. and Lipkin-Edwards, J. (1988) *Secretarial Skills: A Penguin Self-Starter*. London: Penguin.

Coser, R. (1960) Laughter among colleagues: a study of the social functions of humour among the staff at a mental hospital. *Psychiatry*, 23: 81–91.

Cotterill, P. (1992) Interviewing women: Issues of friendship, vulnerability and power. *Women's Studies International Forum*, 15: 593–606.

Crompton, R. (1988) The feminisation of the clerical labour force since the Second World War. In G. Anderson (ed.) *The White-Blouse Revolution: Female Office Workers Since 1870*. Manchester: Manchester University Press.

Crosby, F., Pufall, A., Snyder, R., O'Connell, M. and Whalen, P. (1989) The denial of personal disadvantage among you, me and all the other ostriches. In M. Crawford and M. Gentry (eds) *Gender and Thought*. New York: Springer-Verlag.

Day, A. (1599/1967) *The English Secretorie*. 4th edn. Gainsville: Scholars Facsimiles & Reprints.

Di Tomaso, N. (1989) Sexuality in the workplace: Discrimination and harassment. In J. Hearn, D. Sheppard, P. Tancred-Sheriff and G. Burrell (eds) *The Sexuality of Organization*. London: Sage.

du Gay, P. (1993) Colossal immodesties and hopeful monsters: pluralism and organizational conduct. Paper presented at The Values of the Enterprise Culture conference, Lancaster, October.

Eastlea, B. (1981) *Science and Sexual Oppression*. London: Weidenfeld and Nicolson.

Emerson, J. (1969) Negotiating the serious impact of humour. *Sociometry*, 32: 169–89.

Foucault, M. (1977) *Discipline and Punish*. Harmondsworth: Pelican.

Foucault, M. (1978) *The History of Sexuality: An Introduction*. Harmondsworth: Penguin.

Giddens, A. (1986) *The Constitution of Society*. Cambridge: Polity Press.

Giddens, A. (1990) *The Consequences of Modernity*. Cambridge: Polity Press.

Glucksmann, M. (1994) The work of knowledge and the knowledge of women's work. In M. Maynard and J. Purvis (eds) *Researching Women's Lives from a Feminist Perspective*. London: Taylor and Francis.

Goffman, E. (1961) *Encounters*. Indianapolis, IN: Bobbs-Merrill.

Goffman, E. (1963) *Stigma: Notes on the Management of Spoiled Identity*. Englewood Cliffs, NJ: Prentice-Hall.

Goffman, E. (1967) *Interaction Ritual: Essays on Face-to-face Behavior*. New York: Anchor.

Grice, H.P. (1975) Logic and conversation. In P. Cole and J. Morgan (eds) *Syntax and Semantics 3: Speech Acts*. New York: Academic Press.

Griffin, C. (1985) *Typical Girls? Young Women from School to the Job Market*. London: Routledge and Kegan Paul.

Gruber, J. (1992) A typology of personal and environmental sexual harassment: Research and policy implications for the 1990s. *Sex Roles*, 26: 447–64.

Gutek, B. (1985) *Sex and the Workplace*. San Francisco, CA: Jossey-Bass.

Gutek, B. (1989) Sexuality in the workplace: Key issues in social research and organizational practice. In J. Hearn, D. Sheppard, P. Tancred-Sheriff and G. Burrell (eds) *The Sexuality of Organization*. London: Sage.

Gutek, B.A. and Morasch, B. (1982) Sex ratios, sex-role spillover and sexual harassment of women at work. *Journal of Social Issues*, 38: 55–74.

Habermas, J. (1987) *Theory of Communicative Action, Volume 2*. Cambridge: Polity.

Hakim, C. (1977) *Occupational Segregation*, Department of Employment [Research Paper No. 9.] London: Department of Employment.

Harding, S. (1993) Rethinking standpoint epistemology: What is 'strong objectivity'? In L. Alcoff and E. Potter (eds) *Feminist Epistemologies*. New York: Routledge.

Hartsock, N. (1983) The feminist standpoint: Developing the ground for a specifically feminist historical materialism. In S. Harding and M. Hintikks (eds) *Discovering Reality: Feminist Perspectives on Epistemology, Metaphysics and Philosophy of Science*. Dordrecht: D. Reidel.

Hearn, J. and Parkin, W. (1987) 'Sex' at 'Work': The Power and Paradox of Organization Sexuality, Brighton: Harvester Wheatsheaf.

Hearn, J., Sheppard, D., Tancred-Sheriff, P. and Burrell, G. (eds) (1989) The Sexuality of Organization. London: Sage.

Horn, P. and Horn, J. (1982) Sex in the Office: Power and Passion in the Workplace. Reading, MA: Addison-Wesley.

Jones, C. (1985) Sexual tyranny: Male violence in a mixed secondary school. In G. Weiner (ed.) Just a Bunch of Girls: Feminist Approaches to Schooling. Milton Keynes: Open University Press.

Juliano, A. (1992) Did she ask for it? The 'unwelcome' requirement in sexual harassment cases. Cornell Law Review, 77: 1558.

Kanter, R. (1975) Women in organizations: Sex roles, group dynamics and change strategies. In A. Sargent (ed.) Beyond Sex Roles. St Paul, MN: West.

Kanter, R. (1977) Men and Women of the Corporation. New York: Basic Books.

Kelly, L., Burton, S. and Regan, L. (1994) Researching women's lives or studying women's oppression? Reflections on what constitutes feminist research. In M. Maynard and J. Purvis (eds) Researching Women's Lives from a Feminist Perspective. London: Taylor and Francis.

Konecki, K. (1990) Dependency and worker flirting. In B. Turner (ed.) Organizational Symbolism. Berlin: Walter de Gruyter.

Konrad, A. and Gutek, B. (1986) Impact of work experiences on attitudes toward sexual harassment. Administrative Science Quarterly, 31: 422–38.

Lees, S. (1987) The structure of sexual relations in the school. In M. Arnot and G. Weiner (eds) Gender and the Politics of Schooling. London: Hutchinson.

Lindsay, R. (1976) Secretary Wife. London: Mills and Boon.

MacKinnon, C.A. (1979) Sexual Harassment of Working Women: A Case of Sex Discrimination. New Haven, CT: Yale University Press.

McNally, F. (1979) Women for Hire: A Study of the Female Office Worker. London: Macmillan.

Mahony, P. (1985) Schools for the Boys: Co-education Reassessed. London: Hutchinson.

Martin, S. (1978/1987) Sexual politics in the workplace: The interactional world of policewomen. In M. Deegan and M. Hill (eds) Women and Symbolic Interactionism. Winchester, MA: Allen and Unwin.

Mills, A. (1989) Gender, sexuality and organization theory. In J. Hearn, D. Sheppard, P. Tancred-Sheriff and G. Burrell (eds) The Sexuality of Organization. London: Sage.

Minson, J. (1991) Bureaucratic Culture and the Management of Sexual Harassment. Griffith University Institute for Cultural Policy Studies Occasional Paper No. 12. Brisbane: Griffith University.

Moore, W. (1962) The Conduct of the Corporation. New York: Random House.

Mott, H. (1993) Sexualisation at work: Everyday verbal harassment. Paper presented as part of Nuffield College Women at Work Seminar Series. Oxford University 26 September.

Mowrer, E. (1930) The Family: Its Organization and Disorganization. Chicago, IL: University of Chicago Press.

Nieva, V.F. and Gutek, B.A. (1981) Women and Work: A Psychological Perspective. New York: Praeger.

Office of Population Censuses and Surveys (1994) *1991 Census. Economic Activity: Great Britain*. London: HMSO.

Popovich, P., Gehlauf, D., Jolton, J., Somers, J. and Godinho, R. (1992) Perceptions of sexual harassment as a function of sex of rate and incident form and consequence. *Sex Roles*, 27: 609–25.

Potter, J. and Wetherell, M. (1987) *Discourse and Social Psychology: Beyond Attitudes and Behaviour*. London: Sage.

Pringle, R. (1989a) *Secretaries Talk: Sexuality, Power and Work*. London: Verso.

Pringle, R. (1989b) Bureaucracy, rationality and sexuality: The case of secretaries. In J. Hearn, D. Sheppard, P. Tancred-Sheriff and G. Burrell (eds) *The Sexuality of Organization*. London: Sage.

Rose, N. (1990) *Governing the Soul: The Shaping of the Private Self*. London: Routledge.

Sacks, H. (1974) An analysis of the course of a joke's telling in conversation. In R. Bauman and J. Sherzer (eds) *Explorations in the Ethnography of Speaking*. Cambridge: Cambridge University Press.

Sangster, J. (1994) Telling our stories: Feminist debates and the use of oral history. *Women's History Review*, 3: 5–28.

Schneider, B.E. (1982) Consciousness about sexual harassment among heterosexual and lesbian women workers. *Journal of Social Issues*, 38: 75–97.

Schwarz, N. (1990) Assessing the frequency of mundane behaviors: Contributions of cognitive psychology to questionnaire construction. In C. Hendrick and M. Clark (eds) *Research Methods in Personality and Social Psychology*. Beverly Hills, CA: Sage.

Schwarz, N. and Strack, F. (1991) Context effects in attitude surveys: Applying cognitive theory to social research. In W. Stroebe and M. Hewstone (eds) *European Review of Social Psychology*, Vol. 2. London: Wiley.

Schwarz, N., Strack, F. and Mai, H.-P. (1991) Assimilation and contrast effects in part-whole question sequences: A conversational logic analysis. *Public Opinion Quarterly*, 55: 3–23.

Sedley, A. and Benn, M. (1982) *Sexual Harassment at Work*. London: National Council for Civil Liberties.

Sennett, R. and Cobb, J. (1972) *The Hidden Injuries of Class*. New York: Knopf.

Smith, D. (1986) Institutional ethnography: A feminist method. *Resources for Feminist Research*. No. 15.

Spencer, J. and Pruss, A. (1995). *The Professional Secretary, Volume 2: Management Skills*. London: Cassell.

Spender, D. (1980) *Man Made Language*. London: Routledge and Kegan Paul.

Stanko, E. (1988) Keeping women in and out of line: Sexual harassment and occupational segregation. In S. Walby (ed.) *Gender Segregation at Work*. Milton Keynes: Open University Press.

Stephenson, R.M. (1951) Conflict and control functions of humor. *American Journal of Sociology*, 56: 569–74.

Strack, F. and Schwarz, N. (1992) Communicative influences in standardized question situations: The case of implicit collaboration. In G. Semin and K. Fiedler (eds) *Language, Interaction and Social Cognition*. London: Sage.

Sugg, V. (1966) *Almost a Marriage*. London: Frederick Muller.

Terpstra, D. and Baker, D. (1987) A hierarchy of sexual harassment. *Journal of Psychology*, 12: 599–605.

Thomas, A. and Kitzinger, C. (1990) Sexual harassment: When it doesn't seem that way. *BPS Psychology of Women Section Newsletter*, 5: 4–7.

Turner, B. (1971) *Exploring the Industrial Subculture*. London: Macmillan.

Ullian, J.A. (1976) Joking at work. *Journal of Communication*, 26: 129–40.

Watson, H. (1994) Red herrings and mystifications: Conflicting perceptions of sexual harassment. In C. Brant and Y.L. Too (eds) *Rethinking Sexual Harassment*. London: Pluto Press.

Weber, M. (1968) *Economy and Society*. Berkeley, CA: University of California Press.

Wise, S. and Stanley, L. (1987) *Georgie Porgie: Sexual Harassment in Everyday Life*. London: Pandora.

Zillman, D. and Cantor, J. (1976) A disposition theory of humour and mirth. In A. Chapman and H. Foot (eds) *Humour and Laughter: Theory, Research and Applications*. London: Wiley.

5

'Femininity' and women's silence in response to sexual harassment and coercion

KATHLEEN V. CAIRNS

Most researchers and clinicians working in the area of sexual harassment and sexual coercion have repeatedly heard statements similar to the following: 'We were in his room talking and he started to kiss me and more and I wanted him to stop but I just couldn't say no. I felt terrible and I hated it', or 'when we had a fight . . . he would still want to have sex. It just seemed easier to give in. I'm not sure how he talked me into it and I did not enjoy any of it yet I didn't or couldn't stop him' (Cairns and Wright 1993: 185).

The fact that such incidents still occur over and over in women's lives should not be surprising; research studies of various types and origins have repeatedly indicated that the occurrence rates for sexual assault, coercion and harassment are high in mixed-gender environments and in both casual and committed heterosexual relationships (e.g. DeKeseredy and Kelly 1993; Fitzgerald and Shullman 1993). A study of students' experiences of unwanted sexual behaviour in university residences (Cairns and Wright 1993), from which the above quotations were taken, also confirmed that behaviours which would be classified as sexual harassment under most current sexual harassment policy standards occur routinely at moderate to high levels of frequency in the day to day activities of the student residences.

What we did find surprising, however, was the fact that we still found a very high frequency and intensity of confusion, self-blame, guilt and shame being expressed by female victims of harassment and coercion in response to these experiences. Apparently, neither the university's various efforts to educate its student body about sexual harassment and sexual coercion (for example 'no means no' campaigns, educational workshops and pamphlets), nor the more general adjustments of sex-role attitudes which the university community as a whole has worked toward (such as reduced sex role stereotyping, greater gender equality, workplace equity programs) had made any serious inroads into changing these young women's feelings and beliefs about their experiences. They continued to describe their experiences of harassment and coercion as 'my fault', 'my responsibility', and to report significant losses of self-confidence and self-esteem because of their 'failure' to defend themselves effectively or to behave in accordance with their personal values by refusing men's unwanted sexual advances.

The descriptions women gave of their lived experience of sexual harassment and coercion portrayed a

> paralysis of will, compounded of obligation, service provision, fear of negative repercussions for refusal, and guilt over having possibly given conflicting messages to the partner, all of which combined to make them unable to say no, though they clearly wished to do so.
>
> (Cairns 1993a: 205)

Women in the residence study almost never reported these incidents to anyone in authority, either through legal channels or through the use of the university's sexual harassment complaints procedures, since they could not feel certain either that they had been harassed or that they were not to blame for the harassment.

If, after all our attempts to educate women about harassment and to establish accessible, non-punitive procedures to deal with it when it occurs, women continue to have trouble applying the term harassment to their own experiences, and if, even when they do label their experience correctly, they do not use the means available to them to combat harassment, then we must consider the probability that we still have not fully understood the nature of harassment and of women's responses to it. If we are ever to succeed in substantially reducing the incidence of sexual harassment, let alone in eliminating it, it seems that we will have to expand our understanding in ways that lead to clearer conceptualizations of the causes of women's silence and self-blame, and to consequent changes in our interventions.

Where can we begin in our search to understand this pattern? How can we explain the frequency with which otherwise assertive and self-confident young women experience this paralysis of the will that makes it impossible for them to say no to unwanted sexual activity? What is it that leaves them unable to explain these experiences to themselves in ways that are not self-blaming and self-destructive and that lead to appropriate reporting?

Feminist researchers and theorists have repeatedly described, over the last several decades at least, several potentially relevant social and psychological processes which may be part of the explanations we need. To date, however, their work seems not to have penetrated to theory and applications in the field of sexual harassment. Instead of focusing interventions on the processes suggested by feminist analyses, we have focused on continuing to ask men to please stop harassing us, on educating them about inappropriate, sexist attitudes and about indicators of women's consent to sex, and on producing study after study to demonstrate that sexual harassment, coercion and assault are ubiquitous in women's lives. When we intervene with women, too, we tend to focus on defining the discrete behaviours that characterize harassment, teaching small groups of women assertion skills, and educating them about their 'rights' to own their own bodies and to refuse unwanted sexual attention.

We have been hoping, it seems, that changes in the behavioural skills of the individual women and men who attend our classes and our skill development groups will, over time, decrease the incidence of sexual harassment. However, the best that can be said for the success of our efforts is that they may have assisted some women on some occasions to resist harassment more effectively. Certainly, we cannot claim that they have had any effect on the rate at which women are called upon to use these skills, that is, the rate at which men practise sexual harassment and coercion, since repeated studies show no reduction in the rates of occurrence for these offences. And, if research is to be believed, these interventions have not replaced women's ambivalence and self-blame with certainty and conviction.

It is possible, of course, that this lack of effect is the result of the sheer scale of the problem in contrast to the resources we have with which to fight it. It is also possible, though, that most of our interventions to date are symptomatic of what Naomi Wolf (1993: 65) calls 'victim feminism'. That is, they place more emphasis on 'preventive behaviours for potential victims than on changing the behaviour of potential abusers' (Desaulniers 1994: 15). Interventions such as assertion training may, in the long term, be inappropriate and ineffective ways to combat harassment for two reasons: first, because they are based on individual skill deficit models for explaining what is actually a systemic problem, thus relying on acceptance of an underlying victim blaming rationale; and, second, because they are based on stereotypical male images of the 'conquering boy and [of] the girl as potential conquest, whose responsibility it is to refuse sex, or (where prevention of AIDS is the focus) to refuse unprotected sex' thus placing stronger emphasis on 'female responsibility than on male attitudes' (Desaulniers 1994: 15).

In an effort to find alternative ways to understand these problems and to focus on effective solutions to them, it may be helpful to review three processes which have been identified, primarily by feminist philosophers and educators, as contributing to women's pattern of silence and self-blame in response to their experiences of sexual harassment, coercion and assault. The intention here is not to identify deficiencies in women's responses which can then be addressed through individual psychological intervention, but to understand that these supposedly 'individual' problems are actually products of systemic discrimination against women, and cannot be usefully addressed by prioritizing victim services.

The first of these processes, the fragmentation of women's sense of self, is an essential outcome of the patriarchal socialization of women, achieved through the imposition on women of a pejorative and restrictive definition of what (not *who*) women are. The second process, the development of a psychology of accommodation in women, reflects the internalized, physical and psychological effects of this socialization, including the embodiment of femininity and the development of a circumscribed sense of personal agency. The third process, which coexists with and adds to the effects of the first two, is women's practice of silence as a form of resistance to patriarchy.

These brief reviews can then be used to inform a discussion about how systemic discrimination produces women's limited responses to harassment, and about how incorporating an understanding of these processes into our thinking and practice can assist us to combat sexual harassment and coercion more effectively.

Fragmentation of women's sense of self

Feminist philosophers and theoreticians have, over the last four decades at least, repeatedly provided analyses of the oppressed condition of women, most of which identify the primary mechanism of that oppression as patriarchy's definition of woman as Other. Beginning with Simone de Beauvoir's *The Second Sex* (1952), we have worked progressively towards developing a clearer understanding of how this status as Other, in a world where male experience is taken as the norm, affects the social circumstances in which we live, and makes the psychology of women indistinguishable from a psychology of the oppressed.

De Beauvoir pointed out that the male-defined disciplines, particularly philosophy, religion and psychology, have, on the basis of their perception of woman as Other, uniformly presented an image of woman as being defined by a lack of 'male' qualities. 'Thus, humanity is male and man defines woman not in herself but as relative to him; she is not regarded as an autonomous being . . . He is the Subject, he is the Absolute – she is the Other' (1952: xvi). As a result of the prevalence of this masculinist world view, she suggested,

It is, in point of fact, a difficult matter for man to realize the extreme importance of social discriminations which seem outwardly insignificant but which produce in woman moral and intellectual effects so profound that they appear to spring from her original nature.

(1952: xxvi)

It is these moral and intellectual effects which men then define as the essence of femininity, and prescribe and enforce within patriarchal culture as appropriate stereotypic female behaviour. Feminist theorists hold that the resulting 'subordination of women by men is the hardest form of group oppression, subordination, or subjection to eradicate and . . . will be the last to go' (J. Mill 1970: 168), because it is 'the archetypal oppression, the one upon which all others are modelled' (Johnson 1987: 6).

The psychological effects of women's status as Other, and of their consequent oppression, are profound and pervasive. Because women are required, from their earliest childhood, to understand that they are less than and subordinate to men, not only in their social value, but in their abilities, their characters, and the accuracy of their perceptions of the world, they learn a sense of 'self as fundamentally deficient' and come to understand that:

In actuality the relation of the two sexes is not quite like that of two electrical poles, for man represents both the positive and the neutral, as is indicated by the common use of *man* to designate human beings in general; whereas woman represents only the negative, defined by limiting criteria, without reciprocity . . . A man is in the right in being a man; it is the woman who is in the wrong.

(de Beauvoir 1952: xv)

Women are made to understand and, to varying degrees depending on their individual experiences, to accept, that:

the masculine always defines the feminine by naming, containing, engulfing, invading, and evaluating it. The feminine is never permitted to stand alone or to subsume the masculine . . . Masculine meanings organize social and personal experience, so that women are constantly imbued with meanings not of their own making about appearance, sexuality, psychopathology, and many other crucial characteristics.

(Kaschak 1992: 5)

It is in the interests of men that women should be brought to share this perspective – to understand themselves as deficient and in the wrong, since the resulting devaluing of self makes them more willing to accept their place in the world of men as an underclass, achieving a limited, fragmented self-acceptance only through enacting the male-defined feminine role appropriately: providing services, including sexual services, to men, and keeping silent about their own oppression.

As Johnson (1987: 18) suggests, 'to be born female in patriarchy is to be born behind enemy lines.' To survive there, women must contend with 'living in a split reality – their own and that of men' (Bartky 1990: 31). In men's world, women are, and always have been strangers, both to themselves and to men, placed outside the male moral community, not entitled to the same rights and privileges that are automatically granted to men simply because they are male. Women's rights, to the extent that we have fought for and won them, are still to be understood as gifts from men which, should male necessity or comfort require it, can be withdrawn, or simply ignored and left unenforced.

This marginalized social and psychological position makes women vulnerable to various forms of abuse both by individual men and by the patriarchal institutions through which women are taught their appropriate places and robbed of their voices (e.g. male organized religion and education). When they are sexually harassed or abused, as virtually all women are at some point, their experiences of violation are marginalized by 'an ongoing discourse that legitimates only those ways of making sense or the telling of only those kinds of stories that do not make men "look bad" ' (Lewis 1990: 477). For example, the language descriptive of men's violence against women is altered to make the perpetrator invisible, or to absolve him from responsibility for his violent behaviour: thus '2,000 women are raped each year' is an acceptable expression, couched in passive language, but 'men rape 2,000 women each year' is active 'male-bashing' (Johnson 1987: 10).

In patriarchy, the fact that masculine experiencing and meanings are taken as the objective standard means that women are exposed to 'constant cultural meta-messages [that] inform [them] that their experience is not real, or that it is wrong or bad, or that it is wrong or bad of them to have their own separate perspectives' (Kaschak 1992: 32). Women are obliged to accept men's definitions of them and to experience themselves as *objects* of men's experience rather than as *subjects* of their own experience. In particular, they must accept a definition of themselves which is focused primarily on woman as body and as the object of male desire. Their definition by men, and their subjugation to them, is further reinforced through various male decisions, practices and rituals, both subtle and overt. Relatively subtle practices and decisions might include the limitations on political parties' identification of female candidates for office, the low priority given to 'women's issues' in the business of the nation, men's refusal to accept equal responsibility for family work, or the day to day constant focus on women's appearance regardless of context. More overt practices include the public, ritual shaming of women in the form of catcalls, lewd remarks and so on which serves to demonstrate the fact that 'any man or group of men feels entitled not only to render a judgement on any woman walking along minding her own business, but also to *announce it to her*' (Kotzin 1993: 167, emphasis as original). In the residence study, students of both genders identified such rituals, as in the following quotations: from a male student, 'If some woman is mean enough to enough guys they will dunk her in the tub (with her clothes on) with ice water. Could reinforce her feelings of inferiority'; and, from a female student, 'pranks or jokes that involve a group of six or seven men against one female . . . [the men] taped her ankles and wrists and threw her in the elevator and pressed all of the buttons on each floor' (Cairns and Wright 1993: 178).

In patriarchy, women are taught to accept that their bodies, their femaleness, their simple presence, are responsible for men's behaviour towards them. It is not only what we do or say, but what we *are* that causes us to be mistreated. It becomes women's responsibility to police themselves, to keep their dress, comportment and presence in public places within approved limits to avoid 'provoking' harassment and assault. Women are encouraged to perceive themselves as intrinsically wrong, as the guilty, shameful ones, and made to 'keep the secrets of men, and suffer abuse in silent shame' (Johnson 1987: 18), just as women who have been victims of sexual harassment usually do.

This immersion in a system that denies women's subjectivity and reduces them to object status is psychologically very expensive. In addition to developing a chronically negative perception of self as defective and deficient, as constantly sending sexual messages to men and therefore as shameful, women live with constant awareness of the contradiction between what *they* think they are experiencing and what *men* tell them they are experiencing. They experience a state of paradox, knowing what they are not allowed to say, and conducting their intimate relationships with men in full awareness that, to be found satisfactory as women, they must keep silent about most of their personal experiencing (Miller 1988). We learn to accept praise for 'weaknesses' and to be silent about our strengths and our anger. Under these conditions, it is, as Kaschak (1992: 157) points out, virtually impossible for a woman to 'attain untarnished praise and purely positive self-esteem.'

Women's psychological state under patriarchy, then, is one of 'anguished consciousness . . . an inner uncertainty and confusion' as she attempts to live with 'double ontological shock: first the realization that what is really happening is quite different from what appears to be happening, and second, the frequent inability to tell what is really happening at all' (Bartky 1990: 14). The fragmentation of women's sense of self, and their consequent confusion about how to understand their experiences, are products of patriarchy and constitute essential elements in its maintenance and preservation. The resulting 'chauvinized' woman is likely to be eminently controllable, because she has been taught to control herself. Confused, hurt, demoralized, ashamed, choking down her anger, she is 'eager to please, worried about her weight' (Bartky 1990: 14). She lives 'in a chronic state of bribery and intimidation combined' (H. Mill 1970: 137). Psychologically disempowered, she has been taught to apologize, to distrust and deny her own experiences, thoughts and feelings and to put men's needs ahead of her own. Often she either does not know, or cannot say, what she wants, because for a woman to have serious personal wants is selfish, and to announce them is often dangerous. Her not knowing is, of course, then attributed to her natural deficiency and inadequacy, her femininity. It is proof that she needs to be told what she 'really' needs and wants by male partners and by male experts.

The psychology of accommodation

The goals of gender socialization in a patriarchal system are to produce clearly differentiated, heterosexual men and women who conform to the stringent requirements of their sex roles. This process aims at the development of a psychology of entitlement in men, to support a strong sense of separate individuality, and a psychology of accommodation in women, to support a sense of self which is focused on facilitating the lives of men, and on obtaining and keeping their approval and good will, and which has self-sacrifice as its prime directive.

The psychology of entitlement prepares men for a life of unexamined, and, to individual males, largely invisible privilege in every sphere of life. It demands that males be independent, self-sufficient, autonomous, and focused on building a sense of self which is independent of relationship. The emphasis for entitlement is on personal mastery, power, and the negation of 'feminine' aspects of self in order to avoid any appearance of effeminacy or homosexuality. As a result of this socialization process, few adult men are capable of fully intimate, mutual relationships with others (Jordan 1987; Bergman 1991). The implications of entitlement for the sexual psychology of men include a tendency to experience women primarily as sexual objects. It is generally not the intention of an entitled person to engage in a mutually enjoyable sexual relationship such as might occur between equals; rather, it is to get the woman to comply with what he believes he needs or wants (Jordan 1987). Because the entitled male is attending more carefully to the woman's qualities as a sex object than to her relationship messages, he is likely to overestimate her interest in sex and to perceive her relational signals as indicators of sexual readiness (Muelenhard 1988).

In contrast, the development of a psychology of accommodation in women requires first the fragmentation of the sense of self and then two additional processes which are built on the uncertainty generated by the first: the imposition of embodied femininity, and the reduction of women's sense of personal agency or will.

The embodiment of femininity

Iris Young (1990), in her essay 'Throwing like a girl' describes how women's awareness of their bodies as objects in the culture of men, and of themselves as *shameful* object rather than autonomous subject, becomes embodied and, consequently limits women's physical, psychological and sexual possibilities. Just as the task of learning a first language shapes the physical structures of speech and makes any second language learned after a critical period likely to be accented, for most women, learnings about how to be appropriately feminine are written into their bodies and minds in childhood, limiting their future physical and psychological possibilities.

Learning to experience her body as 'a thing at the same time that she experiences it as a capacity' (Young 1990: 147) is intrinsic to the process of the embodiment of femininity. Women learn to see their bodies as 'fragile thing[s], which must be picked up and coaxed into movement . . . that exist as *looked at and acted upon* . . . thing[s] like other things in the world' (Young 1990: 150, emphasis as original). This perception is reinforced through the constant incidents of physical objectification contained in women's day to day experiences. They learn to move their bodies in ways that take up a minimum of space, to take short steps, to rigidly control the use of their arms and their manner of sitting, avoiding any posture that may be considered vulgar. These bodily habits and positions then announce to the male observer the weakness, physical ineptitude, passivity and narrowly expressed sexuality that are required for acceptable femininity. At the same time, they become 'embedded in every aspect of the body and of the mind' (Young 1992: 48) until eventually:

> Everything about a woman is both grounded in and defined by her female body and, in particular, its sexuality, defined in masculinist society as the ability to arouse, rather than to experience, desire. The measure of woman's sexuality is man's tumescence. What about her is arousing and even whether she intends to arouse, is also designated by the male . . . His feelings become hers, his desire her desirability, his admiration her measure of worth, his disdain her degradation, his ridicule her humiliation.
>
> (Johnson 1987: 55–6)

While the content of the required embodiment of femininity may change across culture, custom and time, the fact that it always represents a male-defined ideal remains constant, since in patriarchy women's bodies are part of the aesthetic environment of men, owned by men and not the possessions of women. The male-prescribed ideal female body in North America currently is thin, hairless, youthful, graceful, physically fit but smooth, soft and silent. Women who do not exhibit these qualities, or who are not preoccupied with trying to achieve them, those who 'escape or transcend the typical situation and definition of women in various degrees and respects' (Young 1990: 144) are labelled unattractive, clumsy, awkward, masculine, lacking self-control, and so on.

The implications of the embodiment of femininity for female sexuality lie in the reduction of women's access to knowledge of self as sexual, the undermining of their identification with their bodies, and the loss of direct access to sensory information through the imposition of a chronic spectatoring position. Women in patriarchy are likely to experience 'a strong tendency to a particular sort of disconnection from their own bodies and their own cognitive / affective / physical experience – that is a tendency to watch themselves through male eyes' (Kaschak 1992: 112).

Michelle Fine also suggests that, 'constriction of what is called [female] sexuality allows girls one primary decision – to say yes or no – to a question not necessarily their own' (1988: 34). The decision about what answer to give to this male question is itself difficult since, as a result of women's 'failure to know themselves as the subject of their own sexuality', they may have difficulty in making decisions about their sexual behaviours and experience that would be healthy for them. 'Struggling not to know or feel her own desire [and knowing] that she "should" say no, [she may] end up having sex "happen" to her' (Tolman 1991: 65). As a result of these embodiment pressures, the experience of male persistence and coercion is complex for women. They experience strong ambivalence and uncertainty about refusing male advances. In the residence study, for example, while it was not a usual part of male experience to engage in unwanted sex due to a woman's persistence or coercion, either within committed relationships or in casual encounters, this pattern was very commonly reported by women in continuing relationships. Although they felt demeaned by such encounters, women expected to have to provide sex as a condition of relationship maintenance with men, and accepted that this 'duty' was not mitigated by their own lack of sexual interest at the time (Cairns 1993a).

All of these problems are further exacerbated by patriarchy's ambivalence about female body functions such as menstruation, lactation, and childbirth. The general atmosphere surrounding these normal processes is characterized by secrecy, control and sanitation, as if women's bodies were naturally dirty and embarrassing. Girls are discouraged, especially at puberty and subsequently, from undertaking physically challenging behaviours that might 'disfigure' their bodies by the development of muscle, or cause them to appear unfeminine by sweating, grimacing or showing other consequences of physical exertion. Their attention is drawn to the male view that they appear ridiculous in sports because of the movement of their developing breasts, and so on. They are kept ignorant of the physical abilities they possess and prevented from forming a strong sense of the body as competent.

Confronted with sexual harassment or coercion, women educated about their bodies through patriarchy are likely to have difficulty experiencing their bodies as their own, even after being 'told' through education that they have the 'right' of ownership. This kind of message, usually given to girls too infrequently, too late, and with too many caveats, cannot be expected to overcome a lifetime of indoctrination into a very different conception of self. We should note that, in contrast to common practice with women, no one feels obliged to tell or try to convince men that their bodies belong to them, since any other conclusion would be patently ridiculous. They need not think of themselves as 'owning' their bodies; they *are* their bodies and everyone assumes this to be the case.

Reduction in women's sense of agency

It is particularly difficult for women, under these conditions, to develop a strong sense of a personal capacity to take action to affect their environments, except in instances where such action can be seen as an effort on behalf of others. To be acceptable, women's agency and achievement, as Carol Heilbrun points out, must usually be 'authorized by that spiritual call to an achievement or accomplishment in no other way excusable in a female self' (1988: 23). Similarly, women 'do not dare to offer themselves as models, but only as exceptions chosen by destiny or chance' (Heilbrun 1988: 25).

The patriarchal view of women's 'nature', and their assignment almost exclusively to Other-oriented roles, has historically been labelled normative by psychology, with the result that its 'consideration of how women develop has been in terms of how well women adjust and function within their restricted roles' (Franks 1992: 28). Self-assertion or strength of purpose is generally reframed in women as selfishness, and as damaging to the well-being of men and children, since women's obligations to and responsibilities for others are expected to override self-interest. The preservation of the female sex role requires that the formation of an agentic sense of self be punished rather than encouraged, so that women will learn to base their self-esteem on sacrifice of self for others. In essence, 'as long as *anyone, anywhere* is suffering, women are selfish to mention that they are suffering too ... everything and everyone should come before women' (Rockhill 1987: 319, emphasis as original).

When women have the responsibility to act as agents on behalf of others, as they often do, especially with reference to children and care of the aged, they cannot usually use this responsibility as an avenue for developing a sense of an effective self. First, service behaviour is held to be 'natural' for women; they cannot expect to be rewarded for what are considered to be 'natural' female behaviours. Second, the services they are expected to perform (housework, childcare) are repetitive, omnipresent, incapable of permanent completion, and are socially devalued. Where some sort of systemic solution could be conceived of for a particular problem, such as child poverty, women do not usually have the power or the resources to get the problem taken seriously, let alone to implement the solutions. Their situation is similar to that of a person moving water from the well to the house in a bucket with a hole in the bottom. They are expected to cope; complaints are redefined as nagging or whining, and there is no money for new buckets.

Women's sense of personal agency is further undermined by the virtually complete absence from public discourse of any positive mention of women's contributions to the creation of our cultures and institutions. They are prevented from seeing the effects of their foremothers' contributions and from establishing role models for agency, while being led to believe that the history of scientific, artistic and social achievement is entirely male. Even women's suffering, such as might be clearly seen in an account of the politics of birth control through the ages, is not part of male-defined history and is therefore not talked about, written about, or presented in educational curricula. In contrast:

> Men's ordeals are recounted and described and depicted in every conceivable way in every media on earth, and have been from earliest history ... [women] are always asked to look at and to listen and to understand and sympathize with men's pain and suffering ... [but] any time women say, 'Look what is happening to us!' someone invariably rises up on the spot – as patriarchy has trained us well to do – and shouts, in order to divert us, frighten us, to remind us of our vulnerability and danger: 'But what about *men*?'
>
> (Franks 1992: 19)

Obstacles to the development of women's personal agency also occur in the day to day interactions of women with the individual men in their lives. The sense of self as subject is achieved through interaction with others, not through isolation. One of the functions of relationship, for men and for women, is the provision of a caring listener: someone who will listen and make an effort to understand, thus enhancing the clarity of the speaker's message and furthering the development of the speaker's sense of self (Jordan 1987). In men's lives, relationships with women are especially productive of male individuality, since women are men's 'designated listeners'. However, listening is not usually reciprocated in women's relationships with men; for women, relationships with men are more likely to be reflective of the personhood of the man and less likely to further the personhood of the woman.

Because of these limitations on women's development of agency, the use of standard psychological concepts such as self-esteem, self-concept, body image, locus of control, assertion, personal boundaries, autonomy and so on to discuss women may obscure, rather than clarify, their experiences. Such constructs, drawn from a male psychology of the male person, pre-suppose an individual acting as an agent. That is, they are formulated from the entitlement perspective and assume that the subject has the free-dom and resources to enact a personalized vision of self. Their use to describe women's experience ignores the reality that most women do not have such freedom or such resources. Rather than being liberating, the use of these terms is, at worst, a straightforward continuation of victim blam-ing, and, at best, an illusory statement of an ideal. Such terminology also emphasizes psychology's efforts to develop supposedly missing skills in specific individuals, usually women, at the expense of focusing on the need for systemic, institutional change. If we must focus on individual change, where are the comparable terms that would describe male skill deficits? Where are the groups teaching men empathy, mutuality skills, and whole-body eroticism, for example? In fact, there is little or no evi-dence that either males or females in sexual harassment contexts are lack-ing skills – they may, in fact, be well able to demonstrate the required skills in other contexts. It is more likely that, in sexually coercive contexts, they either do not consider the specific skills to be applicable at the time or they anticipate sanctions for using them.

Women's learned silence as resistance

Some writers suggest that there is an additional element which may contribute to women's silence in the context of harassment and coercion. They suggest that this pattern may reflect not the absence of knowledge, or a wish to resist, but the absence of 'that hope of success, without which complaint seldom makes itself audible to unwilling ears' (J. Mill 1970: 118), a lack of hope for a positive outcome in response to self-expression. Per-haps the clearest presentation of this view is made by Magda Lewis (1993). She suggests that a harassed or coerced woman does not speak her objec-tions or her refusal because she knows that she will not be taken seriously; she knows that, according to the patriarchal script, she is expected to pro-vide a sexual outlet for the man. She goes along with his use of her body, but refuses to verbally accept it. As long as she has not said yes, has not given her full consent, some part of her is reserved in resistance, in refusal to go along with the cultural expectation that she will *willingly* provide the service. She does provide it, because not to do so would be too expensive, but she will not cooperate in it. She will remove herself from the situation as an agent and remain only as object.

To speak in this situation would only be

> to demonstrate our willingness to participate in the covering over of the scars of our lived subordination . . . to [agree] to participate in the greater exclusion of women from a discursive space that never allows the speaking of our history, our present, or our future; she would be agreeing to participate in creating the illusion of speaking.
>
> (Lewis 1993: 35)

She also points out that,

> The power of phallocentrism may undermine our initiative, it may shake the foundations of our self-respect and self-worth, it may even force us into complicity with its violence. But it cannot prevent us from knowing. Nor do women need to be taught the language through which to speak what we know.
>
> (Lewis 1990: 484)

This pattern may be particularly prevalent in established male/female relationships, where women often feel that their consent is, 'constrained by [a] felt duty to be cooperative, to meet the man's needs, not to be "inconsistent", or to accept a sexual duty towards a man with whom [they are] having a close personal relationship' (Cairns 1993a: 205). Many women in the residence study described interactions with male sexual partners where their refusal went unheard and they simply learned, over time, not to bother expressing it. These women made comments such as:

> My ex-boyfriend always expected me to sleep with him even when I told him I didn't want to . . . no matter what I said he thought he could convince me to get 'in the mood' and wouldn't stop 'til I gave up, so I usually did. I guess I thought he would be mad at me if I didn't . . . he never realized I was really upset.

> [H]e took advantage of me one night after we broke up, I was really drunk so I didn't fight back. I just retreated inside. I felt it was my fault. I let him do it. I mostly keep to myself now.
>
> (Cairns and Wright 1993: 174)

What is required if women's silence is to become unnecessary is that women should live in a context where speaking does not require a choice between betrayal of the other and betrayal of the self, where the truth is accepted rather than punished. Under patriarchy, we speak the truth about our lives only to ourselves, or in whispers to one another.

The effects of these processes on women's responses to sexual harassment and coercion can be clearly seen in female victims' expression of confusion about their role in causing the harassment they experience, about what their reactions to men's unwanted advances and comments should be, and about whether their complaints are valid and can be talked about. Sexual harassment is one form of de Beauvoir's 'outwardly insignificant social discriminations', to which women are exposed through constant 'small, mundane and cumulative incidents committed by ordinary men' (Larkin 1991: 106). This chronic form of harassment occurs much more commonly, and probably causes much more damage to women, than do the dramatic, single incidents on which most attention tends to be focused. Sexual harassment, sex-role stereotyping and sexual coercion are most accurately characterized as being intrinsic to mixed-gender environments. They are a part of the 'normal' day to day interactions between men with women in patriarchal culture, as ever-present and as invisible as the air we breathe, precisely because they are essential to the process of keeping women down.

Patriarchy, as a system of power relations, mounts a constant and unremitting assault on girls' and women's sense of self, producing confusion, demoralization, and ultimately complicity in their own subjugation. Its assaults on women's self-esteem 'are difficult to detect just because they are ubiquitous. They are micro-assaults; they occur every day, everywhere' (Bartky 1990: 170). Custom hardens us to these assaults and deadens our capacity to resist them, replacing the intention to act with demoralization and confusion.

Modern psychology, in the absence of a careful consideration of how 'such issues as discrimination, unequal opportunities, violence against women and other forms of oppression . . . affect women's development', has historically provided a description of women 'that affirms, rather than questions, women's reduced and limited status' (Franks 1992: 28). Naomi Weisstein (1993), in her critique of psychology and psychiatry as disciplines based on the fantasy lives of their male practitioners, argues that: 'there isn't the tiniest shred of evidence that these fantasies of [women's] servitude and childish dependence have anything to do with women's true potential' (p. 197).

When women have turned to psychology for assistance with problems such as depression, anxiety, eating disorders or problems coping with harassment, they have, in effect, been looking to their enemy for assistance. The solutions they have been offered have largely been medication to dull their pain and various forms of treatment drawn from a psychology of entitlement and based on assumptions about women's behavioural or moral deficiencies.

While current work in the psychology of women discusses aspects of the silencing of women, we have yet to develop psychological practice that fully implements feminist theory. Until recently, the development of feminist psychological theory has been largely limited to work on alternative formulations of developmental psychology (e.g. Belenky et al. 1986;

Miller 1988; Brown and Gilligan 1992), attempts to rework masculinist theory in ways that revalorize 'feminine' characteristics and strengths (e.g. Chodorow 1978; Jordan *et al.* 1991), and blends of psychology with religion into 'spiritual' and body-oriented approaches (e.g. Laidlaw and Malmo 1990).

These efforts have been important. They have led to improvements for women through collaboration among feminists from many backgrounds to establish victim services such as the shelter movement, to affirm the reality of women's experiences of sexual abuse and other forms of violence, to outline their profoundly negative effects and to begin to take women seriously as subjects of their own lives. In the case of interventions for sexual harassment, assault and coercion, however, patriarchal resistance to women's progress has been particularly strong, with the result that our interventions have become narrowly focused on epidemiologic studies and on victim services.

Systematic sexual harassment and coercion are invisible to most men because, for them, they are merely a 'natural' way of being in the world, and because to see and acknowledge their presence would oblige men either to give up power or to have it become overt, in which case it could no longer be effectively denied. When sexual harassment is drawn to their attention and they *do* see it, men are generally unable or unwilling to grasp its importance. Forms of harassment such as sexist language and practices in the workplace that women describe as degrading, demeaning, humiliating and sometimes infuriating, are redefined by men as 'a joke', as 'natural male–female behaviour', 'a misinterpretation' or 'just a bit of fun' (Larkin 1991: 107). Women's perceptions of harm, assault and humiliation are assumed to be mistaken, and are attributed to their inability to achieve objectivity, to their oversensitivity to small matters, to their lack of a sense of humour and so on.

Since men's and women's attitudes towards and experiences of sexual harassment remain profoundly discrepant (Cairns 1993b) and since the male experience tends to be reflected in the organizational and administrative view of patriarchal institutions, 'chilly climate' factors become almost impossible for women to 'prove', let alone address. If women persist long and hard enough in their complaints, or if decision-making bodies reach a critical mass level of female membership, some circumscribed changes may be made. Typically, however, these changes are subsequently resented, ignored, sparingly enforced, burdened with endless legalistic and procedural requirements, and named in ways that imply that they are heavy-handed limitations on men's rights and freedoms (e.g. 'politically correct', 'reverse discrimination'). Women's equality, or even their approaches to it, look unfair to men. As a result, women must continue to defend their modest gains at a considerable cost in time and energy, or find themselves back at the starting post.

Other usual tactics used by patriarchal institutions to avoid systemic change include diverting our attention, and their own, from the quality of life for women in general and from the need for systemic change, by presenting the view that sexual harassment, coercion and assault are only a series of individual cases, decontextualized as isolated instances of abuse committed by aberrant men. Simultaneously, popular media presentations and news programmes tend to focus on stories about sexual harassment, coercion and assault which incorporate role reversals, making men the victims and women the perpetrators of harassment (e.g. *Fatal Attraction*, 1987; *Disclosure*, 1994). These approaches allow victim-blaming to continue while simultaneously claiming that 'Women do these things too. It is a human problem, not a male problem', and feeding the apparently endless appetite of male culture for stories of female sexual humiliation and abuse that eroticize women's fear and suffering. They also serve to keep women busy attempting to obtain justice for wrongs committed against individual women, and focusing their scarce resources on one-woman-at-a-time prevention strategies.

These processes add discouragement and despair to women's already strong uncertainty about defining the harassment they experience. They also reinforce and reward women's silence by making it part of demonstrating loyalty to and protection of their oppressors. Women know very well that on the other side of men's pressure for them to accept male definitions of their experience are the omnipresent threats of reprisals for disagreement. Sexual harassment, coercion and assault are central weapons that men use routinely to keep women 'in our place'. While women wait for equality to arrive, they buy their marginalized lives with silence and loyalty to men, and, in the process, are forced to collaborate with their oppressors, reinforcing their self-hatred and confusion in the process (Bartky 1990).

There have been enormous improvements to women's quality of life in this century – the right to vote, the right to be considered legal 'persons', to practice birth control and to access more freely some forms of education – all of these represent giant steps forward for us. Women also have more political power than ever before, though this change has yet to translate into the critical mass of women legislators needed to change government priorities. More women are economically independent of men, though their salaries are often still inequitable. These changes owe a great deal to the earlier waves of the feminist movement, but they are also symptomatic of the fact that patriarchy is failing for other reasons. In the new world economy, for example, no industrialized nation can afford not to utilize its entire population or to have 'throwaway' children. Just as, in the periods immediately following the two world wars, women were essential to nations' capacities to sustain themselves and to compete, we are essential now. We are at 'an open moment' when, if we choose to do so, we can bring our own power to bear on an oppressive system and see its centre of gravity irrevocably shifting towards our full equality (Wolf 1993: xxxvi). This time, with this next wave of feminism, and with the strengths and resources our foremothers bought for us with their lives, we must not back down.

Implications

'It is still much more acceptable for women to complain about what they don't have than to start to propose ways to take hold of what they need' (Wolf 1993: xx). To fight free of our embodied oppression, we need to understand that, now more than ever, our task is no less than to create a 'viable feminist pedagogy of transformation' (Lewis 1990: 467), a 'politics of personal transformation' (Bartky 1990). The feminist revolution will not be complete until women can

> be whole and strong and rise up in that *power that comes from deep within, from knowing who and why we are,* and say, conclusively, 'Stop this wickedness at once. We will not stand for it one more second.'
> (Johnson 1987: 14, emphasis as original)

It is through the development of that certainty of self as subject, as active agent, through anchoring our feet in the history of women that we will come to a place where we 'no longer regard [ourselves] as a living, breathing battlefield where one is damned if one does and damned if one doesn't' (Kotzin 1993: 171). We must become, and remain, aware of the politics of bribery and intimidation practiced by patriarchy against women, so that neither works as effectively any longer, and we must pass that awareness on to other women, to our daughters, to the men who love us, and to our sons. We must remember Hannah Arendt's observation that 'if we do not know our own history, we are doomed to live it as though it were our private fate' (Heilbrun 1988: 71).

For these goals to be achieved, feminist scholarship needs to become much more accessible to girls and women. Our work, of all kinds, needs to be published in the popular press and included in public school curricula. We must also combat the endless presentation of women as victims in the media by publishing and presenting stories of women triumphant: the stories of women who have successfully resisted patriarchal femininity.

Another part of this process is the necessity to return to strengths of the earlier stages of this wave of feminism which, at least in the case of the learnings that are necessary to combat sexual harassment and coercion, we may have left behind too soon. In particular, we need to return to consciousness raising as a form of mutual support and as a way to reach clarity of understanding of the tactics used to keep us down.

We must begin to tell the truth, in groups, to one another. Modern feminism began that way, and we have lost, through shame or fear of ridicule, that important collective phenomenon.

(Heilbrun 1988: 45)

There is still a need for this kind of work, since, for women to develop a strong sense of self and combat the demoralization that follows from their oppression, they must first

acknowledge, then struggle with, and repeatedly work through their feelings about the prejudice and discrimination they experience as women in order to achieve authentic and positive feminist identity.

(Lewis 1990: 695)

We should make every effort to ensure that some of this work goes on through the use of feminist pedagogy with young women in primary and secondary education settings (Brookes 1992), rather than keeping it limited to campus environments.

Another important avenue towards which we should direct more attention if we wish to see meaningful reductions in sexual harassment and coercion is feminist activism and scholarship in the field of sexuality education. Sexuality education 'goes to the very core of personal identity, human relationships, the meaning of life and of love' (Desaulniers 1994: 17), and can provide women with 'the opportunity to gain awareness of their sexual identity and to construct their lives as women . . . to appropriate their sexual identity' (Desaulniers 1994: 13). One of the reasons for the strong, organized opposition to sex education in schools is certainly the fact that sex education for girls is 'an heir of the feminist and social movements' (Desaulniers 1994: 15). We should take our lesson from this opposition; wherever it is strongest we are likely to find critical issues for the dismantling of patriarchy and the freeing of women. Part of the process of influencing sex education is the need to ensure that its curriculum, not simply as prescribed but as actually *taught*, recognizes the history of power relations between the sexes and discusses its current manifestations (Frank 1990: 3).

We should also further explore other, non-traditional approaches to improving women's connection with their bodies, to supplement the work of the 1970s on improving women's knowledge of their reproductive systems. The focus now should be on the role of physical challenge, especially in the teenage years, in women's development of a strong, more separate sense of self. Some studies indicate that women who are less burdened by the limitations that traditional femininity imposes on their use of their bodies may use physical challenge as a means of individuation and identity building (McDiarmid 1994).

In the face of all this work, we must still maintain our support of individual women who have the courage to confront their harassers. No woman should be left to fight such a battle without a team of women to act as her advocates, her place of safety and validation. But we must also involve these women in the continuing struggle to eliminate these problems from the lives of their friends and sisters as well as from their own lives, so that our work with individuals supports our collective efforts.

References

Bartky, S. (1990) *Femininity and Domination: Studies in the Phenomenology of Oppression*. New York: Routledge.

Belenky, M., Clinchy, B., Goldberger, N. and Tarule, J. (1986) *Women's Ways of Knowing*. New York: Basic Books, Inc.

Bergman, S. (1991) *Men's Psychological Development: A Relational Perspective*, work in progress #48. Wellesley, MA: Stone Center Working Paper Series.

Brookes, A. (1992) *Feminist Pedagogy: An Autobiographical Approach*. Halifax, NS: Fernwood Publishing.

Brown, L. and Gilligan, C. (1992) *Meeting at the Crossroads*. Cambridge, MA: Harvard University Press.

Cairns, K. (1993a) Sexual entitlement and sexual accommodation: Male and female responses to sexual coercion. *The Canadian Journal of Human Sexuality*, 2: 203–14.

Cairns, K. (1993b) Sexual harassment in student residences: A response to DeKeseredy and Kelly's study. *Journal of Human Justice*, 4: 73–84.

Cairns, K. and Wright, J. (1993) A survey of unwanted sexual attention in the University of Calgary residence complex. Unpublished report to University Housing, Calgary NS, March.

Chodorow, N. (1978) *The Reproduction of Mothering*. Berkeley, CA: University of California Press.

de Beauvoir, S. (1952) *The Second Sex*. New York: Alfred A. Knopf, Inc.

DeKeseredy, W. and Kelly, K. (1993) The incidence and prevalence of woman abuse in Canadian university and college dating relationships. *The Canadian Journal of Sociology*, 18: 137–59.

Desaulniers, M. (1994) Becoming women: Female students and sexuality education. *Canada's Mental Health*, 42: 13–18.

Fine, M. (1988) Sexuality, schooling and adolescent females: The missing discourse of desire. *Harvard Educational Review*, 58: 29–53.

Fitzgerald, L. and Shullman, S. (1993) Sexual harassment: A research analysis and agenda for the 1990's. *Journal of Vocational Behavior*, 42: 5–27.

Frank, B. W. (1990) Reflections on men's lives: Taking responsibility through sexuality education programmes. *SIECCAN Newsletter*, 25: 2–7.

Franks, B. (1992) Developmental psychology and feminism: Points of communication. *Women's Studies Quarterly*, 1 and 2: 28–40.

Heilbrun, C. (1988) *Writing a Woman's Life*. New York: W.W. Norton & Co.

Johnson, S. (1987) *Telling the Truth*. North Amherst, MN: The Crossing Press.

Jordan, J. (1987) *Clarity in Connection: Empathic Knowing, Desire and Sexuality*, work in progress #29. Wellesley, MA: Stone Center Working Papers Series.

Jordan, J., Kaplan, A., Miller, J., Stiver, I. and Surrey, J. (1991) *Women's Growth in Connection: Writings from the Stone Center*. New York: Guilford Press.

Kaschak, E. (1992) *Engendered Lives: A New Psychology of Women's Experience*. New York: Basic Books.

Kotzin, R. (1993) Bribery and intimidation: A discussion of Sandra Lee Bartky's *Femininity and Domination: Studies in the Phenomenology of Oppression. Hypatia*, 8: 164–72.

Laidlaw, T. and Malmo, C. (1990) *Healing Voices*. San Francisco, CA: Jossey-Bass.

Larkin, J. (1991) Sexual harassment: From the personal to the political. *Atlantis* 17: 106–15.

Lewis, M. (1990) Interrupting patriarchy: Politics, resistance, and transformation in the feminist classroom. *Harvard Educational Review*, 60: 465–88.

Lewis, M. (1993) *Without a Word: Teaching Beyond Women's Silence*. New York: Routledge.

McDiarmid, K. (1994) 'Women and wilderness recreation'. Unpublished MSc thesis. University of Calgary.

Mill, H. (1970) Enfranchisement of women. In A. Rossi (ed.) *Essays on Sex Equality*. Chicago, IL: University of Chicago Press.

Mill, J. (1970) The subjection of women. In A. Rossi (ed.) *Essays on Sex Equality*. Chicago, IL: University of Chicago Press.

Miller, J. (1988) *Connections, Disconnections and Violations*, working paper #33. Wellesley, MA: Stone Center Working Paper Series.

Muelenhard, C. (1988) 'Nice women' don't say yes and 'Real men' don't say no. *Women and Therapy*, 7: 95–108.

Rockhill, K. (1987) Literacy as threat/desire: Longing to be SOMEBODY. In J. Gaskell and A. McLaren (eds) *Women and Education: A Canadian Perspective*. Calgary: Detselig Enterprises.

Tolman, D. (1991) Adolescent girls, women and sexuality: Discerning dilemmas of desire. *Women and Therapy*, 11: 55–70.

Weisstein, N. (1993) Psychology constructs the female: or, the fantasy life of the male psychologist (with some attention to the fantasies of his friends, the male biologist and the male anthropologist). *Feminism & Psychology*, 3(2): 195–210.

Wolf, N. (1993) *Fire With Fire*. Toronto: Random House.

Young, I. (1990) *Throwing Like a Girl*. Indianapolis, IN: University of Indiana Press.

PART II

Sexual harassment as power

6

Sexual terrorism on the street: the moulding of young women into subordination

JUNE LARKIN

> It's a fine spring day, and with an utter lack of self-consciousness I am bouncing down the street. Suddenly I hear men's voices. Catcalls and whistles fill the air. These noises are clearly meant for me; they come from a group of men hanging about a corner across the street. I freeze. As Sartre would say, I have been petrified by the gaze of the Other. My face flushes and my emotions become stiff and self-conscious. The body which, only a moment before, I inhabited with such ease now floods my consciousness. I have been made into an object.
>
> (Bartky 1990: 27)

The sexual harassment of women by men is something I cope with on a daily basis as part of the backdrop of my life as a woman living in a sexist society. Researchers like Liz Kelly (1987: 62) have found that for some women, sexual harassment 'happens so much it's almost a background of what going out the door seems to mean.' To date, the bulk of scholarly attention has been focused on the sexually harassing behaviour men inflict on women in academic or workplace settings. While this behaviour is by no means uncommon, there is strong evidence that women may be more likely to be harassed in other settings.

In her study on women's experiences of male violence, Liz Kelly (1987) found that although a substantial number of women reported having experienced unwanted attention at work (42 per cent), harassment on the street was a routine experience. Similarly, Hanmer and Saunders (1984) reported that the majority of women's violent experiences (67 per cent) were on the street while only 15 per cent of reported incidents were in the workplace. And, yet, as Jaclyn Packer (1986: 331) has noted:

while sexual harassment of women in employment situations has been given a lot of attention lately in sociological and psychological literature, street harassment has virtually been ignored.

It would seem the tendency to view sexual harassment as a problem that occurs primarily in the workplace and/or academic setting has the effect of minimizing its occurrence in other aspects of women's lives. Considering that street harassment may be women's most common experience of males' intrusive and intimidating behaviour, this is a serious omission.

In my own research, I have found that street harassment is such an inevitable part of girls' passage into womanhood that many young women are emotionally worn down long before they ever enter the workplace or academia. Working to eliminate the problem of sexual harassment in institutions is a laudable goal. But unless we expand our focus to include the pervasive forms of harassment that curtail women's ability ever to develop a sense of security and self-assurance in the larger world, it is unlikely that women will have the confidence to confront the abusive and demeaning behaviour in settings where our employment or educational goals are at risk.

What I want to do in this chapter is to explore the reasons why this most pervasive form of harassment is so often overlooked and demonstrate the pernicious effects of the street harassment inflicted on girls and women as they attempt to make their way through the public world.

The broader picture

It's not my intention to criticize the efforts of those who have worked relentlessly to eliminate the hostility that women face in their working and learning environments. In fact, I am proud to consider myself one of these dedicated crusaders. As coordinator of the Women's Sexual Harassment Caucus at the Ontario Institute for Studies in Education (OISE) I funnelled much personal energy into pressuring the administration to develop a sexual harassment policy, lobbying for the hiring of a sexual harassment prevention officer, and doing workshops to educate university personnel about the problem of sexual harassment. No doubt this was important work. But in hindsight I have recognized the limitations of such a narrow focus. Concentrating solely on the sexual harassment that goes on in institutional settings doesn't address the fact that 'sexual harassment is simply what women's experience of life consists of for much of the time' (Kelly 1987: 53).

Women's experience of harassment probably varies from setting to setting and for this reason, it makes sense to examine the nature of women's harassment in specific situations. The discussion should never be divorced, however, from the larger context of a society in which women are routinely taunted, teased and terrorized by men. The way Melanie Randall (1987: 8) sees it, sexual harassment must always

> be seen to include the whole range of intrusive behaviors that are imposed upon women in all spheres of life and on an everyday basis or we lose from its scope and make invisible the many ways that women are threatened and sexually intruded upon by men.

When we deal with this broader picture, the sexual politics that underlie sexual harassment are much more visible. Certainly, some men experience sexual harassment and this is not to be dismissed. But the ubiquitous presence of sexual harassment in women's lives is a constant reminder of our vulnerability to male abuse. For women, sexual harassment is only part of the continuum of violence that restricts our lives. In a society where 27 per cent of Canadian women are sexually assaulted at some point in our lives; where 49.5 per cent of these women are under the age of 17 at the time of their first assault; where 65.5 per cent of female victims are sexually assaulted by males they know; where 60 per cent of college-age men have reported that, under the right circumstances, they would use force, rape, or both in sexual relations with women; and where the degradation and violation of women through pornography is a billion dollar business, every incident of sexual harassment becomes a violent threat (Briere and Malamuth 1983; Brickman and Briere 1984; Larkin 1994). One young woman put it this way, 'Guys might get harassed sometimes, but they aren't in the same boat as we are. We always have to look behind us when we walk down the street' (Larkin 1994).

Historically, men's control of women was assured because women were confined to the private sphere as wives, mothers and domestic workers whose primary purpose was servicing the needs of men and children. But as women have attempted to move into the public sphere, sexual harassment has become a tool men can use to maintain their dominant position by

> ensuring that women will not feel at ease, that we will remember our role as sexual beings, available to, accessible to men. It is a reminder that we are not to consider ourselves equals, participating in public life with our own right to go where we like when we like, to pursue our own projects with a sense of security.
>
> (Houston 1988: 45)

Negotiating the reality, fear and confusion of sexual harassment is part of the everyday content of most women's lives and begins long before we become adults. Elizabeth Stanko (1986: 2) reminds us that

[A]s soon as women begin pubescent development they actually begin to see male behaviour toward them change. Adolescent girls are met with comments, glances, whistles . . . Fending off male sexuality, much of what is initially welcomed, the young girl also learns that she cannot always control sexual encounters she engages in. She also learns that if anything happens, she is to blame.

Young women learn early that they must constantly be on guard as they attempt to manoeuvre their way safely through a threatening world. Eventually, this posture of constant vigilance takes on the illusion of normalcy as they routinely monitor their movements to avoid the threats and intrusions of males. As one young woman explained, 'I just think, "here it comes again" '. When women are enculturated in such a misogynist society, dealing with hostility and intimidation becomes so commonplace they are taken as the norm. The self-doubt and insecurity that can result from years of such mistreatment are then often considered products of women's inherent flaws rather than the outcome of pervasive and persistent abuse by men.

Of course, women's tacit resignation to the kinds of harassment we endure on the streets may have a lot to do with the lack of any recource available to women who are harassed in public places. As Sandra McNeill (1987: 93) points out:

While there are no laws explicitly denying women's free access to public places at all times, in practice their freedom is curtailed by men who attack them, men who threaten them (and) insufficient law enforcement against these men.

In the past decade, the threat of legal liability has pressured many institutions to develop policies to protect their students and employees from sexual harassment. This may be one reason why many feminists, including myself, have targeted these settings in our efforts to confront this problem; the institutional response offers women a mechanism to hold offenders accountable for their harassing behaviour.

But institutional responses offer little more than Band-aid solutions to a few women who have the courage to lodge a formal complaint. The root causes of sexual harassment are not addressed because incidents of sexual harassment are generally treated as isolated and individual cases so that the systemic problem of sexism and misogyny within the institution is obscured (Osborne 1992). When sexual harassment is depoliticized in this way

it is very possible for it to be lifted out of the actual experience of women, out of the social context in which it occurs, and this experience and context then do not find full expression in the definitions (or procedures).

(Dykstra 1982; cited in Osborne 1992: 74)

Before we can begin working from the broader social context we need to acknowledge the many ways and the variety of settings in which we as women adapt our lives to avoid the threats and intrusions of men. Calling into consciousness and labelling as harassment much of the behaviour we have come to accept as standard social practice for males can be both a disturbing and insightful exercise. In keeping with the tenet that the personal is political, I began this work where we all must begin: with ourselves.

Beginning with ourselves

A couple of years ago I kept a record of my personal incidents of sexual harassment over a four-month period. This exercise was part of the preliminary work to my research on the kinds of behaviour adolescent girls labelled as 'sexual harassment' and whether or not their labelling captured the range of sexually intrusive and intimidating behaviour they encountered in their everyday lives. Because the journal-keeping task was part of the research design, I decided to keep an account of my own experiences so I could better understand the process I would be asking my participants to undertake.

In total, I documented 51 incidents. While I was alarmed by the sheer number of incidents of sexual harassment, I was even more surprised when I sorted them by settings. By far, my most common experience of sexual harassment occurred on the street (36 incidents) followed by harassment in public places, such as restaurants (10 incidents) and harassment in my academic setting (five incidents). Contrary to the principle that 'the personal is political', my political work in the area of sexual harassment was not an accurate reflection of my personal experience. In fact, based on my personal record, the university was the safest place for me to be (Larkin 1991).

As is the case for all women, my situation must be examined in a particular context. As a graduate student, my limited economic means restricted my access to the protective measures available to women who can afford taxis or cars; I had no option but to walk or use public transportation and so I often travelled on the streets. However, I studied in a feminist environment where most professors and students were female and where there was a strong focus on issues related to violence against women. For these reasons, most of my sexually harassing experiences occurred outside the academic setting (Larkin 1991).

I treated the pervasiveness of street harassment in my own life as an anomaly until I began to analyse the data I had collected in the focus groups and interviews I had conducted with over 50 young women. The diversity of the adolescent girls in terms of age, class, race and geographical location accounted for many differences in the ways they were sexually harassed. For example, most of the harassment levelled at racialized young women was laced with racist slurs and stereotypes. Comments typically directed at young black women reflected the stereotype of black women's promiscuity and often resonated with the common pornographic image of a Black woman as 'a willing victim of her white master' (Mayall and Russell 1993: 227). Some of the recorded comments included, 'I hear black girls like white guys' dicks'. 'I hear black girls are easy.' For young women in urban settings, harassment on public transit was a pervasive and often threatening problem that was seldom an issue for young women in rural or small town settings.

Despite the variations in their experiences, being harassed on the street was so routine that many hadn't bothered to include these incidents in their journals. Dora told me, 'If I wrote down every little thing that happened on the street, it would take up too much time'. For this reason, any attempt to measure the frequency with which young women were harassed on the street proved to be both difficult and unreliable. Jessica confessed that she hadn't recorded many of these incidents because they were an 'everyday occurrence' and so she 'was less aware of writing them down'. In discussing her only recorded account of street harassment, Sharon told me:

> I wasn't sure if I should put it down because the construction workers hooted and hollered at me every day [that week]; when I went to school and when I came home. Finally, one day I got so ticked off I wrote it in my journal.

In reality, Sharon could have reported 10 incidents of street harassment by this one group of men. The young women usually underreported being hassled on the street because they tended to dismiss this behaviour as normal.

Identifying the ordinary, everyday incidents of male sexual harassment is problematic because we have yet to develop the language to name the intrusions that are considered by male standards as 'acceptable' or 'normal' behaviour. The way Dworkin (1987: 134) sees it:

> male discourse (has become) . . . our language. It is not a second language even though it is not our native language; it is the only language we speak, however with perfect fluency even though it does not say what we mean or what we think we might know if only we could find the right word and enough privacy in which to articulate it even just in our own minds.

Disentangling harassing incidents from what we have come to accept as routine male behaviour can be a difficult task. Fatima explained it this way:

> You don't think about it really . . . because it happens all the time, it

happens so often it's part of life. How can I explain it? It's like you are walking down the street and someone whistles at you. It's as if it's natural for them to do that and if somebody doesn't do that then something's wrong . . . It's like whistles all the time, honks all the time – you don't even pay attention to it. It's part of life.

This tolerance of street abuse does not mean that the consequences of this behaviour are innocuous. Harassing words and gestures are slowly absorbed into girls' developing sense of self and become an essential part of who they see themselves to be (Larkin *et al.* 1996). According to Sue Wise and Liz Stanley (1987: 114), the taunting and teasing that becomes part of the backdrop of a woman's life 'wears [us] down by always sounding in our consciousness so we can never get away from [it]'. It can operate like a 'dripping tap' (Wise and Stanley 1987: 114) that slowly erodes young women's sense of confidence and security. As a result

the sexual harassment girls experience can be a formative influence in terms of their self-esteem and their sense of freedom in the world. Harassment in childhood teaches girls about their subordinate status in a sexist society.

(Langelan 1993: 144)

Street harassment is so pervasive that it is an integral part of 'normal' female development. Because it is almost accepted as a rite of passage, the effect of this behaviour on a young woman's developing identity has largely been ignored (Larkin *et al.* 1996).

Street harassment

Street harassment is part of a system of sexual terrorism that reminds young women of their vulnerability to more extreme forms of abuse (Sheffield 1987; Kissling 1989). Wise and Stanley (1987: 114) point out that most sexual harassment does not involve extreme or 'sledgehammer' male behaviour but consists of smaller, cumulative intrusions that are limiting, demeaning and disempowering. This is the nature of much of the sexual harassment women face on the street. However, the more infre-quent but threatening sledgehammer behaviour that women experience in their lives renders every male intrusion a violent threat because of the fine line that divides men's threatening and non-threatening behaviour. The following scenario, taken from my own journal, demonstrates the ease with which this line can be crossed and how a seemingly non-threatening male intrusion can turn violent:

A man began to walk closely behind me, then finally beside me. He said in a low voice 'Nice day, eh.' He made me uncomfortable and I didn't want to converse with him so I turned to cross the road. He stopped and watched me . . . When I saw him turn and resume walking I began to walk up the street again. He was walking very slowly and I knew I would catch up with him at the light so I slowed down. When I saw the light was green I picked up my pace and crossed the road. He stood on the corner and shouted, 'Want to fuck, slut.' He seemed in a rage . . . I pretended to ignore him but walked quickly into the Board of Education building which was two buildings away. He followed me and when I went in the front door he came right up to the door and started pacing back and forth . . . He finally left but stood across the road watching the building . . . I didn't know what to do. In some ways I wanted to keep him in sight so if we did call the police he would still be there – but I also wanted to hide from him. When I left the building three hours later, I kept checking behind me as I walked home.

According to Stanko (1993: 161) 'women's lives rest on a continuum of danger' so that 'the concrete knowledge that sexual danger can and does occur' evokes a strong sense of fear and vulnerability. In the words of Kissling and Kramarae (1991: 76), this is why

[e]ven ostensibly complimentary remarks and non-violent physical contacts and violations of personal space can remind a woman of her gender identity as woman, subject to evaluation as a sexual object . . . and vulnerable to invasions of privacy and physical space.

Ironically, because women's value in our society is often tied to males' approval of our personal appearance, a young woman may feel flattered at the same time as she feels frightened by males' comments about her body or dress. This conflict can stem from a concern that what she perceives to be a compliment might in fact be a lead-in to demeaning or threatening behaviour. This was true in the case of Alison, whose excitement about being noticed by a group of males was squashed by the crude sexual propositions that followed their initial remarks.

I was wearing a short mini-skirt and I was walking . . . and there were [some] guys. They started whistling. So one guy yelled out, 'Hey you, you in the black skirt.' They kept bugging me. I finally turned around and said, 'What do you want?' They said, 'You got legs that just don't quit.' It made me feel good but it made me feel scared . . . I was afraid they would keep this up. And they did . . . The one [guy] said to my friend, 'Tell her I want to sleep with her.' And I said to my friend, 'I'm not sleeping with him.' The next day my friend came back to me and said, 'Because you won't sleep with him, he wants you to give him a blow-job.

(Larkin 1994: 82)

Women are often leery of male compliments because we are suspicious of the inherent message or agenda behind them. As Beatrice put it, 'You never know what could happen next.'

At a time when young women are in the process of sorting out all kinds of issues around sexuality and identity, the deluge of harassment they experience on the street 'conveys a hostile message about male power and the very meaning of being female' (Langelan 1993: 145). In our work with young women, Carla Rice, Vanessa Russell and myself have observed the process through which harassing comments and gestures can transform adolescent girls' excitement about becoming a woman into anxiety about developing a woman's body (Rice 1995; Rice and Russell 1995; Larkin *et al.* 1996). Almost 50 years ago, Simone de Beauvoir wrote:

> The young woman feels her body is getting away from her, it is no longer the straightforward expression of her individuality; at the same time she becomes for others a thing; on the street men follow her with their eyes and comment on her body. She would like to be invisible; it frightens her to become flesh and show her flesh.
>
> (1974: 346)

It is disheartening to realize that her words continue to carry currency for young women growing up today (Rice 1995).

In many ways, a central dynamic in female development appears to be the loss of individuality and increased objectivity as young women begin to make their way in the larger world (Rice 1995; Larkin *et al.* 1996). In her article 'Growing up in a sexual jungle', Marion Botsford Fraser (1991: 21) points out:

> At some point in their physical development, all female children lose the protection of baby fat and barrettes and become prey in a game in which there are rules only if the law is broken. It is pretty much open season on their self-confidence and propriety . . .
>
> The worst messages come from men. I have watched the way that grown men feel free to look at young girls. A fat white-haired man wheezing and sweating on a bench in a mall lets his eyes slide all over the body of a pretty teenage girl walking by. A man on the street grunts when he encounters two teenagers young enough to be his daughters. A business man in his fifties mutters, 'check out the hot blonde' to his buddy; the hot blonde is not yet 16.

Males' ogling can crush young women's excitement about their developing bodies as they quickly learn the risks that accompany their physical maturation. Often leering is a process used by males to select those females who will be the target of their further sexualized comments and behaviour. So young women learn to watch men watching them and become wary of what may happen next.

This culture of fear becomes the context in which many young women grow into adulthood. Researchers have found adolescence to be a time when girls begin to 'contract' rather than to 'expand', psychologically speaking (Miller 1984; Gilligan 1990). The confident 11-year-old is transformed into an apologetic, hesitant teenager who questions her own knowledge and her own sense of authority (Prose 1990). Sexual harassment may have a lot to do with girls shutting down as they learn to regulate their behaviour to avoid further abuse. In the depressing words of one young woman, 'More and more every year our lives are becoming smaller and smaller, our days are becoming shorter and shorter' (Herbert 1989: 84). In the following section, I describe the ways in which street harassment can contribute to the diminishing world of adolescent girls.

In their own words

For the young women I interviewed, the sexual harassment they suffered on the street was a routine experience that usually involved a combination of whistles, catcalls, horn-honking, flashing, demeaning gestures and vulgar propositions by both adolescent and adult males.

Being followed by individual men or groups of men was commonplace. On one of our group meeting days, Beth had been late for school because she had ducked into a video store to hide from a man who was following her in his jeep.

> A jeep followed me around the Lacroix Street area on the way to school. It honked behind me and then, when it was right beside me, it honked louder. I gave him the finger. Then when I was on Clark Street walking towards James Street . . . the stupid jeep followed me around again, honking at me from behind and then honking really loudly, when [it was] beside me. I still gave him the finger. It even followed me to Grandview Street . . . I really was annoyed this time so I went into the video store on the [corner] . . . I waited there five minutes. I came out. The jeep was gone. So I went to school. It was scary.

When she arrived late for class, Beth was put in the uncomfortable position of having to explain her tardiness (Larkin 1994).

It wasn't uncommon for the young women to be barraged with crude and intimidating questions and comments by males who followed them on the street.

> I was followed once from Wellington to Cumber Avenue. He came up behind me and said things like: 'Where are you going? Where do you

live? Are you a virgin? Do you want to have sex?' . . . I just ran because he scared me so.

Comments such as, 'Hey baby, Oh la la' and 'Wow, you've got great legs. Can I have them?' were standard street remarks that the young women attempted to brush off or ignore. But feigning indifference was more difficult when the taunts came from large groups of males.

Like at night I want to be able to walk down the street with no problems [but] you have these old . . . men that hang out at the billiards [and they yell] 'Hey, baby, come with me' and stuff like that and they whistle. And we'd be walking by and there'd be a [window] in the billiard. All of them would be pounding on the glass [saying] 'Heyyyy.' They're pounding on the glass . . . all the time . . . there's so many . . . like 15 of them, 20 of them.

Although their most common overt reaction to street hassling was to 'look straight ahead and keep walking', there were situations in which the young women were faced with propositions which required some form of verbal or physical response to the harasser. Fending off objectifying comments and gestures was an everyday practice but, in many cases, they were also dealing with sleazy invitations which expressed the idea that their bodies were commodities available for male consumption:

I was walking down the street and I heard a honk from far away . . . I didn't recognize the car so I kept walking and the car pulled up and a guy comes out and I thought he was just going to the phone booth on the corner . . . He comes up to me and he goes, 'What's your name?' and I didn't say anything . . . and he says, 'Do you have a boyfriend?' And I go, 'Yes, I do have a boyfriend.' And he goes, 'OK, why don't you come for a ride with me and my friend?' And I go, 'No, I'm fine, I can walk' . . . After I kept walking he came following behind me . . . He goes, 'Why don't you go out with me?' He pulled out money and I go, 'Money doesn't mean anything.' He goes, 'Oh ya.' And he shoves it back in his pocket. After I kept walking, he goes, 'Come on, come on, come for a ride.' And I said, 'No!' and I just kept walking, walking, walking.

We were in the streetcar and they were outside [on the street]. They were [gesturing to] us if we wanted to give them a blow job for money.

A typical strategy for handling such crude solicitations was to declare ownership by another male. Claiming to have a boyfriend, even when this was not the case, was an attempt to project an 'off-limits' status to invasive and threatening males.

I came out of the subway station . . . I was just standing there and [this guy] looks at the *Sunday Sun* [newspaper] box and says, 'Isn't that girl beautiful on the front page?' . . . I go 'Yah'. He turns around and . . . he says, 'Do you want to come over to my house sometime? . . . Do you live alone?' I go . . . 'No, I live with two other friends' . . . He goes, 'You're coming with me.' I go, 'No, I'm not' . . . He goes, 'I want you to come to my house. I'll give you my number.' I go, 'There's no way I'm going to call you; my boyfriend's going to be coming soon.' He goes, 'I don't care. Come now girl, give me some head.' I go, 'Pardon me.' He goes, 'Yah, you heard what I said. Come girl give me some head.' [I said], 'Sorry, I'm not that kind of girl.'

Sexual harassment in the public sphere reflects a redefinition of women as the public (as opposed to private) property of men. This was apparent in my own experience of street harassment, for although I was hassled when I was alone or in the company of other women, I was never harassed when I was with a man. It seemed that being accompanied by a male provided evidence of 'private' ownership, while a state of 'manlessness' rendered me the potential property of any male (Larkin 1991). This taken-for-granted entitlement of men to women's bodies is the foundation of sexual harassment and perpetuates the notion that women exist for the pleasure of men, that men should be gratified by women, that the public world is a male domain and that women enter this world at some risk to their privacy and personal safety (Larkin 1991).

Flashing is a form of harassment that some men used to assert their territorial rights and to warn young women of the inherent danger they faced as they attempted to move about the public sphere.

We were walking down the street and this guy, he was wearing his joggers. We saw him coming. He was in front of us so we had to move either way . . . because he wouldn't move, he was walking straight, straight, straight. [We tried] to give him some room and the next thing you know he pulls down his pants and he exposes himself . . . Amelia screamed and she jumped off the sidewalk onto the street . . . I got scared so I jumped with her . . . we just looked at each other paralysed like 'Oh, my God, what happened with that guy?' . . . We turned around and the guy just kept walking, didn't turn around, didn't do nothing.

The threatened sense of physical security that young women experienced as a consequence of being harassed on the street was evident in their description of their most common response to this behaviour: fear.

I get scared . . . like don't look at me. [I get] so many feelings, nervous or something, when I'm walking down the street.

Their anxiety stemmed from their concern that even seemingly minor forms of harassing behaviour could escalate to more extreme violence.

I got scared actually [when he was following me] . . . I was walking,

walking . . . I went ahead of him. [I thought], 'Is he going to bother me again?' I thought, 'Oh, no, this and this [can happen].' I didn't want to go home because I didn't want him to follow me, so I went . . . all the way around, just in case he would follow me. I got scared, really scared [that he would] put me in the car, show me a gun or his dink. What else? You know, shove me in [the car].

Some of [them] say, 'Hey baby', or whatever and that's it. It stops. [But] the ones that say, 'Hey, baby. Come in the car, come do this, come do that' and keep following you around or something, then . . . you get more scared. The fear keeps building and building and building and, then, you just feel, 'Oh my God, he is going to kill me or something like that.'

I was going home from work . . . and this guy followed me. He was [saying things like], 'Hey baby. Do you want to take me home?' I ignored him and I kept walking. I walked past my house because I didn't want him to see where I lived. I pretended I was going to the store. I go inside and he's waiting for me outside. So I stayed [in the store] longer and longer and he just eventually left, thank God, and I just went home. [I was afraid that] he was waiting for me to come out and grab me and stick me in a van.

In Canada, the abduction and murder of teen-age girls like Kristen French and Leslie Mahaffy gave depressing validity to the fears and concerns expressed by these young women. The horrifying accounts of physical and sexual torture that led to the deaths of French and Mahaffy sent shock waves through Canadians who followed the trial of their convicted murderer, Paul Bernardo. His estranged wife, Karla Homolka, was found guilty of manslaughter.

Jessica described street harassment as one step in a 'continuous cycle' of violence that could progress from routine comments to sexual assault.

It sorta makes me more uncomfortable, these comments. It makes me very uncomfortable. These men screaming these thoughts out from the car or walking by and commenting on my butt or whatever, and doing these hand gestures at the same time [as] these whooping calls . . . I guess it's one thing to say something but then to actually enforce it with some sort of hand movement makes it more concrete or more dangerous. I guess in a way it's just one more step towards an action taking place [like] assault . . . If they just say something and the guy keeps walking, that's not as severe as the hand gestures and then it just seems like the next step is maybe he'll follow you, next step is to see where you live, you know, follow you in a back alley. It just sorta progresses, it's a continuous cycle . . . After they step over the boundaries, it's like, 'Oh, my gosh'. Do you know what I mean?

Because they realized that comments, leers and gestures could, and sometimes did, progress to more severe abuse, the young women felt they had limited options for responding to the various ways they were harassed on the street; any rebuttal on their part might provoke further violence.

> My friend told off [some guys] cause they were yelling, 'Hey, baby. Come with us' and stuff like that. And she goes, 'Why don't you fuck off, you little bastards?' And then they started getting rude. They go, 'You fucking little bitch . . . I'll fucking kill you.'

Becoming specialists in assessing the violence potential of males' behaviour appears to be a primary task of female development. The costs of young women's wariness on public streets are perhaps immeasurable as they learn to adapt, restrict and regulate their behaviour to minimize the likelihood of a violent encounter with men.

> There is always a sense of watching where you step, watching where you go, watching who you meet . . . You have to be careful, watch out, there are idiots out there, there are creeps, there are weirdos, watch out.

When a young woman must tread so cautiously through the streets, how can she ever develop a sense of security in the public world?

To conclude, then, harassment on the streets is only part of a system of violence that contributes to the moulding of young women's subordinate status. Contending with street harassment is such an inevitable consequence of becoming a woman it often gets taken as the norm. As Beth so poignantly put it, 'That's life.'

Young women's inability to move about safely on the street has the attendant consequence of limiting their potential for power and control in the larger world because so much of their energy is geared to securing their own safety. When a young woman is continually reminded of the risks that accompany her developing body, when she is constantly under the scrutiny and surveillance of males, and when she lives in a state of constant vigilance, it's unlikely that she'll ever develop a sense of herself as a powerful and autonomous person. Unlikely, too, that she'll ever develop the strength to work against the process of her subordination.

Acknowledgements

The author wishes to thank Christabelle Sethna for her helpful comments and suggestions.

References

Bartky, S. (1990) *Femininity and Domination: Studies in the Phenomenology of Oppression*. New York: Routledge.

Brickman, J. and Briere, J. (1984) Incidents of rape and sexual assault in urban Canadian population. *International Journal of Women's Studies*, 7(3): 195–206.

Briere, J. and Malamuth, N. (1983) Self-reported likelihood of sexually aggressive behaviour: An attitudinal vs. sexual explanation. *Journal of Research and Personality*, 17: 315–23.

de Beauvoir, S. (1974) *The Second Sex*. New York: Vintage Books.

Dworkin, A. (1987) *Intercourse*. New York: Free Press.

Dykstra, P. (1982) Review of the Report of the Presidential Advisory Committee on Sexual Harassment, York University. *Resources for Feminist Research*, 10(4): 26–9.

Fraser, M.B. (1991) Growing up in a sexual jungle. *Canadian Woman Studies/les cahiers de la femme*, 11(4): 20-21.

Gilligan, C. (1990) Teaching Shakespeare's sister: Notes from the underground of female adolescence. In C. Gilligan, N. Lyons and T. Hanmer (eds) *Making Connections: The Relational Worlds of Adolescent Girls at Emma Willard School*. Cambridge, MA; Harvard University Press.

Hanmer, J. and Saunders, S. (1984) *Well Founded Fear*. London: Hutchinson & Co.

Herbert, C. (1989) *Talking of Silence: The Sexual Harassment of Schoolgirls*. London: Falmer Press.

Houston, B. (1988) What's wrong with sexual harassment? *Atlantis*, 13(2): 44–7.

Kelly, L. (1987) The continuum of sexual violence. In J. Hanmer and M. Maynard (eds) *Women, Violence and Social Control*. Beverly Hills, CA: Sage.

Kissling, E. (1989) 'Interpreting street remarks'. Paper presented at the 12th annual meeting of the Organization for Study of Communication, Language, and Gender, Cincinnati, OH, October.

Kissling, E. and Kramarae, C. (1991) Stranger compliments: The interpretation of street remarks. *Women's Studies in Communication*, 4(1): 75–93.

Langelan, M. (1993) *Back Off: How to Confront and Stop Sexual Harassment and Harassers*. New York: Fireside.

Larkin, J. (1991) Sexual harassment: From the personal to the political. *Atlantis*, 17(1): 106–15.

Larkin, J. (1994) *Sexual Harassment: High School Girls Speak Out*. Toronto: Second Story Press.

Larkin, J., Rice, C. and Russell, L. (1996) Slipping through the cracks: Sexual harassment, eating problems and the problems of embodiment. *Eating Disorders: The Journal of Treatment and Prevention*, 4(1): 5–26.

McNeill, S. (1987) Flashing: Its effect on women. In J. Hanmer and M. Maynard (eds) *Women, Violence and Social Control*. London: Macmillan.

Mayall, A. and Russell, D. (1993) Racism in pornography. *Feminism & Psychology* 3(2): 275–81.

Miller, J. (1984) *The Development of Women's Sense of Self*. Wellesley, MA: Stone Center Works in Progress.

Osborne, R. (1992) Sexual harassment in universities. *Canadian Woman Studies/les cahiers de la femme*, 12(3): 72–6.

Packer, J. (1986) Sex differences in perceptions of street harassment. *Women and Therapy*, 5: 331–8.

Prose, F. (1990) Confident at 11, confused at 16. *New York Times*, 7 January: 24, 40.

Randall, M. (1987) *Sexual Harassment*. Toronto: Ontario Women's Directorate.

Rice, C. (1995) 'Writing on the body: Exploring the politics of the body in western culture, feminist texts and western culture and women's lives.' Unpublished manuscript, Regional Women's Health Center, Toronto.

Rice, C. and Russell, V. (1995) Embodying equity: Putting body and soul back into equity education. *Our Schools. Ourselves*. 7(1): 14–36.

Sheffield, C. (1987) Sexual terrorism: The social control of women. In B.B. Hess and M.M. Ferree (eds) *Analysis of Gender: A Handbook of Social Science Research*. Beverly Hills, CA: Sage.

Stanko, E. (1986) *Intimate Intrusions*. London: Routledge & Kegan Paul.

Stanko, E. (1993) Ordinary fear: Women, violence and personal safety. In P. Bart and E. Moran (eds) *Violence Against Women: Bloody Footprints*. Newbury Park, CA: Sage.

Wise, S. and Stanley, L. (1987) *Georgie Porgie: Sexual Harassment in Everyday Life*. London: Pandora Press.

7

Men behaving badly? A psychosocial exploration of the cultural context of sexual harassment

ALISON M. THOMAS

Introduction

In spite of the publicity given to the subject of the sexual harassment of men by women by the controversial novel (Crichton 1994) and film (1994) *Disclosure*, it is still generally accepted that male harassment of women is far more prevalent than the reverse. Most of the growing wealth of litera-ture on sexual harassment that has been published in recent years has accordingly tended to concentrate on women as the recipients of harass-ment, documenting the variety of situations in which they may experience it (e.g. Farley 1978; Dziech and Weiner 1984; Paludi 1990), and the effects it has upon them (e.g. Herbert 1989). Yet strangely, as Hearn (1985) first noted some years ago, there have been remarkably few sustained attempts to examine the possible reasons *why* men may behave in this way towards women. There are two likely reasons for this apparent neglect – one broadly 'political' , the other essentially pragmatic.

With regard to the former, feminists have long been insistent that the harasser's motivation and intentions should be irrelevant when it comes to deciding whether or not a given incident constitutes harassment – and that it is the recipient's subjective experience of feeling harassed that should determine whether or not the incident 'counts' as sexual harass-ment (Stanley and Wise 1987). (Indeed, this principle is now widely accepted and has been formally adopted into many anti-harassment poli-cies.) From a feminist standpoint it might therefore be argued that study-ing the reasons why men harass women is not only unimportant, but politically inappropriate, since it provides them with an opportunity to make excuses for this behaviour. This may then explain why feminist researchers have – with a few notable exceptions (e.g. Benard and Schlaffer 1984; Houston 1988; Watson 1994) – largely shunned this as a research topic.

With regard to the second, more pragmatic reason for the lack of research on this subject, it is quite evident from the very diversity of behaviours attracting the label 'sexual harassment' – everything from wolf-whistling and name-calling to sexual assault – that sexual harassment is not a unitary phenomenon (Tangri *et al.* 1982). Clearly then, we should not expect to be able to identify a single kind of harasser, nor come up with a single or simple analysis for such a wide range of behaviours. The difficulties entailed in addressing such a complex phenomenon may therefore provide a second explanation for the relative neglect of this aspect of sexual harassment.

However, as Collier (1995) points out, if we are to make any attempts to prevent sexual harassment from occurring, it is first necessary to examine how and why it happens, and that will involve developing a better understanding of the ways in which men themselves construe harassing behaviour – political principles and pragmatic considerations notwithstanding.

In their important analysis of sexual harassment, feminist sociologists Wise and Stanley (1987) made the useful distinction between 'sledgehammer' harassment (the most extreme cases of physical assault, for example, that make the tabloid headlines), and the so-called 'dripping tap' variety (mundane, everyday instances which occur so frequently that they often fail to be noticed as harassment at all). In so far as there have been attempts to address the reasons for men's harassing behaviour, it appears that psychology has most often been employed in attempts to explain the former kind, while sociological analyses have more often been offered in the case of the latter.

Psychological approaches to understanding harassment

Psychology is traditionally identified with the study of human behaviour at the level of the individual motivations that drive it, and this kind of approach has been popular with journalists speculating on the likely 'causes' of harassment. (As a feminist psychologist, I have on more than one occasion been consulted by a journalist hoping – in vain – that I might identify for them the personality-profile of 'the kind of man who harasses women', as though there were a single, easily identifiable personality type with a predisposition to harass.)

However, there are clear limitations to the value of a strictly psychological approach when examining such 'social problems'; in seeking explanations of social behaviour in the attributes of the individual, there is often a tendency to overlook important sociocultural influences on their behaviour. This of course has the apparent advantage of offering society the possibility of pathologizing and blaming a few individuals for their actions, while maintaining the comfortable illusion that the rest of society is blameless. The study of racial prejudice springs to mind as one very obvious example of this, in so far as many years ago, Adorno *et al.* (1950) pathologized the so-called 'Authoritarian personality', with the implication that, but for such people, there would be no racism. Although few today would apply such a reductionist approach in the analysis of racism, the same kind of approach still clearly retains an appeal for some in relation to sexual harassment (e.g. Pryor 1987; Pryor and Stoller 1994), as also in related areas such as the analysis of violence against women (cf. Groth and Birnbaum 1979; Malamuth 1981).

In the particular context of sexual harassment, this psychologizing approach has tended to have the effect of diverting attention away from the more frequent (though less newsworthy) incidents of everyday harassment and focusing it instead on the more dramatic cases where, for example, the actions of the 'office sex-pest' can be interpreted as revealing either uncontrollable male lust and/or some kind of psychosexual inadequacy. Implicit in this approach, of course, is a basic reluctance to acknowledge as harassment anything other than the sledgehammer cases to which these psychological explanations are applied, and there is a corresponding unwillingness to acknowledge the possibility that the harassing behaviour of men towards women might, just as with racism, have its roots in the sociocultural domain.

This approach is clearly unhelpful therefore, as a means of theorizing the routine kinds of dripping tap harassment – for example, suggestive remarks, being eyed up and down, wolf-whistles and so on – which may be less dramatic than the cases reported in the press, but which are nevertheless the kinds of harassment that women encounter and endure most often. For as Larkin (1991: 106) has observed,

> most of my experiences are small, mundane and cumulative incidents committed by ordinary men. The stereotype of the lecherous professor, the office Romeo . . . does not fit the reality of sexual harassment as I have experienced it.

The kind of psychological approach that seeks to pathologize harassers does not lend itself to explaining the kind of harassment to which Larkin refers. For it is clearly both unnecessary and inappropriate to analyse harassers in this way if, as I contend in this chapter, they are not in fact acting in any 'deviant' manner, but simply overconforming to what is a widely accepted model of masculine behaviour. Indeed, when women talk about their everyday experiences of sexual harassment, one of the most frequent ways in which they explain it is in terms of it being 'just the way men are' (Thomas and Kitzinger 1992).

Sociological analyses of sexual harassment

Sociological analyses, by contrast with the psychologizing approach, focus not on the motivations and feelings of the individual harasser and his 'victim', but on the ways in which harassment stands as a manifestation of a wider system of asymmetrical power relations between men and women in society. They tend accordingly to minimize the significance of any variability in the motivations of individual perpetrators. Feminist sociologists in particular (e.g. Wise and Stanley 1987; Herbert 1989) have argued that the common factor involved in *all* forms of sexual harassment is the exercise of male power over women; in the words of Wise and Stanley (1987) sexual harassment consists of 'the use of male sexuality to reinforce male power'.

Just as with the psychological approach though, sociological approaches also have their limitations, notably the problem of incorporating the idea of individual agency into the analysis of harassment as a social phenomenon. While the reinforcing of male power over women is undoubtedly the principal *effect* of harassment at the sociological level of 'gender-class', should this necessarily be taken to imply that each and every act of sexual harassment of a woman by a man therefore involves a calculated and conscious *intent* to 'do power' over the woman concerned?

Wise and Stanley (1987: 80) do in fact make the uncompromising assertion that 'the purpose [of sexual harassment] is to reduce women to objects of men's whims and wishes', and that this is 'ego-enhancing' for them. Moreover, they identify sexual harassment quite explicitly as 'culpable behaviour' – something that individual men *choose* to do – and thus 'not the determined product of "socialisation" or "capitalism" or "patriarchy" or "psyche" or any other disembodied structure' (Wise and Stanley 1987: 79). Their purpose in taking this position would appear to be to prevent any such excuses being made for men's harassing behaviour.

Yet, while I would agree with them that politically it has been important for feminists to identify men as responsible for their own actions, rather than merely blaming 'the system', this very deliberate separation of individual actors from the social structures they inhabit and perpetuate nevertheless seems to me to be an artificial one to make. To what extent can one reasonably claim that anybody consciously and deliberately chooses a particular course of action, without being influenced in some way by the norms and values of their society? To acknowledge such influences does not, to my mind, let men off the hook; it does, however, make it easier for us to know where to start in our attempts to challenge this kind of behaviour.

A psychosocial perspective on sexual harassment

It is because of the limitations of both the psychological and the sociological approaches to sexual harassment that I have outlined (which themselves stem from the very nature of each discipline and its approach to
theorizing social behaviour), that this chapter instead develops a specifically psychosocial perspective on the subject. Like many feminist sociologists, I see acts of sexual harassment not as the occasional consequences of
uncontrollable male lust, but rather as instances from a continuum of male
behaviours through which men consciously or unconsciously act to assert
and maintain their dominance over women. But for me, as a feminist
psychologist, that is not the end point of the explanation, for where then –
psychologically speaking – does this apparent male need to confirm
superiority come from, and is it inevitable that it should find expression in
this kind of misogynistic behaviour?

By looking more closely at the psychosocial construction of masculine
identities in our society – acknowledging both the psychological and
sociological influences that contribute to this process – I would suggest
that it is possible to see how 'doing power' over women may for some men
represent an important part of forming and maintaining a masculine identity. Hence, much of the everyday sexual harassment that women experience may be seen as a manifestation of the psychosocial pressures on men
to identify with a form of 'masculinity' premised upon misogyny (cf.
Thomas 1993).

Again, I want to stress that by taking this line of approach I am not suggesting that men are the passive 'victims' of these pressures, and my purpose is not to exonerate them from blame for their actions. There are, after
all, various other 'masculinities' with which men may choose to identify
(cf. Hearn and Morgan 1993), which do not entail this kind of antagonistic
self-distancing from women. Rather, I am seeking to understand how men
themselves view what we as women experience as 'harassing behaviour'
in order to be able to tackle this at its source by confronting the attitudes
and expectations that underpin it.

In the following sections I shall develop this approach first by outlining
in more detail the theoretical basis for making connections between
masculinity, misogyny and sexual harassment; and second, through the
use of empirical data drawn from two separate studies (Thomas 1987;
Kitzinger and Thomas 1990).

The idea that 'masculinity' is linked to misogyny is, of course, by no
means a new one; sociologists and social anthropologists, as well as social
and developmental psychologists, have all documented the various ways
in which men seek to distance themselves from women and, at the same
time, to define themselves as superior to them (Ortner and Whitehead
1981). Simone de Beauvoir (1953), in her classic feminist treatise *The Second*

Sex, identified this in terms of women being constructed by men as Other in relation to themselves.

In psychology, a variety of quite diverse theoretical perspectives support the view that the development of a masculine identity entails asserting one's male superiority by derogating all things feminine; the particular approaches I shall refer to here are those of 'social identity' theory (Tajfel 1978), some particular variants on social learning theory (Hartley 1959; Lynn 1969) and the psychodynamic theories of identity development (e.g. Chodorow 1978).

Gender identity and gender antagonisms

I have argued elsewhere (Thomas 1990a, 1990b) that in a predominantly heterosexual society, the two sexes are encouraged to construct their gender identification in terms of difference from each other. (In the English language we find this reflected in the logically unnecessary, yet almost universal practice of referring to the *opposite* sex.) In psychology the social identity model, advanced in this particular context by Abrams and Condor (1984), suggests that identification with one's own gender group is accomplished by means of distancing oneself from (and denigrating) the other. Their analysis would then imply that juvenile male misogyny may simply reflect mutual gender antagonisms.

Indeed, if we look at the numerous studies which have examined young people's gendered interactions (e.g. Lees 1986; Thorne 1993), there is certainly evidence that both boys and girls can be equally disparaging about the 'opposite' sex, putting down and taunting them. Thorne, for example, reports on girls' incursions into boys' playground games or territory (as well as vice versa), and observes that teasing and taunting behaviour was also generally far from unidirectional; girls would tease boys too. She quotes one adult woman who recalled such behaviour from her own schooldays as though it was nothing but 'harmless fun': 'You chased them, yelled at them and called them shocking names, but you really liked the guy' (Thorne 1993: 81).

However other psychological analyses suggest that there is far less symmetry in this process of gender-demarcation than the social identity model would imply, and propose that the male desire to be different may also explicitly entail the wish to be dominant over women.

The fight to be male

Some psychologists (e.g. Hartley 1959; Lynn 1969), theorizing gender identity as learned through identification and modelling, have argued that because boys tend to grow up in settings from which older and adult males are mostly absent, they tend to learn an overrigid masculine identity – in the abstract, as it were. In essence, they learn that being male means *not* being female – and thus seek to be masculine by eschewing all traces of femininity. While girls have the opportunity to model their behaviour on what they see daily in the adult women around them, boys lack the same degree of access to flesh and blood models of their own gender. This means that they are more reliant on other sources (television, for example) in learning what it means to be male and hence tend to imitate more stereotypically gendered role models than do girls. (Note that these theories remain equally valid today, as has been documented by Silverstein and Rashbaum 1994, since the care of young children, whether in the home, in day-care or in junior school is still predominantly undertaken by women.) According to this model, then, the imperative to differentiate oneself from the other gender is much stronger for boys than it is for girls.

Psychodynamic perspectives on the male 'need' to assert difference from women (e.g. Greenson 1968; Chodorow 1978) place particular emphasis on what they theorize to be its source in the boy's early struggle to separate from his mother. It is this fight for autonomy against the all-powerful figure of the mother that is seen as responsible for leading him, later on, to seek to distance himself from and seek mastery over all females (Forcey 1987), as well as to compete with other males. In the words of a male psychotherapist:

> Masculinity, then, can be viewed as a defensive construction developed . . . out of a need to emphasise a difference, a separateness from the mother. In the extreme this is manifested by machismo behaviour with its emphasis on competitiveness, strength, aggressiveness, contempt for women and emotional shallowness, all serving to keep the male secure in his separate identity.
>
> (Ryan 1985)

Making connections: sexual harassment, masculinity and misogyny

If, then, as so much of the psychological literature suggests, this need to differentiate the male self from all things female is fundamental, and leads to more or less overt expressions of misogyny, it is not difficult to see that the sexual harassment of women represents an obvious way of acting all of this out. Two research studies of my own, the first, Study 1, on the social construction of gendered identities (Thomas 1987), and the second, Study 2, (carried out jointly with Celia Kitzinger) on understandings of sexual harassment itself (see Kitzinger and Thomas 1990; Thomas and Kitzinger

1994; Kitzinger and Thomas 1996), offered opportunities to explore this possible link between 'doing masculinity' and sexual harassment.

Together the two studies showed up a number of similarities between the present-day accounts of teenage boys (in Study 1) and the retrospective accounts of adult men (in Study 2) regarding their attitudes and behaviour towards women, and these lend strong support for the interconnectedness of masculinity and misogyny in the construction of a male identity (cf. Thomas 1993). In the next section, I draw upon some of the findings of these two studies in order to elaborate on this theme and to show how harassing women can become part of a particular repertoire of masculine behaviour.

Study 1: the social construction of gendered identities

Research design

The first of these two studies (Thomas 1987) involved a Q sort investigation of three discrete aspects of gender identity (gender self-representation, gender salience and gender ideology respectively) and sought to explore the ways in which people construct accounts of their personal identities as men and women in relation to the wider discourses of gender politics current in contemporary society. Q methodology, now in common use in feminist research (e.g. Kitzinger 1987; Senn 1996), requires research participants to sort a set of propositions or attitudinal items (the Q set) to fit a particular (normally quasi-normal) distribution, in such a way as to map out their construction of the subject in question. In this particular study the 77 items in the Q set were sorted into a distribution ranging from –5 (strongly disagree) to +5 (strongly agree).

For each of the three Q sets used in this study, items were drawn from a variety of sources (e.g. modified from newspaper and magazine articles on gender topics, as well as the orthodox psychological literature) and they were designed to cover as wide a range of potential perspectives as possible – from extreme radicalism to extreme conservatism, for example, in the case of the gender ideology Q set.[1] It is important to note that in Q methodology (unlike conventional psychometric scaling) no *a priori* meanings are attached to any items, the idea being rather that participants should interpret them in their own terms, and that the pattern of meanings associated with particular items by different participants will then emerge in the course of the subsequent analysis.[2]

Factor analysis of the resultant Q-sorted data clusters together Q sorts which show high positive intercorrelations, and the factors so derived therefore represent the common response of the participants who sorted them. Each such factor is then reconstructed for interpretation by forming a single composite Q sort – representing a collective account – from the appropriately weighted individual Q sorts that best define it (i.e. those that have a strong positive loading on that factor alone). From this, the values assigned to each Q-set item (in this case from +5 through to –5) can then be compared with those from other factors and their accounts.[3]

Forty-five of the 93 participants in this research were male, ranging in age from 15 to 81, and coming from a variety of different occupational backgrounds.[4] Elsewhere (Thomas 1987; Thomas 1990a) I have presented a comparative discussion of several of the different accounts that emerged for each of these three dimensions of identity, but here I am focusing on one particularly distinctive account which emerged as Factor II in the analysis of both the gender salience and gender ideology Q sorts. In each case it was best defined by the Q sorts of the three youngest male participants in the study, all in their mid-teens.

Research findings

What is distinctive in both these identity accounts (gender salience and gender ideology) is their generally disparaging view of women as Other from, and implicitly inferior to, themselves as young men.[5] Indeed, significantly, women seem only to be of interest to them in so far as they are seen as providing an outlet for male sexual drives. From the placings given to several of the items in the *gender salience* Q sort it is apparent that conformity to conventional standards of (macho) masculinity is paramount:

Item number	Q sort placing
4 The photographs of me that I like best are those that seem to capture my masculinity.	+4
36 I enjoy doing things that other people would regard as unconventional for a man.	–4
38 I dislike effeminacy in men.	+4
55 How masculine or feminine I am doesn't worry me.	–5
71 Being a man is not the most important thing about me.	–4

It would also appear that one way that this can be achieved is via a form of 'conspicuous consumption' of sex, as can be seen in the placings given to the following set of items:

Item number	Q sort placing
34 I generally understand sexual jokes and stories.	+5
44 To me, losing interest in sex means losing interest in life.	+3
47 I enjoy sexually explicit books and films.	+4
59 I don't often have sexy or erotic dreams.	–5
66 My fantasies tend to be erotic rather than romantic.	+5

According to this account, relations with women appear somewhat ambivalent: on the one hand there is the claim that flirting is enjoyable (item 46), as is testing one's sexual attractiveness (item 9). Yet there is also a feeling of some discomfort in the company of women (items 24 and 67), who are seen as very different from men (item 58).

Item number		Q sort placing
46	Flirting has no appeal for me.	−3
9	It's important to me to know whether the people I meet find me sexually attractive or not.	+5
67	By and large, I tend to get on better with women than with men.	−4
24	My behaviour with my own sex is very different from my behaviour with the other sex.	+3
58	I do not see the emotional life of men and of women as being different in any important respects.	−4

Examining the account generated from the *gender ideology* Q sorts of these same teenage boys, it is clear that the feelings towards women expressed here are founded upon the general view that the two sexes are innately and irreconcilably different (see items 8 and 34). There are some rather stereotyped notions of what women are actually like (see, for example, item 10); commenting on this item, one of the boys summed up his own view of girls as 'just interested in clothes and babies'. There is firm opposition to the principle of gender equality (item 5), and this is bolstered with the view that it is men's superior physical strength which gives them the power to dominate women (item 60).

Item number		Q sort placing
8	The 'psychological' differences between the sexes cannot be denied or wished away – they are part of our biological make-up.	+5
34	Children learn to behave appropriately for their sex in much the same way as they learn anything else – it doesn't just 'come naturally'.	−5
10	The assumption that women are only interested in clothes, cooking and 'getting a man' has more than a a grain of truth to it.	+5
5	Seeing men and women as equal is central to my beliefs.	−5
60	As long as men remain physically stronger than women, they will continue to be able to dominate them.	+3

A more worrying display of male chauvinism is apparent in the ratings of another set of items: women seem to be expected to make themselves attractive in order to seek male approval (items 40 and 45) – this being something they are assumed to want, if only subconsciously; yet they are likely to be blamed for inviting sexual harassment (item 30). Wolf-whistling, it transpires, is not seen as a form of sexual harassment, but as 'just a bit of fun', as one of these boys commented in relation to item 33. In addition, it is also suggested that some women may actually enjoy being dominated by men, in spite of their claims to the contrary (see item 42).

Item number	Q sort placing
40 Women should free themselves from the dictates of fashion.	−4
45 Even women who claim to dress for themselves, or other women, really still like their appearance to be noticed by a man.	+4
30 Much of the sexual harassment women experience they bring on themselves.	+2
33 Men whistling at women is a form of sexual harassment.	−5
42 No matter what they say, there's no doubt that many women actually enjoy being dominated by a male partner.	+3

Once again, there is also a conspicuous emphasis on the importance of enjoying sex, as seen in the placings given to the following items:

Item number	Q sort placing
26 There's nothing wrong with appreciating sexual beauty, whether in an art gallery, in a strip-club, or on the beach.	+3
73 The ideal of remaining a virgin – or 'saving oneself' – for the right person is still a worthwhile one.	−4
4 It's perfectly possible to base a good relationship on a mediocre sex life – other things are much more important.	−3
16 Too much importance is attached to sex in our society.	−4

All of these sentiments can be seen to form part of a discourse of macho (and somewhat misogynistic) masculinity, whose essence is perhaps best summed up by one of the youths himself, who commented: 'I think it's better to be a man and I don't want anyone to think I'm soft.'

These data from the Q sort study of gender and identity present a vivid picture of many of the concerns of teenage males with regard to their developing sense of masculine identity; it is particularly notable that this seems to revolve around a sense of distance from women, who are treated predominantly as sex objects and generally disparaged. The accounts obtained from these young men can thus be seen to project a particular

Jack the Lad image of their own masculinity with which – at this moment in their lives at least – they are choosing to identify.

Further evidence of the way in which putting down girls may form an accepted part of establishing a masculine identity in adolescence comes from the following, more recent study of the social construction of sexual harassment (Kitzinger and Thomas 1990; Thomas and Kitzinger 1994; Kitzinger and Thomas 1996).

Study 2: the social construction of sexual harassment

Research design

This study involved interviews with both women and men about their experiences of situations which might be construed as harassment. Although we were most concerned with exploring women's experiences of such situations, we were also interested in men's ideas about what 'counted' as sexual harassment, both in relation to their own experiences of being harassed (mostly by other men, as it turned out) and with regard to whether or not they thought they had ever harassed women in this way themselves.

Six of our 21 interviewees were men; all were white, and five of the six were in professional occupations (e.g. university lecturer, computer programmer) while the sixth was a mature college student, who defined himself as working-class.[6] Their ages ranged from around 30 to over 60, and all identified themselves to us as heterosexual.

In our interviews, which were semi-structured and informal, we asked participants to talk about their understandings of the term 'sexual harassment', and also sought descriptions of experiences they themselves had had which might be defined in this way. Before the actual interviews took place we gave each participant a sheet listing the broad topics we proposed to discuss, in order to give them an opportunity to reflect in advance on potentially relevant experiences. We first asked them how they would define sexual harassment and what they would consider to be a typical example of it. We then went on to ask about situations which were in some way ambiguous: ones in which either they themselves might now construe the situation differently, or in which different people might have had different ideas as to whether or not it was a case of sexual harassment. In the case of two of the men in particular, this led them to recall and talk about how, as teenagers, they used to behave towards girls and women.

Research findings

Interview extract 1: Chris (university lecturer)

> *AT*: If you look back on your own experience of relationships in a
> very general sense, do you think there are ways in which you

behaved, perhaps when you were younger, that now you would see as harassing women, but you didn't then?

C: Of course. Oh yes ... I don't even want to think about it, I'm totally embarrassed about it ... As a teenager, I used to tease women – much more than I do now. I used to do it to a degree which was ... well now I'd like to crawl into a hole in the ground ... but I rationalize it by saying that we all do things that we grow out of ... I used to pick on women in groups and tease them ... I do it now ... but I don't do it on an overtly sexual basis ... well, it might be something to do with hormones, but – well, like it or not, I think that ... adolescents, because of pubertal changes, are much more prone to that sort of thing, particularly when they're sexually naive, as in this case ... I mean ... If you go through puberty not knowing about sexual relationships (which most people do) and then you find yourself attracted to women yet unable to recognize that as an attraction, then you're more likely in those circumstances to channel your sexual attraction through ways which are potentially pathological but defensive.

AT: Like?

C: Well, I always used to tease women or girls (I'm talking about when I was 13 now) – I always teased the girls that I fancied, but I'd never admit to myself that I fancied them and that was what I was doing ... I was immature, as I think most boys are at that age.

AT: Are you suggesting that most boys sexually harass girls at that age?

C: Of course they do – they do it as part of the power relations between boys and girls in schools or wherever – but girls put down boys as much as boys put down girls, so I wouldn't call it harassment – well, you *could* call it harassment – I would say that young teenage boys and girls may be unaware completely of what they're doing in teasing, cajoling members of the opposite sex.

Interview extract 2: Andrew (college student)

AT: What about when you were younger – can you recall incidents in which you acted towards a woman in a way which now you would construe as sexual harassment?

A: Well I'm sure I have done, but I don't really remember ... erm ... it was different then, in the 60s. I can't recall thinking I was sexually harassing them, I was just ... Well I don't know, I mean we used to chat up girls or women on the street ... but I never really thought of it as ... I think things were less defined then ... I think it was more sort of being in a male role and stereotype than sexual harassment. There wasn't any real consciousness of it, from my point of view.

Talking later about whistling and cat-calling as forms of harassment, the same interviewee again made reference to the idea that this was part of acting out a macho male role, performing to an audience of one's peers.

A: Well I think I'd define it [wolf-whistling] as not looking at the person really . . . not looking as if that woman was a person but more like an object . . . to be ridiculed, really . . . and I suppose it's not honest . . . it's like it's only a group thing – I don't think I've ever seen one man do it; I think there's something wrong here, it's sort of an act without any point . . . I think it's just sort of proving like – 'I'm one of the lads', I suppose, 'I'm OK', sort of thing. It's probably tied up with not being seen as an OK man . . . you've got to be as macho as the rest and er, you're certainly not gay if you erm sort of . . . it's a sort of a way of keeping a male sort of . . . your heterosexual identity.

In both of these accounts there is a denial of any conscious awareness of harassing women as an adolescent – though that may partly reflect the absence of a cultural notion of harassment at that time, as Andrew points out. Andrew claims that 'chatting up' girls was an important way of affirming one's masculinity, while Chris suggests that, as a youth, he (like many others) was too socially inexperienced to know how to relate to girls and hence resorted to what he here construes as playful teasing of them.

Clearly, these have to be seen as the accounts of adult men now seeking to distance themselves from their earlier behaviour: 'I don't even want to think about it, I'm totally embarrassed by it'. In doing so they draw, for the most part, on the familiar 'boys will be boys' discourse, and suggest that this was all part of acting out a masculine role: 'I think it was more sort of being in a male role and stereotype than sexual harassment'. Hence if they were in any way to be considered guilty of harassing girls in their youth, their account seeks to suggest that their behaviour was the result of ignorance, immaturity and youthful insensitivity, rather than deliberate intent; as Chris says, 'We all do things that we grow out of'. In the following section I shall examine the connections between these accounts, and those of the young men reported from Study 1.

Discussion

Taken together, these two quite different studies present contrasting, yet complementary, perspectives on the sorts of behaviour that many adolescent boys (and some grown men) are often seen to show towards girls and women. On the one hand, we have the blunt and derogatory appraisals of girls and women that emerge from the distinctly misogynistic accounts of some of today's teenagers, complete with the view that what others might label sexual harassment is – in their words – 'just a bit of fun'. On the other hand, we have the accounts of two adult men, in which they present somewhat embarrassed recollections of their own youthful participation in similar 'fun' (though now conceding that this was at the expense of the girls concerned), while asserting that this was all part of learning a masculine role.

Data from these two different studies thus indicate that one of the main ways in which men may choose to explain the sexual harassment of women and girls is by claiming that this kind of behaviour is what is expected of them as a demonstration of their masculinity. The youths in Study 1 signal via their somewhat defiant identity accounts that conforming to masculine norms is something that is important to them, while for the adults in Study 2, looking back on themselves as teenagers, the importance of conforming to masculine roles then, now provides a way of retrospectively rationalizing their teenage 'pranks'.

It is therefore apparent that both studies provide substantial support for the link between sexual harassment and 'doing masculinity' that was proposed earlier. Study 1 also provides evidence that this kind of behaviour may go in tandem with a juvenile misogyny, formulated here in a youthful macho discourse expressing a general contempt for women. This thereby also offers empirical support for the theoretical link between masculinity and misogyny, as discussed previously. In practical terms, it appears from the accounts in Study 1 that conformity to the perceived 'rules' of masculinity necessitates both drawing attention to one's difference from women, and the conspicuous display of one's heterosexuality – both of which are easily combined in acts of sexual harassment, such as wolf-whistling. The adult accounts in Study 2 further suggest that proving one's masculinity in this way, by objectifying women, is a way of reinforcing a heterosexual identification with other men: as Andrew says, 'You've got to be as macho as the rest . . . it's a sort of a way of keeping a male sort of . . . your heterosexual identity'.

In the final part of this chapter, I shall look at how the findings of these two studies complement those of other researchers, and trace the links between masculinity, misogyny and patriarchal power.

Misogyny, masculinity and male bonding

The findings from Study 1 in particular clearly correspond to those of various other researchers, who have similarly reported young men expressing antagonism towards girls and women. Wood (1982: 41), for example, describing the teenage boys he interviewed, claims that

For the boys I worked with, it was clear that learning to inhabit their form of masculinity invariably entailed, to a greater or lesser extent, learning to be sexist: being a bit of a lad and being contemptuous of women just went 'naturally' together.

From Wood's research, as well as my own, it would seem that an important way of establishing one's masculinity is through the conspicuous display of chauvinistic attitudes and behaviours, which may often include harassing behaviours. As Andrew (in Study 2) confirmed, wolf-whistling, for example, is an act performed predominantly for an all-male audience, using women as mere stage props; the purpose of such a performance is to demonstrate one's credentials for membership of the men's club. Houston (1988), indeed, quotes a male university student who claims that wolf-whistling at women 'is something that men do to impress other guys'. Lees (1986) has likewise remarked upon such behaviour as a means of promoting solidarity among 'the lads'; as she notes, 'Sexism appears to be one feature of male bonding, where denigrating girls and women builds up a kind of camaraderie between them' (Lees 1986: 31).

The fact that in many of the everyday kinds of sexual harassment that women encounter there is some kind of conspicuous evaluation of them as sexual objects – whether through wolf-whistling, making crude comments or simply eyeing up and down – further underlines the connection for men between 'doing masculinity' and proving one's heterosexual credentials by publicly commenting on women in this way. This, of course, should hardly seem surprising in the context of the messages boys pick up from their society about women's role as sexual objects or commodities, and their own role as sexual consumers. As Kagan and Moss (1962: 167) observed, boys soon learn that:

> one of the concomitants of maintaining a traditional masculine identification is a preoccupation with and an ostentatious display of sexual ideas. The individual gains support for his masculinity by announcing his concern with sexuality.

(Here, as elsewhere, the identification of sexuality with *hetero*sexuality is taken for granted.)

There was certainly ample evidence of this form of display in the Q sort accounts of the boys in Study 1, and I would likewise argue that it is this which is going on when groups of men whistle at or otherwise harass women on the street. They are, in effect, asserting their position as male 'consumers' of female bodies. The comments made by Andrew, in Study 2, ('it's . . . a way of keeping your heterosexual identity') would appear to support such an interpretation.

The teenagers of Study 1 of course indicated that in their view women actually enjoy being the object of male attention in this way, and as both

Benard and Schlaffer (1984) and Houston (1988) report, this is frequently mentioned by men as a defence of whistling and other similar forms of harassment. However, the objectification of women that occurs in sexual harassment is by no means as benign as men imply when they construct it in this way as a simple act of 'appreciation' of the female form. Rather, acts such as wolf-whistling are premised upon 'the taken-for-granted entitlement of men to women's bodies' (Larkin 1991), and consist of asserting the male right to comment on them (Bartky 1990). Thus, in Larkin's (1991: 114) analysis,

> every incident of sexual harassment is an expression of men's power, a systematic reminder to women that we are seen not as human beings but primarily as sexual objects for the pleasure of men.

Here again, then, we are brought back to the central connection between sexual harassment and the male desire to wield power over women. Yet men and women alike consistently find ways of denying this connection and of generally minimizing the significance of sexual harassment (Kitzinger and Thomas 1996).

'Normalizing' sexual harassment

As we have seen in Study 2, one way of 'normalizing' sexual harassment is to treat wolf-whistling and similar kinds of 'everyday' harassment as manifestations of the normal process of establishing a masculine identity – and hence to dismiss them as something that young men will in due course grow out of. Nor is this discourse confined to men seeking to excuse their own behaviour, as is the case here. Again and again in women's accounts of everyday harassment the notion that 'boys will be boys' is mentioned, even when the 'boys' in question are in fact adults.

As an illustration of this apparent tolerance of male misbehaviour, we need only to look at the popularity of the British television hit comedy *Men Behaving Badly* which offers a distinctly benign view of male boorishness. This sitcom invites the viewer to participate in laughing at what the *Radio Times* (20 June 1996) referred to as an 'excruciating (and accurate?) portrayal of laddish behaviour', in the form of the loutish and juvenile antics of two adult men, Gary and Tony. Their characters are based (according to the creator of the series) on 'an amalgam of students I knew at university in London', and although their behaviour is of course contrived to be excessive – a parody of 'masculinity' – it none the less appears sufficiently recognizable to strike a chord with many viewers. Significantly, most of the humour is derived from the tensions between the two men's relationship with each other as 'good mates', and their inept attempts at managing relationships with women (towards whom they express considerable ambivalence).

The fact that this comedy has become so popular suggests two possible interpretations: first, if we take it simply at face value, its popularity implies that as a society we are prepared to tolerate a considerable degree of 'bad behaviour' from men without stigmatizing it as deviant. A second, somewhat different reading is that making humour out of some fairly repellent and loutish behaviour may function as a way of sanitizing it, and thereby defusing it of potential menace. For, in common with much else in popular culture (such as the 'Carry On' films of the 1970s), *Men Behaving Badly* leads us to construct acts such as wolf-whistling as the actions of lovable prats such as Gary and Tony – i.e. as a source of humour, rather than as problematic – and this thereby reinforces the view that this kind of laddish behaviour is not really the same as 'serious' sexual harassment.

Seen, then, from the psychosocial perspective advanced in this chapter, the most common forms of everyday sexual harassment cannot be attributed simply to the deviant behaviour of a few sexually inadequate individuals. Rather, the roots of this kind of harassment are culturally embedded in the dominant definitions of masculinity with which young men grow up. For, far from being the product of individual pathology, it is recognizably 'normal' behaviour, in so far as most men at some point in their lives are likely to practise it in some form or other (even if, like Chris and Andrew, they will later come to denounce it); and, as Wise and Stanley (1987: 72) claimed, 'all women have been sexually harassed at some time or another'. Under these circumstances, we might therefore conclude that 'everyday' sexual harassment is an act of conformity, rather than one of deviance.

Brant and Too (1994) have suggested that conclusions such as these are inappropriately dramatic and despairing; as such, they argue, they can lead to charges of exaggeration and fear-mongering, which then provide the justification for society to continue ignoring sexual harassment. While sharing some of their fears in this regard, I do not myself feel that that should lead feminists to back down from pointing out the insidious all-pervasiveness of sexual harassment. Nor can I identify with the view expressed by many of the women I have interviewed, that we simply have to resign ourselves to sexual harassment on the cynical grounds that it is 'just the way men are' (cf. Thomas and Kitzinger 1992). Unless we seriously believe that 'the way men are' in this context is governed by their biology (in the form of an insatiable sex drive for example; cf. Tangri *et al.* 1982); or that it is in some other way 'determined' (as a product of their psyche for instance; cf. Person 1980), such that men's harassing behaviour towards women is beyond their voluntary control, then it can only be interpreted as the outcome of the way we, that is society, permit (or encourage) them to behave. That, of course, is something that we do have the power to change, provided that there is the collective will to do so.

Challenging patriarchal practices

A close examination of the connections between masculinity, misogyny and sexual harassment has here revealed that the common factor linking all three is patriarchal power. It therefore seems that in order to be effective, any strategy for tackling sexual harassment must be made part of a much wider project of resistance to patriarchal practices, confronting misogyny and challenging the dominant forms of masculinity that are founded upon it. Of course, feminists have for a long time been seeking to do just that – to wean men from their attachment to some of the more pernicious forms of 'masculinity' – and even today, many still remain committed to the belief that it is possible to bring up boys to reject patriarchal practices, including sexual harassment (cf. Rowland and Thomas 1996). Critically, though, it appears that this is a project that will only work in the long term if it has the support of men as well as women. Yet there are clearly grounds for scepticism about the likelihood of men supporting this or any other feminist campaign which threatens to undermine their position of power over women.

Historically, the primary obstacle to gaining male cooperation in this way has always been the basic refusal on the part of most men to recognize that they possess any such power. Thus, as we have seen here, even though men may often admit to participating in the kinds of everyday harassment discussed in this chapter, they tend to play down the power dynamics involved. They are also at pains to avoid labelling it as 'sexual harassment', since that would imply acknowledging their own behaviour as oppressive to women (Kitzinger and Thomas 1996). In these ways, most men thereby continue to avoid making the important links between the personal and the political; between 'just having a bit of fun' at women's expense, and its political symbolism as an expression of male dominance over women.

Nevertheless, what an increasing number *do* recognize is that what impels men to behave in this way towards women may actually be fear as much as anything else (cf. Hearn 1985). For, as we have seen in the two studies discussed here, there is an openly acknowledged fear of failing to conform to the rules of masculinity – a fear of not being accepted as one of the lads. (As one of the young men in Study 1 explained, 'I would worry about the ridicule from others if I turned femanine [sic]'.) Indeed, it is significant that more and more men are now becoming aware of the various negative consequences for them of conforming to patriarchal expectations of what it means to be a man (e.g. Connell 1987; Hearn 1987; Seidler 1989; Morgan 1992). As Seidler (cited in Eardley 1985: 98) observes: 'Masculinity is never something we can feel at ease with. It is always something we have to be ready to prove and defend.'

As men begin to recognize the damage that this constant pressure inflicts on them, they may start to realize that conformity to norms of masculinity predicated upon misogyny not only perpetuates fear among men but also engenders a climate of mistrust and mutual antagonism between men and women, which – in the long run – benefits nobody. In this way, by acknowledging the coercive and corrosive aspects of patriarchal power that they themselves experience, men may at last be in a position to understand that rejecting the patriarchal imperative could in fact be liberating for all. Only then, when men themselves start to resist hegemonic masculinity, will there be any real likelihood of progress towards eliminating sexual harassment.

Notes

1 The first Q set, dealing with self-representation, consisted of descriptions of personality traits and behaviours commonly associated with masculinity and femininity, e.g. 'Is confident and self-assertive'; 'Is warm and gentle'. The second Q set, on gender salience, tapped self-perception in terms of masculinity and the consciousness of male identity, e.g. 'I don't think of myself as particularly masculine'; 'Being a man is not the most important thing about me'. The third Q set, on gender ideology, concerned the network of basic attitudes and beliefs about men and women used in accounting for gender roles, e.g. 'The "psychological" differences between the sexes cannot be denied or wished away – they are part of our biological make-up'; 'There's nothing to stop a talented woman from "getting to the top" in our society today, if she has the ambition and drive to do it.'.

2 To give an example, one item in the gender salience Q set – 'I do not see the emotional life of men and of women as being different in any important respects' – elicited strong disagreement (–4) in both a radical feminist account and in two different men's accounts, one of which was extremely traditional. In other words, the significance of how this item was treated in these different accounts can only be interpreted in the context of the overall response to the Q set as a whole.

3 As a way of checking the interpretation of the account emerging from each statistical factor, Q sort researchers frequently invite the participants to comment either on their response to individual items in the Q set (e.g. Stainton Rogers 1991), or on the researcher's interpretation of the account as a whole (e.g. Kitzinger 1987). In this research, I asked those participants whose Q sorts best defined each factor to comment on the particular items that marked it as distinctive from others, and I draw on some of these comments in my discussion of the data.

4 Note that in Q methodology the number of participants does not affect the validity and significance of the resultant data in the same way as it does with most other research methodologies. (For a detailed technical explanation of this, see Kitzinger 1987; Thomas 1987; Brown 1980.) In terms of the general principles involved, Q methodology seeks simply to establish the variety of perspectives that are expressed within a given population, rather than making claims regarding the proportion of the population expressing them. As a result, large numbers

of participants are not required – merely sufficient (and sufficiently diverse) Q sorters 'to establish the existence of a factor for purposes of comparing one factor with another' (Brown 1980).

5 The items reported here are some of those which best characterize the distinctive features of these particular accounts, in so far as they were most significant in discriminating between these and the identity accounts generated by other participants.

6 As with the first study, the research emphasis here was simply on identifying the presence of different accounts concerning gender identity, gender relations and sexual harassment in contemporary discourse, not on making any claims that these discourses could be identified with particular sections of the population. In terms of the arguments advanced in this chapter, what is significant is that such discourses exist in contemporary culture, and that they are employed to warrant the kinds of disparaging behaviour shown towards women discussed earlier. The representativeness of the participants in this study is therefore not in itself an important issue.

References

Abrams, D. and Condor, S. (1984) 'A social identity approach to the development of sex identification in adolescence'. Paper presented at the International Interdisciplinary Conference on Self and Identity, University College, Cardiff, July.

Adorno, T.W., Frankel-Brunswick, E., Levinson, D.J. and Sanford, R.N. (1950) *The Authoritarian Personality*. New York: Harper and Row.

Bartky, S.L. (1990) *Femininity and Domination: Studies in the Phenomenology of Oppression*. New York: Routledge.

Benard, C. and Schlaffer, E. (1984) The man in the street: Why he harasses. In A. Jaggar and P. Rothenberg (eds) *Feminist Frameworks*. New York: McGraw-Hill.

Brant, C. and Too, Y.L. (1994) Introduction. In C. Brant and Y.L. Too (eds) *Rethinking Sexual Harassment*. London: Pluto Press.

Brown, S.R. (1980) *Political Subjectivity: Applications of Q Methodology in Political Science*. New Haven, CT: Yale University Press.

Chodorow, N. (1978) *The Reproduction of Mothering*. Berkeley, CA: University of California Press.

Collier, R. (1995) *Combating Sexual Harassment in the Workplace*. Buckingham: Open University Press.

Connell, R.W. (1987) *Gender and Power*. Cambridge: Polity Press.

Crichton, M. (1994) *Disclosure*. London: Century.

de Beauvoir, S. (1953) *The Second Sex*. London: Jonathan Cape.

Dziech, B. and Weiner, L. (1984) *The Lecherous Professor*. Boston, MA: Beacon Press.

Eardley, T. (1985) Violence and sexuality. In A. Metcalf and M. Humphries (eds) *The Sexuality of Men*. London: Pluto Press.

Farley, L. (1978) *Sexual Shakedown: The Sexual Harassment of Women on the Job*. New York: Warner Books.

Forcey, L. (1987) *Mothers of Sons: Towards an Understanding of Responsibility*. New York: Praeger.

Greenson, R. (1968) Disidentifying from the mother: Its special importance for the boy. *International Journal of Psychoanalysis*, 49: 370–4.

Groth, A. and Birnbaum, H. (1979) *Men Who Rape: The Psychology of the Offender*. New York: Plenum Press.

Hartley, R.E. (1959) Sex-role pressures and the socialization of the male child. *Psychological Reports*, 5: 457–68.

Hearn, J. (1985) Men's sexuality at work. In A. Metcalf and M. Humphries (eds) *The Sexuality of Men*. London: Pluto Press.

Hearn, J. (1987) *The Gender of Oppression*. Brighton: Wheatsheaf.

Hearn, J. and Morgan, D. (eds) (1993) *Men, Masculinities, and Social Theory*. London: Unwin Hyman Ltd.

Herbert, C. (1989) *Talking of Silence: The Sexual Harassment of Schoolgirls*. London: Falmer Press.

Houston, B. (1988) What's wrong with sexual harassment? *Atlantis*, 13(2):44–47.

Kagan, J. and Moss, H. (1962) *Birth to Maturity*. New York: Wiley.

Kitzinger, C. (1987) *The Social Construction of Lesbianism*. London: Sage.

Kitzinger, C. and Thomas, A.M. (1990) 'Asymmetry and ambiguity in gender relations: Constructing sexual harassment'. Paper presented at the British Psychological Society London Conference, as part of a Psychology of Women Section symposium on 'Gender relations and the social construction of gender difference', December.

Kitzinger, C. and Thomas, A.M. (1996) Sexual harassment: A discursive approach. In S. Wilkinson and C. Kitzinger (eds) *Feminism and Discourse: Psychological Perspectives*. London: Sage.

Larkin, J. (1991) Sexual harassment: From the personal to the political. *Atlantis*, 17(1): 106–15.

Lees, S. (1986) *Losing Out: Sexuality and Adolescent Girls*. London: Hutchinson.

Lynn, D.B. (1969) *Parental and Sex-Role Identification*. Berkeley, CA: McCutchan.

Malamuth, N. (1981) Rape proclivity among males. *Journal of Social Issues*, 37: 138–57.

Morgan, D.H.J. (1992) *Discovering Men*. London: Routledge.

Ortner, S.B. and Whitehead, H. (1981) *Sexual Meanings: the Cultural Construction of Gender and Sexuality*. Cambridge: Cambridge University Press.

Paludi, M. (1990) *Ivory Power: Sexual Harassment on Campus*. New York: State University of New York Press.

Person, E.S. (1980) Sexuality as the mainstay of identity. In C.R. Stimpson and E.S. Person (eds) *Women: Sex and Sexuality*. Chicago, IL: University of Chicago Press.

Pryor, J.B. (1987) Sexual harassment proclivities in men. *Sex Roles*, 17: 269–89.

Pryor, J.B. and Stoller, L.M. (1994) Sexual cognition processes in men high in the likelihood to sexually harass. *Personality and Psychology Bulletin*, 20(2): 163–9.

Rowland, R. and Thomas, A.M. (eds) (1996) Mothering sons: A crucial feminist challenge. *Feminism & Psychology*, 6(1): 93–154.

Ryan, T. (1985) Roots of masculinity. In A. Metcalf and M. Humphries (eds) *The Sexuality of Men*. London: Pluto Press.

Seidler, V.J. (1989) *Rediscovering Masculinity*. London: Routledge.

Senn, C.Y. (1996) Q methodology as a feminist methodology: Women's views and experiences of pornography. In S. Wilkinson (ed.) *Feminist Social Psychologies: International Perspectives*. Buckingham: Open University Press.

Silverstein, O. and Rashbaum, B. (1994) *The Courage to Raise Good Men: A Radical Reassessment of the Mother–Son Relationship*. London: Penguin.

Stainton Rogers, W. (1991) *Explaining Health and Illness*. Hemel Hempstead: Harvester Wheatsheaf.

Tajfel, H. (ed.) (1978) *Differentiation Between Social Groups: Studies in the Social Psychology of Intergroup Relations*. London: Academic Press.

Tangri, S., Burt, M.R., and Johnson, L.B. (1982) Sexual harassment at work: Three explanatory models. *Journal of Social Issues*, 38(4): 33–54.

Thomas, A.M. (1987) 'Cultural representations and personal meanings in the social construction of gender: A psychological study. Unpublished PhD thesis. University of Reading.

Thomas, A.M. (1990a) The significance of gender politics in men's accounts of their 'gender identity'. In J. Hearn and D. Morgan (eds) *Men, Masculinities, and Social Theory*. London: Unwin Hyman.

Thomas, A.M. (1990b) 'Defining difference: The social construction of gender in contemporary discourse'. Paper presented at the British Psychological Society's London Conference, as part of a Psychology of Women Section symposium on 'Gender relations and the social construction of gender difference', December.

Thomas, A.M. and Kitzinger, C. (1992) 'Contesting "sexual harassment": An analysis of the rhetoric of denial'. Paper presented at the British Sociological Society's Annual Conference, University of Kent at Canterbury, April.

Thomas, A.M. (1993) 'Masculinity' as misogyny: An exploration of the cultural context of sexual harassment. Paper presented at the Annual Women and Psychology Conference, University of Sussex, July.

Thomas, A.M. and Kitzinger, C. (1994) It's just something that happens: The invisibility of sexual harassment in the workplace. *Gender, Work and Organisation*, 1(3): 151–61.

Thorne, B. (1993) *Gender Play: Girls and Boys in School*. Buckingham: Open University Press.

Watson, H. (1994) Red herrings and mystifications: Conflicting perceptions of sexual harassment. In C. Brant and Y.L. Too (eds) *Rethinking Sexual Harassment*. London: Pluto Press.

Wise, S. and Stanley, L. (1987) *Georgie Porgie: Sexual Harassment in Life*. London: Pandora.

Wood, J. (1982) Boys will be boys. *New Socialist*, May/June: 41–43.

8

Keeping them in their place: hetero/sexist harassment, gender and the enforcement of heterosexuality[1]

DEBBIE EPSTEIN

Introduction

Since September 1991 I have been engaged in a research project in which we set out to explore the experiences of lesbian and gay students, teachers, and parents in relation to the English system of education.[2] In the course of the project, we have interviewed or held group discussions with some 30 lesbians and gay men, as well as carrying out ethnographic work in four schools and in a lesbian and gay youth group.[3] While the majority of our respondents have been white, we have also spoken with lesbians and gays of African and of South Asian descent.[4] My own contribution to the field work for this project has been that of interviewing many of our lesbian and gay respondents and participant observation in one of the schools. Doing the research, I have been struck forcibly by the various forms of harassment experienced by our female respondents as well as by those men and boys who identified as and/or were perceived as gay or effeminate by their peers and/or teachers. During the same period, and partly because of the research findings, I have found myself reflecting on my own experiences of harassment and those of my students in both the recent and more distant past. This chapter is, in large part, the result of these reflections and of discussions I have had with students, colleagues, and friends about the issues involved.[5]

In this chapter, I will argue that the term 'sexual harassment' is misleading. I do not wish to suggest that the term has not been useful, particularly in the way that it has been used to make women aware of the sexual content of gender inequality. However, I believe that the more or less orthodox feminist view of sexual harassment, which argues that sexism is, by definition, sexual (see, for example, MacKinnon 1979; Wise and Stanley 1987), is now due for reconsideration. I will also argue that, within this reconsideration, it is imperative to pay close attention to the harassment of gay men as well as that of women, since both can be understood as a kind of pedagogy of heterosexuality and a key way in which heterosexuality is institutionalized. Indeed, it may seem that this chapter is overweighted towards the consideration of the harassment of gay men. This is deliberate, precisely because I believe that it is an important area of sexist harassment which has not been considered in detail.

Definitions of sexual harassment in policy documents often refer to a range of activities that extend well beyond the obviously sexual. Despite these wide-ranging definitions of what constitutes sexual harassment, this term is usually used in more limited ways that appeal to certain common-sense notions of what it is to be sexual. This limiting of the term may, indeed, be a key factor that hinders women from taking formal action against their harassers. I will therefore propose that the term 'sexist harassment' may well be more useful to those at its receiving end. I will also suggest that, to develop a fuller understanding of sexist harassment, we need to see it within the context of what Adrienne Rich (1980) calls 'compulsory heterosexuality' – that is, the ways in which heterosexuality is rewarded (for example through social approval, the legal institution of marriage with its manifold material and other benefits) while lesbianism (and gay sexuality) is punished (for example through social stigmatization, the frequent loss of custody of children, the impossibility of having one's relationship recognized in law). More fruitful for my purposes in this chapter is, perhaps, Judith Butler's (1990) notion of the 'heterosexual matrix' which she conceives as including not only the institutionalization of compulsory heterosexuality, but also the wider discursive field which shapes our understandings of gender in terms of binary opposites tied together through (presumed heterosexual) desire.

Defining sexual/sexist harassment

The bulk of my research has taken place in schools or has asked interviewees to reflect on their experiences of school life in relation to sexuality. It seems appropriate, therefore, for me to use the definition of sexual harassment given by the National Union of Teachers' (NUT) pamphlet on *Dealing with Sexual Harassment* (1986). It is important to note that this definition is typical of those employed in institutions (educational or otherwise) that have policies pertaining to sexual harassment:

> any uninvited, unreciprocated and unwelcome physical contact, comment, suggestion, joke or attention which is offensive to the person

involved, and causes that person to feel threatened, humiliated, patronised or embarrassed.

(cited in de Lyon 1989: 122)

De Lyon points out that the wide range of actions covered by such a definition and the subjective nature of its terms 'can cause certain difficulties' (p. 122). I would suggest that not least among these difficulties is the fact that it can be difficult to define harassment as 'sexual' when, in common-sense terms, it is not.

Rebecca, for example, described to me the ways in which a more senior colleague in her university department, a sociologist who both taught and wrote about inequality, would frequently invade her space.[6] But, she explained, his touches could not really be said to be 'sexual'. She perceived them more as an infantilizing process than as 'touching up'. They would occur if she disagreed with him and he would touch her in a way that indicated that he found her immature, not to be taken seriously. Rebecca was neither young nor inexperienced. She was, however, on a temporary contract and a lesbian, and felt totally unable to take any official action against her harasser, feeling that this would:

1 be countered by William becoming angry and denying any form of harassment; and
2 result in her failure to become a permanent member of staff.

The point here is that the wide-ranging definition of sexual harassment in operation in Rebecca's university, which is almost identical to that quoted from the NUT, did not help her report the harassment or take official action against William. Her difficulty was, in part, due to her particularly vulnerable position as a lesbian on a temporary contract. It also fits into a frequently reported picture of the underreporting of sexual harassment (see, for example, de Lyon 1989). It was, moreover, clearly about the term 'sexual harassment' itself. She felt that in the course of a disciplinary hearing she would have to agree that the touches she had endured while being harassed were not specifically sexual. At no time had William made sexual advances to Rebecca. This deterred her from taking action against what she clearly perceived as his sexist actions.

This story is representative of stories which have been told to me over and over again by students and friends. In addition, such stories have come up in relation to the experiences of both lesbian and gay respondents in our research. The point of all these stories is that the very term *sexual harassment* constrains the action these people have felt able to take. In this context, the term *sexist harassment* may well have been more helpful to them. Language is a powerful force in the making of meanings. Over the years feminists have, for example, argued that the use of the word 'man' to subsume women constitutes an erasure of women. Similarly, the term 'sexual harassment' erases the experience of *sexist* harassment which is not overtly or obviously sexual in content or form. A consequence of this is that it becomes even more difficult for many women to have recourse to official procedures than it might otherwise have been – a recourse which would, in any case, be difficult simply because of the patriarchal hierarchies of educational and other institutions. I would, therefore, suggest that the term 'sexist' rather than 'sexual' harassment, may be more helpful to those who experience this kind of behaviour.

Sexism, heterosexism, and the heterosexual matrix

Drawing on the work of Rich (1980) and Wittig (1980, 1981), Judith Butler uses the term *heterosexual matrix* 'to designate that grid of cultural intelligibility through which bodies, genders and desires are naturalized' (1990: 151). She argues that gender (and its instabilities) need to be understood in the context of the heterosexual matrix. Butler suggests that gender is a constructed and excluding category which is put in place through its connection, via desire (culturally assumed to be of the opposite sex) to heterosexuality. She also argues that a great deal of cultural work goes into the maintenance of the oppositional, binary 'gendered possibilities' available to us and that this work rests on the presumption of heterosexuality as both 'normal' and normative (see also Epstein and Johnson 1994). I will suggest below that sexist harassment constitutes a significant part of this cultural work.

The limits of what is permissible for each gender are framed within the context of compulsory heterosexuality. This is established very early in childhood and is part of the way in which the education of young children is structured. It is clear, for example, that the meanings both of being a 'good girl' and of being a 'real boy' are constituted within a silent heterosexuality, which is made all the more powerful by its very silence.[7] Clarricoates (1987: 156), for example, in her much cited work on primary school teachers and children, offers the following quotes from teachers:

> the girls seem to be typically feminine whilst the boys seem to be typically male . . . you know more aggressive . . . the ideal of what males ought to be.

> I think the boys tend to be a little more aggressive and on thinking about it the male is the same in the animal world . . . we are animals basically.

Clarricoates' paper is concerned with the gendered ways in which teachers treat children and the gendered ways that children behave, having learnt their gender-appropriate sex roles. However, nowhere does she point out that these roles are not simply about the genders of the children, but also about the assumed heterosexuality of those genders. Being 'typically feminine', for example, does not make sense except in a heterosexual relationship to its binary opposite, the 'masculine'. Women are supposed to show their femininity by dressing and behaving in ways which are attractive to men (see also Lees 1986, 1993). Indeed, it is this (presumed heterosexual) relationship of femininity to the masculine which is often parodied by drag queens, who adopt stereotypically ultra-feminine ways of dressing and behaving.[8] Equally, the notion that 'boys tend to be a little more aggressive' provides a basis for later discourses of the male sex drive (see Hollway 1984, 1989), which assume that men will take the lead in sexual encounters with women and have strong needs for (instant) gratification of their sex drive.[9] The underlying assumption here is that men are (biologically) programmed to pursue women in more or less aggressive ways while women will wait to be pursued, their most active agency involving putting out signals of availability. Within this discourse, sexual harassment is seen to be simply the expression of men's (biological) needs to pursue potential sexual partners in the search for immediate sexual satisfaction. In this way, feminist discourses of sexual harassment can be appropriated by and incorporated into an inherently anti-feminist framework.

Feminists have not generally explained sexual/sexist harassment in these biological terms. Rather, most feminists have argued that biology is not destiny and feminist explanations of harassment have therefore been in terms of the relative power of men and women and of the ways in which sexual/sexist harassment serves to reinforce and preserve this power relationship (see, for example, MacKinnon 1979; Hanmer and Maynard 1987; Wise and Stanley 1987). What I would like to suggest is that this relationship of power is not simply one in which men oppress women, and in which women are marked as Other. Rather, building on Butler (1990), I would suggest that it is one in which:

1 gendered and sexualized relationships are complexly constructed in relation to other differences, such as those of age, race, ethnicity, class, and/or disability;
2 heterosexuality is presumed and deviations from heterosexual norms are punished;
3 the harassment of gay men (and of men perceived to be gay) is not a separate issue, which is of relatively minor importance in understanding the harassment of women but is, rather, an important aspect of policing culturally produced boundaries of both gender and sexuality; and
4 sexist harassment can be seen as a pedagogy which schools women and men into normative heterosexuality (but not always successfully).

The next sections of this chapter explore these four points in more detail.

The complexity of social relations and sexist harassment

The gendered power relations which are constructed in part through sexist harassment are themselves complex and somewhat fluid. It would, therefore, be a mistake to assume that the sexist harassment of black women, for example, takes exactly the same forms as that of white women, for there are particular racialized constructions of black women's sexuality and their gender-appropriate behaviour which impact upon the forms of sexist harassment which they might experience.[10] There are, therefore, likely to be differences in the forms of (racialized) sexist harassment experienced by black women from those experienced by white women, and in the forms of (sexualized) racist harassment experienced by black women from those experienced by black men. The case of Anita Hill and Clarence Thomas provides ample evidence of the complexity of the ways in which sexist harassment becomes racialized in a racist society and, conversely, in which racism becomes sexualized in a sexist society (see Morrison 1993). Indeed, as Morrison argues, the case could not have happened in the absence of particular racist/sexist tropes which gave rise to the case in the first place (p. xvii).

It is important to note here that neither the category 'black' nor the category 'white' should be considered to be monolithic. Within the category 'white' there are different constructions of WASP (White, Anglo-Saxon Protestant) and other heterosexualities, *vide* the stereotypical 'Latin lover'.[11] Equally, there are different versions within Anglo-American popular culture (both white and ethnic minority) of the sexualities of (to adopt American terminology) 'people of colour'. They are, nevertheless, versions of heterosexuality and the experiences of harassment of lesbian and gay people of colour are shaped both by racist and by heterosexist assumptions.[12]

For disabled people, the assumptions about sexuality take a somewhat different form. Even more than 'nice girls', disabled people are not supposed to be sexual. However, the presumption is, almost invariably, that any sexual desire that exists or any sex which takes place will be hetero, as will any loving or romantic relationships. Hence the well-publicized cases of the sterilization of mentally and physically disabled women (and sometimes men) who, it is feared, might become sexual but fail to take precautions against pregnancy. Moreover, people who become disabled as the result of illness or accident may find that their relationships with same-sex partners are denied by doctors, families of origin, and legal institutions.[13] While the denial of sexuality to disabled people might, on the face of it, appear to rule out harassment, this very denial can be experienced as harassing in itself.[14] Furthermore, when hetero/sexuality *is* recognized as being part of the lives of disabled people, it may be medicalized, with disabled people being offered physical assistance for mechanical versions of sexual intercourse in which the 'release' of orgasm is assumed to be the only issue and closeness in and through sexuality disappears. Here, hetero/sexist assumptions about sex and penetration being identical are writ large. This, too, can be experienced as a form of 'official hetero/sexist harassment'. Finally, an important aspect of the experience of visible disability is being seen as undesirable, ugly, and unsexy. In a society where the necessity of having a 'body beautiful' is stressed, disabled people may be harassed about their appearances in ways which do not constitute sexual approaches (wanted or unwanted) but are most definitely harassing. For those disabled women and men identifying as lesbian or gay, then, the struggle to express themselves sexually is shaped both by constructions of disability as a/anti-sexual and by constructions of sexuality as heterosexual.[15]

In this section I have explored two aspects of the complexity of social relations in and through which sexuality and gender are constructed and within which sexist harassment takes place. However, the argument could be extended to cover other inequalities. The point here is that there is not one, univocal form of hetero/sexist harassment but, rather, that the forms of harassment experienced shape and are shaped by the particular social locations of those who are harassed and, indeed, their harassers.

The presumption of heterosexuality and the punishment of deviance

Richard Johnson and I have argued elsewhere that the almost universal presumption of heterosexuality is part of what makes it compulsory (Epstein and Johnson 1994: 198). Furthermore, deviance from normative heterosexuality is regularly punished in a myriad of ways too numerous to be fully documented. Most obvious are, perhaps, the legislative discrimination against gay men in relation to the age of consent and other sex 'crimes'. Furthermore, as Evans (1993: 123) points out, neither European (including British) nor American legislation generally protects lesbians and gay men from discrimination in employment.

Similarly, there is juridical and bureaucratic discrimination against lesbians in relation to issues of child custody, adoption, and fostering (effectively endorsed by the Save the Children Fund when they dropped Sandy Toksvig from speaking at their annual conference after she came out as co-parent of her female partner's children).[16] The prevalence and increase of violence against gay men and lesbians, particularly those on the 'scene', is also indicative of punitive action against those who dare to deviate from the heterosexual path. Other punishments include the bullying of boys and men found to be 'sissy', 'wimpish' and/or gay and the taunting of certain girls as 'lezzie' (see Alistair et al. 1994; Rogers 1994; Mac an Ghaill

1994). Throughout our interviews with lesbians and gay men, respondents reported to us a combination of the experience of being harassed because they were perceived as being, in some way, not sufficiently like 'real boys' or were not 'feminine' enough. They also reported the experience of fearing such harassment and taking avoiding action, often through a heightening of their own homophobic behaviours and even heterosexual activities. Thus, for example, Alistair talked about having a 'pretend girlfriend', while several of our lesbian respondents spoke about seeking to have boyfriends in order to avoid both being labelled as lesbian and to avoid other forms of sexual harassment. In other words, heterosexist harassment can be seen as one form of punishment of deviance from the straight and narrow.

The harassment of gay men and those perceived as gay

Herbert (1992: 12) argues first that men cannot be sexually harassed because harassment can take place only if the harasser has both institutional and personal power over the person harassed. Second, she also posits that

> sometimes a gay person sexually harasses a straight person, sometimes a gay person is sexually harassed by a straight person, and sometimes a gay person is sexually harassed by a gay person.
>
> (p. 23)

What is noteworthy here is that her first statement (that men cannot be harassed) must logically, in the light of her second (that gay people can be harassed either by straight people or by other gay people), apply only to heterosexual men (unless, of course, gay men do not count as men). In addition, her suggestion that gay people can harass straight people seems not to make sense within her own terms since, in relation to sexuality at least, gay men and lesbians lack 'institutional and personal power' over straight people.

In fact, most writing about sexist harassment assumes that the harassment of boys and men who appear to be gay or effeminate is different in kind and in effect to the harassment of women. Sometimes, as in the case of Herbert, the heterosexist or homophobic harassment of lesbians and gay men is mentioned in passing. Sometimes, as in the work of Mahony, it may be pointed out that:

> When a boy gets 'pushed around' it is not, I would suggest, in virtue of being a boy but because he is not the right sort of boy. Perhaps he is perceived as possessing qualities which run counter to dominant notions of masculinity. In this case he may also be subject to verbal abuse, 'poof', 'queer' and 'you've got AIDS'.

> For him the lesson to be learnt is how to become a *real* man, dominant and not subordinate.
>
> (1989: 162–3; original emphasis)

However, even Mahony's very clear description of girls' experiences of sexual harassment, including violence, in mixed schools does not make explicit the extent to which such harassment is directed towards the production of *heterosexual* girls and boys, that is, girls and boys for whom heterosexuality is inherent in their sense of themselves as gendered. Thus, for Mahony's boy to learn to be a 'real man, dominant and not subordinate', he will also, as is clear from the range of insults directed towards him, have to constitute himself as heterosexual (and specifically not a 'poof' or a 'queer'). Similarly, Julian Wood's (1984) quite shocking account of the horrendous sexism of boys' sex talk (which includes fantasies of violent rape), takes for granted that this talk will be entirely and aggressively heterosexual. Indeed, reading his article, it is difficult to see how a gay, or even a less aggressively heterosexual, boy could begin to survive (or, at any rate, to thrive) within this context.

The gay men with whom we spoke during the course of our research project mentioned that they experienced several different kinds of harassment while they were still at school: first, they spoke about being harassed for being gay and/or effeminate; second, they spoke of harassing other men; and third, they recalled harassing women. With regard to the first point, the harassment which they endured was part of school cultures which seemed to be designed to punish those boys who were not stereotypically masculine, or, indeed, macho. Thus, Michael recalled a friendship with another boy, Alan:

> we became really good friends and I remember one day actually just completely spontaneously, um, the bell went and we were off . . . And we just grabbed each others' hands and ran off, together, holding hands and all the other people in the class started shouting homo, homo, yurgh, homo, and I didn't understand what it meant, um, but I just realized that, you know, they were sort of shouting something abusive, and it was obviously something to do with Alan and something to do with us holding hands, so we stopped, and, um, felt quite guilty about it actually. I didn't really understand why and then a couple of days later there was this joke going around . . . Um, somebody would come up to you and say, so are you a, and you know this idea of homo somehow had stuck in my head as something bad and then somebody came up to me . . . and said are you a homo sapien [*sic*] and I didn't know what that meant, but I just heard the word homo and I thought, no no no, I'm not a homo sapien and everyone laughed at me.

In this case, Michael's friendship with Alan was made the subject of verbal harassment in such a way that both of them felt constrained to cool the friendship. Furthermore, the later teasing of Michael by others whose vocabulary allowed them to play on the word 'homo' was an additional punishment for his deviations from the norms of heterosexual masculinity. Michael was then made to feel guilty about being 'homo'(sexual) in the first instance and through the later teasing, he was put in a situation whereby the denial of being 'homo' meant that he had also to deny being human. The joke was not only about his naiveté, but about the Catch-22 situation in which he was placed – a situation made more significant because the denial of full humanity to particular groups has, historically, been one of the ways in which a variety of oppressions have been held in place.

Gay men also spoke about their own harassment of other gay men. Such harassment was often entered into in an effort to defend their own masculinity. Thus Alistair recalls:

> I remember, when I was about 15 or so, people at school who were, kind of, singled out as queer, who, um, I don't know, were just, kind of, a couple of camp men that spring to mind, who, um, I kind of befriended, um, in a detached kind of way . . .
>
> I mean, I did use, y'know, I did call people queer and that kind of stuff, but I didn't do it to them. I did it to, uh, um, people who probably were, y'know, not people who were maybe unsure, um to, um, kind of protect myself from them, I think. I mean, looking back on it, that wasn't why I did it at the time, so, if somebody was saying something about a bloke, y'know, or something, I'd say queer, y'know, in order to protect myself from them, whereas these, kind of, um, nellies in the woodwork, or whatever, I could be nice to them and keep my masculinity intact.[17]

This story of Alistair's was told in response to a story told by one of the women taking part in this group discussion. Teresa had talked about how she and a gang of other girls used to call a boy 'queer' and 'poof' because, she said, he was different:

> He was, like, really quiet and he was, um, he always used to get his homework done, used to have his school uniform on and then, none of us had a school uniform. He did. And this sort of thing. So he was just different I think, just different.

Alistair's stress, in his response to this, was on keeping his masculinity intact. He recognized that the difference Teresa described was specifically a difference in the form of masculinity which her target had inhabited. In her story, being clean, quiet, and academic (an 'ear'ole' in Paul Willis's 1977 terms) was seen as equivalent to being 'queer'. Alistair was able to avoid this label, despite befriending some 'nelly' (that is effeminate) boys, primarily by joining in the harassment of those who were not his friends. Thus he was able to present himself as masculine, and *feel* masculine, by virtue of behaving homophobically; his masculinity, in the school context, was, in part at least, constituted by and through the expression of homophobia.

The third way in which the gay men we spoke to recalled being involved in harassment was when they joined in, or were urged to join in, with the harassment of women or girls. In one group discussion, for example, David explained how:

> one day, um, just out walking with the gang of four boys, y'know, we decided that it was time for [getting together with a girl] . . . Yeah, they spotted these women, these young women, right, and there was a woman . . . and she's really good-looking. I liked her because she looked good, right. She carried herself well. Because . . . this woman had all the qualities that my sisters had and my mother, y'know, and I liked her for that. But it was perceived by the other guys as being, y'know, attracted to this woman and of course, it was, like, *behaving like men*, y'know, 'Go on, go on, go on, go on'.
>
> [my emphasis]

Here the pressure on David was not only to be heterosexual, but to be heterosexual in a particular way ('behaving like men') which involved the harassment of women. The fact that he thought about the young woman in terms similar to those in which he thought about his sisters and mother was, it seems, illegitimate within the heterosexualized homosocial context he describes. The imperative to 'go on' is an urging to objectify and harass thereby constituting himself as a (heterosexual) man. Furthermore, implicit within this statement (and confirmed later in the interview), is David's fear that if he did not take part in harassing this young woman, he would himself become the subject of homophobic abuse.

Similarly, Michael recalls how he:

> went to sixth form, where you're supposed to be able to be who you want to be, theoretically, and of course nobody is, they're all trying so hard, desperately hard to prove that they've slept with as many people as, you know, they're always bragging about how many girl-friends they've had and this, that and the other. And I was always the odd one out . . . They'd all start talking about tits and, look at the jugs on that, and that's not something I've ever been able to do. I find it quite difficult to talk about men in those terms, let alone women. Um, no, I do, but you know in that sort of really derogatory way, which it is when you start talking about, oh, jugs on her, oh what I'd like to do, I've never been like that.

Here, Michael notes that the difference between him and the other men in his sixth form was as much to do with his failure to enter into abusive and objectifying discussion of women as to do with his being gay. In these situations, masculinity is constituted both by misogyny (and the associated harassment of women) and homophobia.

Sexist harassment as a pedagogy of heterosexuality

I have focused above on the experiences of gay men partly because (as I pointed out above) they are often ignored in discussions of harassment, which are thereby rendered incomplete. More importantly, however, I have tried to show how the harassment of gay men and of those perceived to be gay or effeminate is one of the ways in which heterosexuality is rendered compulsory through the punishment of deviance from heterosexual norms of masculinity. In this sense, the heterosexist harassment of gay men can be understood as a pedagogy of heterosexuality. Similarly, the harassment of women can be understood as one of the ways in which we are schooled into gender-appropriate, that is, heterosexual, sexuality. Thus Rebecca's experience of harassment, for example, can be read not just as sexist, but also as heterosexist in that the fact she was a lesbian made her doubly vulnerable to William's harassment. Furthermore, most (if not all) out lesbians will recognize the experience of being sexually harassed precisely as a result of coming out. The 'all you need is a good fuck' phenomenon is alive and kicking within the experience of all our lesbian respondents. Moreover, the terms 'lesbian', 'lezzie', and 'dyke' are common forms of abuse in and outside of schools. Indeed, it is a common experience for women and girls who resist sexual/sexist harassment to be labelled 'lesbian' (particularly if they associate themselves with feminism), regardless of how they identify themselves. Indeed, the term 'feminist' has, in some quarters, become a synonym for 'lesbian'.[18]

The point here is that the options open to women in response to sexist harassment are limited in ways which tend to reinforce heterosexuality. Strategies of resistance are often contradictory and strategies for avoidance are also mixed in their effects. For example, women often comment that shouting back at men who harass them on the street appears to be taken as a form of provocation from which the men seem to derive pleasure. On the other hand, ignoring harassing men, remaining silent and 'well-behaved' can feel like allowing them to trample all over one's sensibilities and as if one has, indeed, colluded in one's harassment in some important ways.[19] Furthermore, if women adopt styles and behaviours which try to avoid harassment through being quiet and 'well-behaved', this can seem to signify a particular kind of heterosexual femininity in which women are seen to be passive, waiting for men's attentions. Furthermore, as Sue Lees says:

> The danger of avoidance is that you can then get the reputation for being a lesbian or too tight . . .
> Girls also talk about the need to avoid boys if a girl begins to get a reputation. *Better still, getting engaged is a greater protection.*
>
> (1993: 274–5, emphasis added)

The safety achieved through getting engaged (or married or living with a man) is a dubious form of safety at best, given that most sexual violence is carried out by men known to their victims. Sexual harassment by other men is, indeed, less likely when a woman is in the company of a man who seems to be her partner, no doubt at least partly because she is seen as belonging, in some sense, to him. Similarly, women are able to feel safer on the streets when they have a man with them. Again, these are double-edged rewards for heterosexuality.

Another possible strategy for dealing with sexist harassment is to try to treat the whole thing as a joke, but this often ends up in the kind of flirtatious banter which characterizes much social contact between women and men, particularly in ultra-heterosexual spaces like (straight) clubs, discos, and pubs. Within these contexts it is often expected that men will 'pull' women (and sometimes vice versa). One purpose of going to such events is to find potential sexual partners and those who go simply because they like music or dancing may well be seen to be deviant. In order to keep control of these situations, women may well enter into jokey teasing with underlying hetero/sexual content. Indeed, in my own (long distant) experience of working as a barmaid, it was effectively part of the job description to be able to take 'teasing' and joke with male customers in this heterosexual way (though similar banter with other women would, almost certainly, have been a dismissable offence). In this context I was not expected to have sex with male customers, but was certainly expected to behave hetero/sexually with them in order to keep them happy and under control (but still drinking). Judging by recent discussions with students doing this kind of work, there have been few changes in the expectations of barmaids in heterosexual pubs and clubs (see also Adkins 1995).

Interestingly, in discussions about ways of dealing with harassment, accounts of successful resistance often involve the woman concerned taking up what might be seen as a 'super-feminine' position. Jane, for example, told me about a woodwork teacher at her school who had a reputation for regularly harassing the girls in his class. There were rumours among the pupils that he had previously been complained about and been given a verbal warning about his behaviour. However, he continued to invade their space, including touching them up, and the girls had no confidence that any further complaint would make any difference to his behaviour. It was with delight that Jane told me how, in her year, some of the girls had made a pact to wear stiletto heels to school. As she commented:

> Then, if he touched us, we could stamp hard on his feet, which would really hurt, but he couldn't do a thing. It was always 'Sorry, sir, that was an accident'.

The teacher had retreated defeated (at least for the moment), but the solution was not permanent. Furthermore, in order to achieve this respite from constant harassment, these girls had had to adopt a style which signified heterosexuality. Of course, it may well be the case that wearing stiletto heels was particularly satisfying because it was against the school rules. However, this does not negate the use of the device as a form of resistance, and one which rendered the girls hyper-feminine (not to mention hurting their feet and making it difficult for them to stand or walk for long periods and impossible for them to run!).

Conclusion

The harassment both of women and of gay and/or 'effeminate' men, then, seems to be related to the enforcement of heterosexuality. It is difficult for women to find responses to harassment which do not reinforce heterosexuality, either directly or by invoking the stigmatization of lesbianism. For men, both the avoidance of stigmatization and the production of acceptable masculinities seem to depend, at least in part, on harassing women and other men. It seems, therefore, that harassment is strongly implicated in the production of heterosexual gendered identities and can, therefore, be seen as not simply sexist, but heterosexist in nature. This indicates the potential for developing new feminist ways of thinking about sexist harassment – ways which I have only begun to open up here.

Earlier feminist analyses of sexual harassment had implications for, and influence on, the development of policy, however unsatisfactory the implementation of such policy has proved to be. Equally, my analysis here calls for a rethinking not just of the ways in which we understand hetero/sexist harassment but for policy development. It is beyond the scope of this chapter to develop the policy implications of my argument fully. However, I would like to end with some questions about policy:

- Is there a case for policies and codes of practice on sexual harassment to be rewritten so as to take account of hetero/sexist harassment?
- If this were to happen, should the concept of sexual harassment be retained as a specific kind of hetero/sexist harassment, or should it simply be subsumed under the wider terminology?

- If harassment is, indeed, hetero/sexist, what are the implications for practices of, in particular, anti-sexist and girl-friendly schooling?
- Finally, and perhaps most importantly, what would anti-hetero/sexist policies and practices actually look like?

Like earlier feminist thinking about sexual harassment, the argument I have presented here, however convincing in theory, will only achieve its objectives when such theorization is taken on board in policy and practice.

Notes

1   I would like to thank Joyce Canaan for her detailed comments on an earlier draft of this paper. I would also like to thank Diana Leonard, who chaired the BSA conference session at which I gave this paper and Janet Holland for her editorial comments in relation to the publication of the article in Holland and Adkins (1996). Thank you also to Richard Johnson, Deborah Lynn Steinberg, and Gaby Weiner for their comments on earlier drafts of the paper.
2   This project has been carried out in collaboration with Richard Johnson (Epstein and Johnson in press). Part of the project, concerned specifically with sex education, was carried out with Peter Redman. We are grateful to the Universities of Birmingham and Central England and to East Birmingham Health Authority for their support for our work. Other people who have been involved in our work are Louise Curry, Mary Kehily, Gurjit Minhas, Anoop Nayak, and Shruti Tanna.
3   Louise Curry was responsible for the work in/with the youth group.
4   Shruti Tanna was responsible for the interviews with all our South Asian respondents. Some of the interviews with African Caribbean respondents were carried out by myself. However, the bulk of the information from them comes from group discussions which they themselves taped, without any of the research team present but using a number of stimulus questions which I suggested.
5   Discussions which have taken place within the meetings of the Politics of Sexuality Group, Department of Cultural Studies, Birmingham University, have particularly influenced my thinking. See Steinberg *et al.* (1997).
6   Names of respondents, and, where necessary, some other details have been altered in order to maintain anonymity. The exception to this is where respondents have specifically requested their names be used.
7   It is interesting to note, here, that these are the adjectives most often applied by teachers (and other adults) to children's stereotypically gendered behaviours. Furthermore, children constitute themselves as gendered through these discourses. For example, in BBC1's *Panorama* programme 'The Future is Female' (broadcast on 24 October 1994) one little boy commented that if a boy worked hard at his schoolwork this would mean that he was not a 'real boy' – a point echoed by older, secondary age boys and their parents later in the programme.

8　See Tyler (1991) for an interesting discussion of the politics of drag.
9　Kerr (1991) points out that gay men often also operate within discourses of male sex drive.
10　bell hooks (1991, 1992) gives particularly detailed and rich accounts of the racist sexualization of black women. See also, Patricia Hill Collins (1990). See Bhattacharyya (1994) for a discussion of racist sexualization of Asian women in the UK.
11　See also, Cohen (1988) for a discussion of the ways in which Jews have been sexualized within Anglo-American and West European cultures.
12　See, in particular, the work of Julien and Mercer (1988) and Isaac Julien's *Arena* programme broadcast on BBC2 in February 1994 for discussions of the racist and heterosexist sexualization of people of African descent.
13　For a discussion of this case and of the position of disabled lesbians more generally, see Appleby (1994).
14　See Morris (1991) for a discussion of disability and hetero/sexuality and related issues.
15　I would like to thank David Colley for his help with this paragraph.
16　See the *Pink Paper* (1994a, 1994b).
17　See Alistair *et al.* (1994) for an edited version of the discussion during which this statement was made.
18　Sue Lees (1993), for example, notes the association made by young women between lesbianism and feminism.
19　I would like to thank Joyce Canaan for pointing this out to me.

References

Adkins, L. (1995) *Gendered Work: Sexuality, Family and the Labour Market*. Buckingham: Open University Press.

Alistair, Dave, Rachel and Teresa (1994) So the theory was fine. In D. Epstein (ed.) *Challenging Lesbian and Gay Inequalities in Education*. Buckingham: Open University Press.

Appleby, Y. (1994) Out in the margins. *Disability and Society*, 9(1): 19–32.

Bhattacharyya, G. (1994) 'Offence is the best defence? – Pornography and racial violence. In C. Brant and Y.L. Too (eds) *Rethinking Sexual Harassment*. London: Pluto Press.

Butler, J. (1990) *Gender Trouble: Feminism and the Subversion of Identity*. London: Routledge.

Clarricoates, K. (1987) Dinosaurs in the classroom – the 'hidden' curriculum in primary schools. In M. Arnot and G. Weiner (eds) *Gender and the Politics of Schooling*. London: Hutchinson/Open University.

Cohen, P. (1988) The perversions of inheritance: Studies in the making of multiracist Britain. In P. Cohen and H.S. Bains (eds) *Multi-Racist Britain*. Basingstoke: Macmillan.

Collins, P.H. (1990) *Black Feminist Thought: Knowledge, Consciousness, and the Politics of Empowerment*. London: HarperCollins Academic.

de Lyon, H. (1989) Sexual harassment. In H. de Lyon and F.W. Migniuolo (eds) *Women Teachers: Issues and Experiences*. Milton Keynes: Open University Press.

Epstein, D. and Johnson, R. (1994) On the straight and the narrow: The heterosexual presumption, homophobias and schools. In D. Epstein (ed.) *Challenging Lesbian and Gay Inequalities in Education*. Buckingham: Open University Press.

Epstein, D. and Johnson, R. (in press) *Schooling Sexualities*. Buckingham: Open University Press.

Evans, D.T. (1993) *Sexual Citizenship: The Material Construction of Sexualities*. London: Routledge.

Hanmer, J. and Maynard, M. (eds) (1987) *Women, Violence and Social Control*. Basingstoke: Macmillan.

Herbert, C. (1992) *Sexual Harassment in Schools: A Guide for Teachers*. London: David Fulton.

Holland, J. and Adkins, L. (eds) (1996) *Sex, Sensibility and the Gendered Body*. Basingstoke: Macmillan.

Hollway, W. (1984) Gender difference and the production of subjectivity. In J. Henriques, W. Hollway, C. Urwin, C. Venn and V. Walkerdine, *Changing the Subject: Psychology, Social Regulation and Subjectivity*. London: Methuen.

Hollway, W. (1989) *Subjectivity and Method in Psychology: Gender, Meaning and Science*. London: Sage.

hooks, b. (1991) *Yearning: Race, Gender and Cultural Politics*. London: Turnaround.

hooks, b. (1992) *Black Looks: Race and Representation*. London: Turnaround.

Julien, I. and Mercer, K. (1988) True confessions: A discourse on images of black male sexuality. In R. Chapman and J. Rutherford (eds) *Male Order: Unwrapping Masculinity*. London: Lawrence & Wishart.

Kerr, E. (1991) 'Perversion and subversion: A study of lesbian and gay strategies of resistance'. Unpublished MA dissertation. Department of Cultural Studies, University of Birmingham.

Lees, S. (1986) *Losing Out: Sexuality and Adolescent Girls*. London: Hutchinson.

Lees, S. (1993) *Sugar and Spice: Sexuality and Adolescent Girls*. London: Penguin.

Mac an Ghaill, M. (1994) (In)visibility: Sexuality, race and masculinity in the school context. In D. Epstein (ed.) *Challenging Lesbian and Gay Inequalities in Education*. Buckingham: Open University Press.

MacKinnon, C.A. (1979) *Sexual Harassment of Working Women*. New Haven, CT: Yale University Press.

Mahony, P. (1989) Sexual violence and mixed schools. In C. Jones and P. Mahony (eds) *Learning Our Lines: Sexuality and Social Control in Education*. London: Women's Press.

Morris, J. (1991) *Pride against Prejudice: Transforming Attitudes to Disability/A Personal Politics of Disability*. London: The Women's Press.

Morrison, T. (1993) Introduction: Friday on the Potomac. In T. Morrison (ed.) *Race-ing Justice, En-gendering Power: Essays on Anita Hill, Clarence Thomas and the Construction of Social Reality*. London: Chatto & Windus.

National Union of Teachers (1986) *Dealing with Sexual Harassment*. London: NUT.

Pink Paper (1994a) Staff split over Toksvig row. 14 October: 5.

Pink Paper (1994b) 'Apologise' Save the Children told. 21 October: 6.

Rich, A. (1980) Compulsory heterosexuality and lesbian existence. *Signs: Journal of Women in Culture and Society*, 5(41): 631–60.

Rogers, M. (1994) Growing up lesbian: The role of the school. In D. Epstein (ed.)

Challenging Lesbian and Gay Inequalities in Education. Buckingham: Open University Press.

Steinberg, D.L., Epstein, D. and Johnson, R. (eds) (1997) *Border Patrols: Policing the Boundaries of Heterosexuality*. London: Cassell.

Tyler, C.-A. (1991) Boys will be girls: The politics of gay drag. In D. Fuss (ed.) *Inside/Out: Lesbian Theories, Gay Theories*. London: Routledge.

Willis, P. (1977) *Learning to Labour: How Working Class Kids Get Working Class Jobs*. London: Saxon House.

Wise, S. and Stanley, L. (1987) *Georgie Porgie: Sexual Harassment in Everyday Life*. London: Pandora Press.

Wittig, M. (1980) The straight mind. *Feminist Issues*. 1(1): 103–11.

Wittig, M. (1981) One is not born a woman. *Feminist Issues*, 1(2): 46–54.

Wood, J. (1984) Groping towards sexism: Boys' sex talk. In A. McRobbie and M. Nava (eds) *Gender and Generation*. Basingstoke: Macmillan.

9

Daughters in danger: the case of 'campus sex crimes'

LINDA MAHOOD and BARBARA LITTLEWOOD

The first time I took sculpting I just loved it, and he was a good teacher. We had a very professional relationship and he encouraged my work . . . He asked me a number of times if he would be able to draw my face . . . He asked me to come to his studio and I did . . . So I started to read, he started to draw and before I knew it he was sort of coming on to me. He was putting his arm around me and saying how pretty I was . . . I felt sorry for him, so I didn't fight him off, and when it began to get out of hand, I began to panic.

(Solomon 1993: 3)

The feminist understanding of 'sexual danger must be seen as part of a system in which women were participants, sometimes willing, sometimes unwilling, sometimes conscious and sometimes unaware' (Dubois and Gordon 1984: 36). In their study of nineteenth-century feminism, Ellen Dubois and Linda Gordon argue that the feminist movement has played an important role in organizing and even creating women's sense of sexual danger over the last 150 years. They explain that while the main focus of Victorian feminism was prostitution the focus of modern feminism has shifted to rape. To different generations, each of these has been 'the quintessential sexual terror' (Gordon and Dubois 1984: 32). In the decade since 'Seeking ecstacy on the battlefield' was written a new sexual terror has emerged. Now, the media coverage of 'campus sex crime' suggests that our daughters are in danger not only on the city streets, but in places which are on the borders of the public and private divide, such as the university campus.

This chapter examines some historical and contemporary perspectives on sexual harassment. The problem of direct comparison between contemporary culture, which has a language naming sexual harassment and date rape and nineteenth-century culture which lacked this, will be tackled by a more general analysis of what we call narratives of sexual danger. Such narratives appear in a wide variety of both historical and contemporary sources, and they are evident not only in feminist writing, but also in media reports, novels and plays. This chapter concentrates on two of these sources, nineteenth-century melodramas which revolved around the 'seduction scenario' (Rahill 1967; Clark 1986; Davis 1991) and late twentieth-century press coverage of incidents of campus sex crime. We would like to suggest that there are many ways of telling these tales, and many forms these tales can take. By selecting these two very diverse and historically distinct forms, one fictional and the other factual, we will highlight both what they have in common and where they diverge. We also want to suggest that both forms, melodramatic fiction and the press report, are particularly effective ways of reaching a wide audience, but there is something else that relates them. Historian Judith Walkowitz (1982–3), writing of the tabloid press reporting on the Ripper murders in 1888 notes how the linking of the facts to a well-established formula for telling stories, served to fix the story in the minds of the audience – to make it more easily comprehensible. Through the survey of a number of widely publicized cases of sexual assault and harassment that occurred on Canadian university campuses between 1985 and 1992 we will argue that they replay elements of seduction melodramas mixed with standard journalistic conventions. By tracing the codes and conventions which structure the telling of these tales, in which women's bodies are both the currency and at stake, some of the processes by which bodies and spaces are made and remade are identified.

'She tried to push him off': Problems of naming and definition

We are familiar now with the idea that feminism has provided women with a voice and a language to name their experiences, and to clarify their analysis either through adapting existing terms, such as 'patriarchy', or through forging new terms: 'sexual harassment' and 'date rape', and slogans such as 'no means no' and 'zero tolerance' are just a few examples. Before these terms were available to name certain experiences, how might these have been understood? The following account is taken from the criminal trial record of a teacher of acting in 1892.

> On one occasion he came into her room after a lesson . . . she was putting her shoes on. Roberts sat on her knees . . . put one arm around her neck, and asked if she would go to Brighton with him the following Saturday. She said, 'Certainly not'. She tried to push him off. He asked if he could come up to her room.
>
> (quoted in Davis 1991: 88)

Today this scenario would serve as a textbook example of sexual harassment, and though the perpetrator was accused of conspiracy, fraud and sexual assault many Victorians would have called the incident 'seduction'. This case raises a number of questions concerning the use of criminal records in historical comparative research on sexual crimes, which is limited due to changes in terminology and classification of offences. An alternative method is to examine popular narratives from novels and plays relating to illicit sexual encounters.

Narratives are common to a variety of written and spoken forms of communication, whether we are talking about factual or fictional accounts. Many of the popular themes of early Victorian melodrama featured standard narratives which turned upon familiar and recurrent plot lines such as the 'seduction scenario' (Clark 1986: 48–9), where the poor but honest servant girl or village maiden is relentlessly pursued by an upper-class rogue. The villain might be given some motivation such as vengeance for an ancient wrong, and the heroine might be tricked by false marriage promises, but like *Lucy Lisle, the Cottager's Daughter*, her end was predicted in the play's subtitle, *The Maid, the Mother and the Maniac* (Rahill 1967). These simple village maids all begin by personifying virtue, but virtue is reduced simply to sexual virtue: 'morality ... has nothing to do with ethics; it means sexual morality and nothing but sexual morality' (Carter 1986). Her simplicity and her innocence, though, put her at risk and leave her susceptible to charms and promises, even when she is ready to die rather than submit to force. It is for this reason that she had to be protected, not only from rapacious squires whom she recognized for the villains they were, by their sinister looks and rude gestures; but also from their handsome sons, with their smooth cheeks and winning words. Anna Clark (1986: 51) has pointed out that few of the stories distinguished between seduction or rape. This is in part due to the perception of female sexuality dominant at the time, where any sexual activity that occurred outside of marriage was defined as immoral and marked the women involved as 'fallen'. It was a woman's loss of innocence and reputation which mattered, and not whether the incident was voluntary or forced (Mahood and Littlewood 1994). These stories then, function as morality tales with lessons for gullible maidens. They are reversals of the Cinderella story. The kitchen girl does not get to marry the prince. If her father allows her to consort with princes, ruin and remorse, not a wedding ring await her.

'Is your daughter in danger?': Journalistic narratives

Melodramatic themes and warnings of sexual danger provided an immediately recognizable framework that can also be found in both nineteenth and twentieth century newspaper reportage. Historian Debra

Gorham (1978: 353) argues that journalist William Stead's exposé of juvenile prostitution, as a 'veritable slave trade', was part of a larger mid-1880s campaign for protective legislation which was directed at all young women. Judith Walkowitz (1982–3: 55) suggests that the journalistic accounts of the mutilation of prostitutes by Jack the Ripper in 1888 were designed to warn women who strayed beyond the protection of their homes. Modern studies have also noted the role of the media in constructing a climate of sexual danger. Carol and Barry Smart (1978: 90–91) observed that the

> stock-in-trade press coverage [of the British press] continues to be the novelette style . . . [T]he general form and content of rape reporting . . . serve as both a form of sexual titillation and as a veiled 'warning' to non-conforming 'independent' women.

Sophia Voumvakis and Richard Ericson's (1984: 47) study of the press in Toronto in 1992 also noted a standardized news format: 'If the victim had taken care not to place herself in perilous circumstances she could have avoided victimization.'

Since the late 1980s a number of widely publicized cases of sexual violence and harassment on Canadian university campuses has propelled the issue of 'campus sex crime' onto the front pages of newspapers and popular magazines, as journalists have publicly linked certain features of campus life, such as Lady Godiva rides and panty raids on dormitories with more than simply time-honoured initiation rituals or 'boyish pranks'. Consider these headlines: 'Rape on campus: Is your daughter in danger?' 'Leers from professor, jeers from the media', 'Abusive prof . . . got off scott-free', 'Campuses "hunting grounds" for sexual assaults'.

> *The Reality of Campus Rape*: she's young and on her own for the first time. They've both been out drinking at the campus pub. It could be a recipe for disaster . . . .
>
> *(University Affairs* 1993: 18)

On her television talk-show, host Shirley Solomon asked her Canadian viewers: 'Is your daughter in danger when you send her off to college or university? The answer is yes':

> An alarming number of young women are being raped on college campuses across the nation – and they're not being raped by some stranger. They're being raped by friends, acquaintances and sometimes even by their teachers . . . Today, the truth about date rape on college campuses.
>
> (Solomon 1993: 1)

Many feminists would argue that while media coverage such as this is fairly recent and due to women's growing self-confidence in reporting offences, these forms of behaviour have always been with us. Following this argument we would like to suggest that the press reporting on sexual violence on campus can be read as a re-run of the old melodramatic seduction scenario – with, as we shall see, a few new twists.

Gary Tuchman (1978) has described the process whereby journalists attempt to provide a balanced view of a story by presenting opposing points of view. Cases of campus sex crime prove to be more difficult to report than similar cases among the general public for three main reasons. First there is a reluctance by university authorities to involve the police and a preference for dealing with cases internally. This may simply be due to the institution's fear of adverse publicity, or it may stem from their assumption of family-like responsibilities for their members. One journalist described university administrators as benevolent, but neglectful father figures. It was his perception that an unspoken understanding 'exists that sexual abuse on campus is not a problem for society at large to solve but for the campus family to solve, the not-yet-adult society of the school, with its own special code of behavior' (*Harper's Magazine* April 1991: 62). Second, internal grievance and discipline procedures on campuses are not only private (thus excluding the press), but commonly have confidentiality clauses which protect the identities of complainants and respondents. Third, the laws governing reporting of civil and criminal trials do not extend to such private hearings, so journalists are able to comment and speculate on cases in ways which would be ruled out during criminal trials. A content analysis of 51 newspaper stories and eight magazine articles where incidents of sexual assault and harassment were linked to a Canadian university or college community between 1985 and 1992 revealed that of the 388 sources quoted in the stories surveyed 61 per cent had little or no direct knowledge of the case apart from what they had heard in the campus gossip-mill (Mahood 1996). Thus, without access to the drama of the courtroom to structure their narratives, journalists instead draw upon other conventions. In this case, they deploy the narratives and characters of Victorian melodrama. The 'voluptuous co-ed', the lecherous professor and the stern-faced feminists who appear as stock characters in the journalistic exposé would be immediately recognizable to their Victorian counterparts as the village maiden, the upper-class rogue and the bluestocking or the suffragette.

Virtue rewarded? Lessons for gullible maidens

Studies of Victorian theatre stress that there were both disjunction and parallels between what was presented on stage and myths about what went on behind the curtain. While the stage heroines were often innocent maidens, the actresses who portrayed them on stage were rarely seen in this way off stage. In spite of social purity feminists' campaign to 'raise the tone' of popular entertainment by creating better working conditions and more roles for young women in serious drama and comedies of manners (Maitland 1986), the theatre remained at best a dubious career option for women, morally compromising if not actually corrupting. Nevertheless the stage appeared to offer job opportunities for certain women. It had a magic and a glamour. In the popular imagination, actresses were the embodiment of beauty, fashion and independence.

In the fullest study of Victorian professional actresses, Tracy Davis (1991) argues that certain features of the job made acting a particularly 'dangerous' profession for women. A successful career required training, introductions and patronage. When women competed for parts which men were in a position to allocate, it was a short step to assume that getting work involved the nineteenth-century version of the casting couch. Once in this man's world, survival depended upon the actress enduring a certain amount of horseplay and innuendo in rehearsal, backstage and on tour. This was the popular understanding of the profession though individual actresses were often at pains to publicize their blameless and harmonious domestic lives. The actress then, was part of a sexualized profession. By this we mean that it was ordered by a set of assumptions about the sexuality of the women who engaged in it (analogies were constantly made between performing and prostitution). The features which made women vulnerable to sexual advances, though, were turned back upon the women themselves, stigmatizing them as 'those kind of women' who would not mind familiarity and advances.

Female students today are often sexualized in a similar way. This is illustrated in the following description of campus life offered by a reporter for *Maclean's* magazine:

> In the late 1960s and 1970s higher learning often went hand in hand with getting high – on sex, drugs and rock 'n' roll. Monogamy fell from fashion. And bodily fluids were exchanged as freely as ideas.
>
> (*Maclean's* 1992b: 41)

In their book, *The Lecherous Professor*, Billie Wright Dziech and Linda Weiner claim that assumptions about the sexual behaviour of college women are largely the product of popular films, fiction, advertising and journalism. In films and fiction

> the college woman overwhelms men with her irresistible loveliness and cheerleader voluptuousness ... [She] uses the classroom or lab to meet men and appears to be on campus primarily ... to improve the scenery ... [These] images also foster the fantasy of

coeds as wriggling seductresses. The voluptuous coed image is promoted by advertising which portrays college women as ultimate consumers of beer, liquor, and the leering men who surround them. The
portrait . . . on the evening news is equally one-dimensional. Whether
at an NCAA basketball game, a nuclear disarmament rally, or an ERA
march, the news camera focuses on college women as pretty faces in
the crowd.

(Dziech and Weiner 1984: 62)

This sexualization makes it difficult for young students to personify
innocence in the way melodrama's heroines did. Instead, it is their naiveté
which makes them vulnerable.

It was weeks before I could grasp that [professor] was definitely
following me and staring at me . . . At first I thought I must be overreacting, but he was always there. I became so uncomfortable that I
changed my swim times, first to weekends, then to lunch time. But it
wasn't long before he showed up too.

(*Toronto Star* 1990: F1)

Frosh think they're invincible . . . You never think that anything will
happen to you . . . Date rape happened to other women, women who
drank and went out with the wrong guys . . . I had done nothing . . . I
hadn't kissed him. I hadn't held his hand. I did resist, and I said 'no'
in no uncertain terms. But he just kept forcing me, and I was afraid of
being hurt. Then, I gave in to avoid embarrassing us both . . . I'm sure
he didn't think he was raping me . . . I'm sure he thought, 'She'll have
a nice glow on her face when it's all over, just like Vivian Leigh in *Gone
with the Wind.*'

(*Maclean's* 1992a: 45)

Accounts in newspapers and magazines of these and similar incidents
are not, though, straightforward factual representations of real events.
They, like novels and dramas, construct a narrative which, by linking
character and action, attempts to create meanings for the events. Media
accounts cannot, therefore, be regarded as objective commentaries or
pictures of reality, but are part of the chain of significations in stories of
sexual danger. This is not simply just another example of bias in the
media, but rather part of a process whereby journalistic techniques
enable a story to be told. This does not mean that each and every story
has to be balanced; there are differences between stories coded as news
reports, and those coded as opinion pieces, documentaries or editorials,
in which there is a greater licence for journalists to comment. But overall, media accounts typically present themselves as plausible and
authoritative.

Feminist journalists have joined feminist critiques of the media by raising questions about the representations of women in the media. Do, for example, degrading stereotypes of women contribute to discrimination and exploitation? Reports of sexual harassment in general and campus sex crime in particular provide an interesting test case for assessing the news media from a feminist perspective. These issues have been raised by feminists, who have had some success in shifting media agendas. Press reports such as the following appear at first sight as if they are counter-weights to media hostility and the trivialization of feminist issues.

Incidents of campus sex crime: 'Too gross to be repeated here'

In 1988 *Maclean's* magazine reported that a McGill University fraternity called Zeta Psi held one of its notorious parties in honour of the women's rugby team, which was initiating 20 of its rookies. As part of their initiation the young women were required to obtain men's signatures on their stomachs. At 8:00 they arrived at the packed fraternity house where they were treated to all the beer they could drink. The men's team had 25 of its own initiates pay a naked visit to the party. Later, a 19-year-old initiate of the women's team told a reporter that 'she was sexually assaulted by three men while as many as ten others looked on' (*Maclean's* 1988: 56). At Wilfrid Laurier University in September 1989, the *Toronto Star* reported that first-year male students raided a women's dormitory. The next morning, students arriving for breakfast in the main hall were astounded to see walls plastered with crude hand-painted posters flaunting women's underpants, some of which had been decorated with ketchup and other gunk to represent blood and faeces. Each panty was captioned. One example: 'Do you take VISA?'. The *Toronto Star* claimed that other insults were 'too gross to be repeated here' (*Toronto Star* 25 October 1989, cited in Wise Harris 1991: 38).

On 11 October 1990 at the University of British Columbia, 30 fraternity brothers from Caribou House congregated to write invitations to the women at a residence called Vanier Place, inviting them to a tug-of-war and dance. As the night of invitation-writing and power drinking progressed 'a competition started to see who could write the "best" invitation'. At 4:00 a.m. ten men obtained the front-door key to Vanier Place and delivered the invitations to approximately 300 women. The women awoke the following day to find that the invitations had been slid under their doors. The notes included overtures to the women to engage in acts of oral sex and sexual intercourse (*Vancouver Sun* 1990: A1–A2; *Vancouver Sun* 1990: B1–B2). '[S]everal women said the authors of the notes wrote that they would "pound your cervix to a pulp", or "suck your nipples until they bleed" ' (*Globe and Mail* 1990c: A4).

In January of 1990 a student, quoted above, filed a complaint against a

61-year-old engineering professor, who was staring at her at the university pool. Witnesses stated that the professor's staring was 'way beyond normal'. Three lifeguards recalled that he 'stared so hard at women walking on the deck that he actually bumped into pillars' (*Toronto Star* 1990: F1). In February 1990 two female medical students at the University of Calgary told a reporter that five of their professors regularly hosted drinking parties in their labs and used the tub for testing body temperatures as a party toy. 'The breasts of women students thrown into the tub were photographed through their wet clothing and the photos posted on the lab bulletin board' (*Calgary Herald* 1990b: A1; *Calgary Herald* 1990c: B1). On the other side of the country, the *Montreal Gazette* reported that in response to a date rape awareness campaign at Queen's University on 2 November nine male residents of Gordon House responded to the 'no means no' poster campaign with posters of their own, notably; 'no means kick her in the teeth', 'no means on your knees bitch', 'no means tie her up', 'no means more beer', 'no means she's a dyke' (*Montreal Gazette* 3 November 1990, cited in Wise Harris 1991: 38).

These detailed and grim cases covered in the Canadian press can be read as evidence of the extent of male violence and illustrate the way in which popular stereotypes of sexy co-eds are translated into a licence for assault, for example, during initiation rituals. According to the investigative journalists this is what happens when women try to make it in the male dominated culture of the university campus. They also, like the early Victorian narratives, appear to contain a critique of the abuse of power relations, but nevertheless reinforce notions of women as victims, in need of protection, if not by their parents, then by the surrogate parents – the university authorities. There are, though, departures from this pattern which are worth noting.

We have cautioned that these reports are structured by certain narrative and journalistic conventions, and are open to a different interpretation. One strategy, which justifies much of the media's claim to objectivity, is to juxtapose various opinions or interpretations of an event. In the case of sexual harassment, the reader is typically offered two opposing interpretations: harmless prank or sex crime? The reporting of different perspectives creates an appearance of balance, offering the reader a full and 'fair' account of the incident from multiple points of view. Rarely, though, are readers left without some hints as to how they should weigh opposing versions. The reporting of a feminist issue does not necessarily deliver a feminist message. As one feminist columnist for the *Toronto Star* put it: 'when it comes to questioning male privileges, or asking that a woman's experiences be given serious and equal consideration, most of the mainstream media are – alas – wilfully, complacently, blind and deaf' (*Toronto Star* 1990: F1). So although incidents and events may be reported we also must consider how they are framed. How meaning (including blame) is attributed.

One typical strategy is to leave the incident open to 'expert' comment. The image of objectivity or neutrality in the press has received considerable criticism by sociologists and feminists. Media critics argue that the media do not simply repeat the facts of the case but shape and structure the meaning and content of the event through the selective use 'of who gets to speak' (Wise Harris 1991: 39). What emerges is a striking similarity in the range of sources used by journalists because they systematically overemphasize the opinions of accredited spokespersons of state institutions and certified experts, whose journalistically interpreted thoughts appear in the media. These 'authorized knowers' serve to reproduce symbolically society's 'hierarchy of credibility', while persons who lack positions of authority are less frequently called-upon sources (Becker, 1967). In Canada this has resulted in the reproduction of a 'patriarchal point of view' (Malette and Chalouh 1991: 1). Feminists, who are seen as having an axe to grind, rarely feature as impartial experts (Stone 1993). Take, for example, this report of an incident at the University of Alberta when Celeste Brousseau, an engineering student, was booed off stage while performing in a 'light hearted' skit night. Male cast members appeared on stage wielding toy guns and members of the audience began to chant 'shoot the bitch, shoot the bitch' in reference to her feminist activism. A professor, who watched the production told a reporter that Brousseau 'should have known better than to take the stage when she knew she was unpopular'. A professor who was not present claimed

> 'The anger directed at [Brousseau] was no more severe . . . than that directed at perceived male traitors from time to time' at the university. He also stated that female speakers at the University of Alberta have been guilty of their own 'anti-male diatribes . . . For the sake of those who don't care about harm to men, however, let me also point out that hatred has a way of being returned . . . It would not surprise me if one of the demons that tortured Marc Lepine was the steady torrent of abuse directed at men in general by too many feminists.'
>
> (*Globe and Mail* 1990b: A2)

The reference to Marc Lepine, who murdered 14 female engineering students and female staff at the Ecole Polytechnique on 6 December 1989 (his suicide note stated that he hated feminists) indicates another strategy which can be used to defuse the feminist message. Feminist journalists Louise Malette and Marlene Chalouh (1991: 1) observed that the mainstream journalists who covered the 'Montreal massacre' scrambled 'to ignore or down play the significance of the victims being women and the analysis of feminists was ignored or ridiculed and rejected with hostility'.

Instead, psychological imbalance or individual aberration were the preferred interpretations, rather than one which would see this as indicative of more general male attitudes.

Rather than contributing to an exposé of the continuum of male violence the reporting of campus sex crimes can also contribute to a further sexualization of female students. Graphic descriptions of incidents walk a fine line between exposé and titillation. Reports of the photos of female medical students, in wet T-shirts (taken after they had been dunked in tubs used for taking body temperatures), which were posted on lab walls at the University of Calgary, recall similar photos in tabloids and soft porn magazines (*Calgary Herald* 1990b: A1; *Calgary Herald* 1990c: B1). The reports of the UBC Caribou House / Vanier Place incidents invite the (male) reader to thrill to the invasion of the women students' dorm in the dead of night, while ostensibly also condemning the brutality of the 'invitations' slid under their doors.

Thus, the press reports and continual warnings that 'our daughters are in danger' recall the lessons of early Victorian melodrama. As we can see, the myths about college women told and retold in these narratives can be read in a number of ways: they serve to explain away sexual violence and harassment; they serve to diminish the damage to victims; and they suggest that the women deserve what they get, especially if they associated themselves with the feminist movement. Like the Victorian melodramatic tales these stories function as morality tales, but the moral of the story is not that virtue conquers vice. The message to the women who follow these cases is that those who protest do so at great personal cost. The medical students who objected to participating in the 'party games', confided that the light reprimand the professors received 'is simply a signal . . . that their behavior . . . is approved of' (*Calgary Herald* 1990c: B1; *Calgary Herald* 1990d: B2). They left the university fearing that 'they had been blacklisted' as 'troublemakers' (*Calgary Herald* 1990c: B1). The young woman who 'blew the whistle on . . . the former frogman of the University of Toronto pool' was publicly named by the professor (who violated the confidentiality rules). She became 'the butt of merciless media ridicule'. She told a reporter, with tears of outrage welling in her eyes, 'I was determined to fight dirt with dignity' (*Toronto Star* 1990: F1). Celeste Brousseau would tell a *Globe and Mail* reporter 'people who care about me have told me not to talk to the media or anyone' (*Globe and Mail* 1990b: A3).

'The campus witch hunt': victims and villains

The accounts above illustrate that while the telling of 'sexual harassment situations are sordid, like the melodrama of a bad soap opera' (Dziech and Weiner 1984: 90), to the terrified or inexperienced student the campus sex crime is a form of melodrama that is real. Realism is also a literary convention. It is most often analysed in films and novels, but journalism shares important narrative and representational conventions with this genre. It offers us a slice of life, presents us with a world characterized by a struggle between good and evil, personified by the villain and heroine, it can be given added force by its reference to a recognizable and credible social world outside the story. 'Strangers lurking in dark corners aren't the problem', a journalist wrote, 'friends and acquaintances who don't understand what "no" means are' (*University Affairs* 1993: 18).

There was more to early Victorian melodrama than a moral message for gullible maidens; these tales can also be read in another way. Clark argues that while these stories present coercive sex as a personal tragedy they were also a form of political criticism. Typically, the innocent village maiden was the victim of an upper-class villain and the plot worked as a radical critique of the libertinage of the aristocracy and the brutality of capitalist class relations. The seduction scenario, she concludes, owed its popularity (its wide manifestation in novels, drama, pamphlets and songs) to the way it linked personal crisis and structural change. The focus, though, was on men's experience; the upper-class rogue seduced or raped a poor man's woman, thus seduction became a vehicle for dramatizing exploitation and oppression (Clark 1986: 48). The drama might have been radical in terms of class politics, but it was conservative in terms of its sexual politics. It was structured by a set of patriarchal assumptions which emphasized women's passivity – they were victims to be rescued – and safe only when firmly located under the protection of men in their family.

Over the past decade university administrators have responded to growing concerns about sexual discrimination and harassment or what we call 'climate issues', by establishing what Veronica Strong-Boag calls 'feminist bureaucracies' (*British Columbia Report* 1991: 32). To this troubled family, then, is brought the healing touch of the feminist administrator. But regularly, more power and influence is attributed to feminists on campus than they actually have. Consequently the accounts of sexual harassment that do appear in the press, indicate that in contrast to feminists, most women are not troubled by sexist comments or rituals. One fourth-year nursing student informed a *Maclean's* reporter that 'we were just killing ourselves laughing' during her initiation in the late 1980s. She was required to lie on the ground while a male student did push-ups over her. She complained though: 'If I were to say something like that on campus now, they'd massacre me. They'd say . . . "you're looking at women as mattresses" (*Maclean's* 1992b: 45). In contrast to 'feminist' Celeste Brousseau, who was reduced to tears, the other female engineering students 'who appeared in skits endured crude chants from men urging them to bare their breasts. But none seemed bothered by the remarks.' One female student allegedly told a reporter, 'If you are going into a male dominated industry you have to learn to live with men' (*Calgary Herald* 1990a: A7).

Many women faculty and students offer rationales for what male students and colleagues do. In defence of the medical professors found guilty of creating a 'sexually offensive workplace', 21 female students and colleagues circulated a petition defending the character of the professors (*Calgary Herald* 1990e: A5). While investigating the obscene tug-of-war invitations at the University of British Columbia, one journalist suggested that the majority of note recipients were 'generally sympathetic to the men. "It's hard on the guys . . . I don't think the guys should be evicted from residence. They didn't sexually attack us; they verbally attacked us"' (*Globe and Mail* 1990c: A4). '"If they get kicked out or get a sex assault on their record, it ruins their life" . . . They were drunk . . . they were in a group and "this is normal for guys when they get together in a group like this"' (*Vancouver Sun* 1990: A2). Debbie Wise Harris (1991: 40) argues that gender bias and the goal of journalistic balance combine to create a politics of overreaction. 'The strategy of divide and rule is used to mark out feminists as extremists who have blown everything out of proportion.' Unlike feminists, 'normal' women react to sexual harassment with grace and dignity, and best of all humour, like the Queen's University women who responded to the 'no means tie her up' posters with signs of their own, notably, 'no means too small!'. Humour, incidentally, may serve to excuse, rationalize and even encourage harassment (see McDaniel and van Roosmalen 1991: 5).

A consequence of feminism's struggle to raise the issue of sexual harassment has been a backlash against the supposed hegemony of 'political correctness'. Now, in a curious reversal of the staple plot of melodrama, it is the men – the smooth-cheeked sons and the lecherous professors – who personify 'innocence'. The leering professor at the University of Toronto swimming pool, whom the press nicknamed 'the Frogman', claimed the sexual harassment board 'is dominated by people identified too closely to the feminist movement and is therefore unable to differentiate between leering at women and looking at them'. His female colleague accused 'some of the women students who testified . . . [of] heading a witch hunt' (*Globe and Mail* 1990a: A3). A male student from Queen's University told a *Maclean's* reporter,

> [We] got bombarded by all this 'no means no' stuff . . . It's a girl's role to say no, and the guy's role to get into her pants. She says no, and you kiss her back a little harder. You go slower and faster. With 'no means no' you can't even play the game.
>
> (*Maclean's* 1992a: 44)

The new villains, then are the 'feminazis' who are limiting freedom of choice, freedom of speech, and most seriously, spoiling everyone's fun.

The new victims of the 'campus witch hunt' are the young men, who after all are only engaging in pranks, and the professors, those jolly old rogues, whose friendly pats and hugs are misinterpreted. The new melodramatic plot, as told by contemporary narrative, works as a reactionary critique of feminist politics – not a critique of gender relations or male privilege.

Transcending limitations: conclusion

According to Gordon and Dubois (1984: 43) it is crucial that modern feminists grasp the link between current debate and historical analysis. '[W]ithout an appreciation of these legacies . . . we cannot have much historical insight into our own concerns . . . political movements like ours swing back and forth endlessly, reacting to earlier mistakes and overreacting in compensation.' In this chapter we have concentrated on the way stories of sexual danger are told, the role the protagonists fill, the way certain marginal spaces involve special rules of conduct, and the lessons which are drawn for audiences who consume these stories. The stock settings and characters of nineteenth-century popular drama have been updated in the campus sex crime, and the conflicts given a modern twist for the drama to work for a modern audience. Journalism is the mode *par excellence* for the telling of a 'true' story. The publicity given to sex crime functions as a warning to those young women who venture into a man's world without parental or male protection. It can imply that she is unable to keep herself from danger – or to even recognize the danger she is in. Campus women are vulnerable to sexual harassment by the structural features of the fact that many may work, study, and live on campus and are stigmatized by cultural myths about how some women get on, such as the 'casting couch' or 'A's for lays'. When women object to these myths they are presented as traitors, bad sports or 'feminazis'. Whether the narrative is told in its 'daughters in danger', 'harmless prank' or 'campus witch hunt' version, the moral of the story retains echoes of older ones. While we may have abandoned the belief that a stalwart father (or Dean) will burst through the door in time to save us from the clutches of Sir Jasper (or Professor Jasper) we must also keep in focus the highly conservative antifeminist ends to which historical and contemporary narratives of sexual danger are put, that is, to keep us in our place.

References

Becker, H. (1967) 'Whose Side are We On'? *Social Problems*, 14: 239–47.
British Columbia Report (1991) UBC's feminist bureaucracy, 32–3.
Calgary Herald (1990a) Female engineer jeered, 12 January.

Calgary Herald (1990b) U of C probes prof's conduct, 17 February.

Calgary Herald (1990c) Sexual harassment profs keep jobs, 2 August.

Calgary Herald (1990d) U of C dogged by sex scandal, 30 August.

Calgary Herald (1990e) Rally on campus uncovers differing harassment view, 12 September.

Carter, A. (1986) Introduction. In A. Carter (ed.) *Wayward Girls and Wicked Women*. London: Virago.

Clark, A. (1986) The politics of seduction in English popular culture, 1748–1848. In J. Radford (ed.) *The Progress of Romance: The Politics of Popular Fiction*. London: Routledge.

Davis, T. (1991) *Actresses as Working Women: Their Social Identity in Victorian Culture*. London: Routledge.

Dubois, E. and Gordon, L. (1984) Seeking ecstasy on the battlefield: Danger and pleasure in nineteenth century feminist thought. In C. Vance (ed.) *Pleasure and Danger: Exploring Female Sexuality*. New York: Routledge.

Dziech, B.W. and Weiner, L. (1984) *The Lecherous Professor: Sexual Harassment on Campus*. Boston, MA: Beacon Press.

Globe and Mail (1990a) Professor seeks review of ogling conviction, 9 January.

Globe and Mail (1990b) University fights outbreak of sexism 'virus', 25 April.

Globe and Mail (1990c) Brothers no more at UBC, 18 October.

Gorham, D. (1978) The 'maiden tribute of modern Babylon' re-examined: Child prostitution and the idea of childhood in late-Victorian England. *Victorian Studies*, 21: 353–79.

Harper's Magazine (1991) The second revolution: sexual politics on campus, April, 58–62, 64–72.

Maclean's (1988) Rape on campus: Wild parties and fears about walking alone, 31 October, 56.

Maclean's (1992a) Campus confidential, 9 November, 43–6.

Maclean's (1992b) Taking the campus pulse, 9 November, 38–41.

Mahood, L. (1996) Campus sex crime, journalism and social control. In B. Schissel and L. Mahood (eds.) *Social Control in Canada: Issues in the Social Construction of Deviance*. Toronto: Oxford University Press, 352–72.

Mahood, L. and Littlewood, B. (1994) The 'vicious girl' and the 'street corner boy': Sexuality and the gendered delinquent in the Scottish child saving movement, 1850–1940. *Journal of the History of Sexuality*, 4: 549–78.

Maitland, S. (1986) *Vesta Tilly*. London: Virago.

Malette, L. and Chalouh, M. (1991) *The Montreal Massacre*. Charlottetown: Gynergy Books.

McDaniel, S. and van Roosmalen, E. (1991) Sexual harassment in Canadian academe: Explorations of power and privilege. *Atlantis*, 17: 3–18.

Rahill, F. (1967) *The World of Melodrama*. London: Pennsylvania University Press.

Solomon, S. (1993) *Shirley: Shirley Reports, Date Rape on Campus*. PS# 10440-1, CTV, Toronto, Canada, 19 January.

Smart, C. and Smart, B. (1978) Accounting for rape: Reality and myth in press reporting. In C. Smart and B. Smart *Women, Sexuality and Social Control*. London: Routledge.

Stone, S. (1993) Getting the message out: Feminists, the press and violence against women. *Canadian Review of Sociology and Anthropology*, 30: 377–400.

Tuchman, G. (1978) *Making the News: A Study in the Construction of Reality*. New York: Free Press.

Toronto Star (1990) Leers from professors, jeers from the media, 20 January.

University Affairs (1993) The reality of campus rape, January.

Vancouver Sun (1990) UBC harassment investigated, 16 October, A1; A2.

Vancouver Sun (1990) UBC women reluctant to complain officially, 17 October, B1; B2.

Voumvakis, S. and Ericson, R. (1984) *News Accounts of Attacks on Women: A Comparison of Three Toronto Newspapers*. Toronto: Centre of Criminology.

Wise Harris, D. (1991) Keeping women in our place: Violence at Canadian universities. *Canadian Woman Studies*, 11: 37–41.

Walkowitz, J. (1982–3) Jack the Ripper and the myth of male violence. *Feminist Studies*, 8(3): 542–74.

10

Sexual violence in India: 'Eve-teasing' as backlash

BARBARA BAGILHOLE

Introduction

Independent India has a long tradition of having 'relied heavily on legislation to eradicate social evils which had an adverse effect on the status of women' (Sarkar 1995: 1). On Gandhi's symbolic representation of a spinning wheel, one of the major spokes representing his principles was the liberation of women. He strongly endorsed a role for women outside the home (Karlekar 1995). Following on from this philosophical position, the new Indian Constitution 'gave a mandate to the State to ensure equality for women before the law and an equal protection of the laws' (Didi 1995). Article 51 placed a duty on every citizen to renounce practices derogatory to the dignity of women. The first signs of this were introduced by the first Prime Minister Nehru as the Hindu Code. This granted rights of property to Hindu women, outlawed polygamy and legalized divorce. The Code was introduced against considerable male opposition and at a time when there was no women's movement in India, although women had played a very significant and equal role in the freedom movement. Nehru staked the future of his government on these policies and they became law.

However, India has major problems with the implementation and enforcement of legislation. This is in part because of its size and deep social, economic, religious and political diversity; it has a population of just under 900 million with about 58 per cent (521 million) in the economically active age group (15–64) with an addition of 90 million to this age group expected by the turn of the century (Mathur 1995). Legislation supporting the equality of women has in many cases been ineffective because of traditional values and attitudes towards women that remain common and the fact that very few mechanisms have been put in place for its implementation. Legislation becomes a shallow husk if there is a lack of enforcement by the authorities and the police force. Kumar (1995: 72) argues that 'little and faulty connection between the enactment and the implementation of laws left many [feminists] feeling bitter that the government has easily side-tracked their demands by enacting legislation'.

The situation in India today is that a small section of women are playing a significant role in different fields of activity, while the rest are deprived of gender equality by discrimination, bias and continuing violence (Didi 1995; Singh 1996).

> While the vast majority of Indian women continue to be illiterate, given away in marriage without being consulted, ill-treated by husbands and mothers-in-law, shunned as outcasts when widowed, a very small educated minority has availed itself of the windfall in their fortunes by getting into the legislatures, becoming chief ministers, governors, ambassadors and senior civil servants. In no other country in the world do so few women wield so much power as they do in the India of today.
>
> (Singh 1996: 186)

Despite legislation being passed on women's rights during the 1960s and 1970s, including the Maternity Benefit Act, 1961, the Minimum Wages Act, and the Equal Remuneration Act, 1975, the All-India Democratic Women's Association (AIDWA 1995: 63) argues that the present laws relating to women's rights at work are 'extremely inadequate and insensitive to their problems'. The government itself has acknowledged the 'tardy implementation of the Equal Remuneration Act' and maternity benefits and minimum wages continue to be denied to women workers (AIDWA 1995: 63). It has been calculated that women earn on average 56 per cent of the male daily wage, therefore having 'to work twice as long to achieve the same level of earnings as men' (Oughton 1993: 108).

Didi (1995: 1) argues that the vast majority of Indian women are vulnerable to increased levels of violence 'premised as physical injury and intimidation, with many forms and dimensions such as witnessed during custodial situations and widespread communal carnage and many variants of domestic violence escalating year after year'. As the mainstream model of the Indian family is traditionally patriarchal, it should not be surprising that much of the violence women suffer is 'executed within the family' (AIDWA 1995: 50). However, this increase has happened not only in the private sphere but, with the increasing participation of women in the public sphere, there has been an increase in attacks against women in the workplace and in political life.

The women's movement in India gained impetus from the 1970s onwards, since the report of the Committee on the Status of Women in India, which highlighted the inadequacies in the women's rights legislation as remaining largely ineffective. The Women's Decade began in 1975 with hundreds of seminars, conferences and workshops on women's issues held across the whole country. These focused on women's equality and development, and on the question of social oppression and crimes against women in particular. At that time, crimes resulting from dowry demands were the main concern of the various women's organizations. The issue of violence in general, central to feminists' concerns, became and remains a rallying point for the women's movement (Kumar 1995).

Violence against women

Violence against women is both severe and pervasive in India and operates against women from their conception onwards. Sexual harassment in India can only be understood in the context of violence against women more generally. In this section, I briefly outline some of the major forms this violence takes: female foeticide; dowry harassment and violence; rape, molestation and 'Eve-teasing'; and sexual harassment in the workplace.

A crucial area where violence against women is perpetuated and continues, albeit one not recognized in the legislation, is where sex determination of foetuses through amniocentesis is used to facilitate female foeticide (Sarkar 1995). There has been a proliferation of clinics for this purpose due to the continued preference for male children because of the continuance of the illegal dowry system. In 1986, the state government in Maharashtra, after pressure from the women's movement in Bombay, passed the Maharashtra Regulation of Prenatal Diagnostic Techniques Act to attempt to stop abortions being used to abort healthy female foetuses, but remaining legal on the grounds of genetic abnormalities. However, central government has dragged its feet in passing a national law and the practice still continues (AIDWA 1995). In the early 1990s, of 8,000 abortions in Bombay, opted for after parents learned the sex of the foetus through amniocentesis, only one would have been a boy (New Internationalist 1992). The census figures for 1991 reveal a rising imbalance in the male–female sex ratio. In 1981, the ratio was 934 females to 1000 males, and by 1991 this had reduced to 929 to 1000 for the whole of India. The state of Haryana showed the lowest ratio at 870 females per 1000 males (Reddy 1995).

Dowry harassment and violence has remained and possibly increased, despite legislation and intensive campaigning by women's groups. The National Commission for Women reports that during 1991 there were 55,127 cases of dowry death – up by a staggering 170 per cent from 1987.

According to the Crime Records Bureau of the Home Ministry 17 women in India are killed for dowry reasons every day. This appears even more incongruous set against 'the growth of feminist organisations, the expansion of educational and economic opportunities for women, and some societal questioning of traditional gender roles' (Stone and James 1995: 125). The Dowry Prohibition Act, 1961 was amended in 1984 and 1986. It makes the giving and taking of a dowry an offence with a minimum punishment of five years in prison and fine of 15,000 rupees. (The size of this fine can be put in context by the fact that the minimum wage rate in India is set at 30 rupees per day and many in the unorganized sector of the workforce receive wages well below this. There are roughly 50 rupees to the UK pound). Welfare organizations have the right to complain under the legislation. Also, further amendment through the Evidence Act provides that if a wife dies within seven years of her marriage there will be an inquiry into the death. However, the National Federation of Indian Women (NFIW) claim that the police are unsupportive of women victims of domestic violence. Complaints are treated lightly and as a family affair: 'Wife-beating is treated as a male privilege' (Didi 1995). Stone and James (1995) argue that violence against women is not only linked to women's relative lack of economic power, but its more recent increase, including dowry deaths, is related to the diminishing value of women's traditional power base in Indian society, their fertility.

Indian legislation recognizes three different forms of sexual assault against women: rape, molestation and Eve-teasing,[1] each of which has a technical definition. Rape is forcible penetration of the vagina by a penis, penetration by any other object is molestation, and Eve-teasing is sexual assault that does not involve penetration.

During 1991, 10,410 cases of rape were reported in India, up 26 per cent from 1987; 1099 incidents of child rape (below 10 years) up from 394 in 1990; and 20,611 cases of molestation, up by 36 per cent from 1987 (Didi 1995). In the past two decades reported rape cases have increased by nearly 400 per cent, from 2962 in 1974 to 11,117 in 1993 (Didi 1995). Even in the state of Gujarat, where there was an annual improvement in the crime figures in 1994, with no major incident of communal violence, a rise of 14 per cent in the incidence of rape was recorded (CWDS 1995). According to the Crime Records Bureau of the Home Ministry, a woman in India is raped every 47 minutes (cited in AIDWA 1995). There were 10,283 cases of Eve-teasing reported to the authorities in 1991 and figures for Delhi show that in 1993, Eve-teasing accounted for 60 per cent of all the recorded crimes against women (Sarkar 1995).

Eve-teasing is the closest to the concept of sexual harassment in the West, but it is commonly and popularly defined in India as verbal or gestural teasing only, with no physical contact. Anagol-McGinn (1994) gives us an official definition from the New Delhi Prohibition of Eve-Teasing Act, 1984:

When a man by words either spoken or by signs and/or by visible representation or by gesture does any act in public space, or signs, recites or utters any indecent words or song or ballad in any public place to the annoyance of any women.

However, the harassment that women experience often includes physical actions, such as touching and grabbing of breasts or jostling against them. Distinguishing features of Eve-teasing are that it is performed in public places, such as in streets and parks or on buses, mostly by groups of men who may come from any strata of society but have been identified as coming mostly from the middle and upper-middle class (Dave 1994).

As examples of what is understood by Eve-teasing take two examples reported in the newspaper, *The Calcutta Telegraph* (Dave 1994). In the first case, a young woman was travelling in a crowded suburban train with her father and a friend. She got separated in the crush and found herself surrounded by a group of men playing cards. She was pushed around by them while they made obscene comments and gestures. When she slapped one of their faces she was slapped back harder. None of the other passengers intervened. The second case involved a prospective student who visited Jadavpur University for her admissions tests. She was sexually assaulted by a male student who touched her breasts. Later, it was revealed that other students had bet him to touch the breast of any girl in public and offered him a reward.

There has been a growth of aggression against women in the public sphere (Gandhi and Shah 1991; Datar 1993) and many Indian feminists argue that the present definition of Eve-teasing 'is adequate and antiquated' (AIDWA 1995: 69). This is because it fails to acknowledge the incidence of physical harassment and continues to obscure its recognition as a violent act. The term is seen to trivialize the issue. One of the reasons for this is that the name Eve conjures up images of a temptress or seductress. As Dave (1994) wittily points out, 'whoever called it Eve-teasing should be bitten by the serpent'. She argues that what is labelled Eve-teasing is nothing less than harassment and should be called this. Also, Eve-teasing is viewed by the police almost benignly, as its name implies, and the term is used as a label by them for acts of physical assault against women, even serious assaults such as acid throwing (Dave 1994). Molestation, according to police records, is much more common than rape, but is generally regarded as Eve-teasing and rarely punished (Kumar 1995).

Despite difficulties with statistical data, the participation of women in economic life and activities in India is acknowledged to be greater than ever before (Bardhan 1995) and their contribution to the income of the household is significant (Oughton 1993). In the light of this, AIDWA (1995) argue that work-related violence, specifically sexual harassment in the workplace, is a problem that demands urgent attention. NFIW claim that the problem of sexual harassment in the workplace is widespread and has serious consequences for women, which adversely affects their ability to work and earn a living. Many women leave work under threat of sexual harassment. As the economic crisis deepens in India more and more women are concentrated into the unorganized sector of the economy, employed as casual labour on low pay and at low skill levels. Also, ever-increasing unemployment reinforces the need to hang on to even ill paid jobs. There is no social security system in India to maintain even subsistence level existence. 'The need for survival drives women repeatedly to what has been referred to as "rape situations", i.e. where the scope for sexual harassment is built into the pressure on the women to somehow earn a living' (AIDWA 1995: 53). At the extreme end of this, the NFIW state that there are two million women forced into prostitution in the major Indian cities as a consequence of rape and sexual harassment – despite the Suppression of Immoral Traffic Act.

Despite the fact that incidents of sexual harassment in the workplace are on the increase, attempts to focus on the problem have met with a negative response from the government. Where women have reported specific incidents, there has been a lack of action by the authorities which 'has had an adverse reaction, reinforcing the belief that raising a voice against crime only causes further harassment, trauma and a revictimisation' (AIDWA 1995: 53). In the absence of legislative protection 'women in dire need of employment are forced to compromise' (AIDWA 1995: 64).

Sexual violence as backlash

The increase in violence against women is seen by many as a backlash in response to women assuming new roles.

> Thus violence against women continues to be seen as being 'provoked' by acts of transgression on the part of women rather than crimes committed to silence them and prevent them from fuller participation in social development.
>
> (AIDWA 1995: 59)

As the extent of violence against women increases, 'the forces which glorify and glamorise the secondary status of women acquire greater strength on the ground' (CWDS 1995: 20).

This backlash is linked to the rise in fundamentalism in the religions in India: Hindu, Muslim, and Christian. The fundamentalists in the different religious communities, though ostensibly hostile towards each other, have as their common denominator their antagonism and opposition to women's rights (Joint Delegation of National Women's Organisations 1993; Nadkarni and Awate 1994; CWDS 1995; Mazumdar 1995; Reddy

1995). 'Central to the claims of most contending groups is a militant masculinity and the demand for an acquiescent femininity' (Karlekar 1995: 61). One extreme example of this is the call from Hindu revivalists for the recognition and worshipping of *sati*, widow burning, which is still illegally practised in some parts of India, contravening the Sati Prevention Act. In 1987, a famous case was reported in Rajasthan where an 18-year-old widow, Roop Kunwar, allegedly voluntarily threw herself on her husband's funeral pyre (Kumar 1995). 'Sati' actually means good, virtuous and devout, and is seen by fundamental Hindus as symbolizing the feminine ideals of sacrifice, dedication and subordination (Karlekar 1995).

On a recent three-week study trip to India, I met and engaged in debates with women academics at an independent centre for women's development studies, women's studies academics teaching and researching in universities, and women activists in both the trade union movement and women's movement in Bombay, Ahmedabad and Delhi. They talked to me at great length about the issues that they were fighting and campaigning on, which centred on girls' and women's educational, economic, political and social progress. They gave me two important examples of cases that the women's movement, alongside the trade union movement, is fighting. These two prominent campaigns, I would argue, illustrate the way in which sexual harassment and sexual violence control Indian women and work to prevent them from asserting their rights.

Significantly, the first example also illustrates the continuing existence of caste injustice in India. Child marriage is illegal in India but is still carried out, particularly in the rural areas. The Child Marriage Prohibition Act can only be acted upon if someone registers a complaint. Bhanwari Devi, a woman government rural development worker in Bhateri, a village in Rajasthan, complained to the police about an influential local family who were breaking the law. As a consequence of this, she was publicly raped by five police officers. The women's movement supported her in her prosecution of the police. The court was unwilling to admit that rape had been committed because the accused were from an upper caste and she was from a lower caste. However, after substantial pressure from the women's movement, the culprits were arrested and Bhanwari Devi was later awarded compensation. This example is 'indicative of the ways in which women's voices have been silenced, by using rape as a weapon of intimidation' (Didi 1995: 5).

The second example has developed out of the recent introduction of legislation aimed at the political empowerment of women. A radical quota system has been established for 30 per cent of all local government (*panchayat*) seats to be filled by women in the Gram Panchayat Act, 1994. The National Federation of Indian Women (NFIW) is already calling for a change to procedures to draw out and encourage women to take these positions and to force the Panchayat not to ignore their voices. Activists feel that there are real possibilities for power for women at this grass roots level, and they are calling for similar reservation of seats for women in the Assemblies, Parliament and other decision-making bodies. However, this legislation has proved to be a major challenge for the women's movement in some states where women are not sufficiently educated or empowered to take advantage of it. In some cases, traditional political families have put up their daughters or wives to maintain their power. In other cases, women have been elected onto local governments and at the first meeting of the newly elected councillors their husbands turn up instead and say, 'Talk to me, she is at home looking after the children'. Some women have experienced sexual harassment and assault in taking up their rights. The women's movement is at present supporting a young Muslim woman, who despite strong opposition, stood and won a reserved seat on her local council. The day she turned up to claim her seat she was surrounded by a crowd outside and her sari was torn off as a warning to other women.

Didi (1995) tells us that there have been 'a spate of cases of stripping women in public and parading them naked to avenge caste, family, political or communal feuds' (1995: 18). 'Sexual violence is being used as a weapon of political intimidation' (CWDS 1995: 28).

Conclusion

The majority of women in India experience substantial inequality and are vulnerable to an increasing level of violence in both the private and the public domains from the time of their conception. Even now, the 'empowerment of women in a just social order is a distant dream despite the growing number of women in the Parliament, Assemblies and local bodies' (Didi 1995: 24). This is because sexual violence in its many forms is being increasingly used to control Indian women and to prevent them from claiming their legal rights. This is true internationally for women, but the problem in India is exacerbated by the fact that the present legislation preventing sexual harassment is so inadequate, rarely enforced, and – in terms of the workplace – non-existent.

Sarkar (1995) argues that the Indian women's movement has been over-reliant on legislation, which is a legacy from the past. It has taken a path which has given success in getting relatively radical laws passed. Where it has been let down is in the enforcement and implementation of these acts. However, there are still 'vast areas where rights do not exist at all as in the areas of unorganised women workers or in the area of sexual harassment at work or in the area of sexual assault which have not been defined as yet' (AIDWA 1995: 74). Therefore, the NFIW is calling for legislation that makes sexual harassment in the workplace an offence, which would result in action against an offender ranging from censure, loss of bonuses and/or fines, to losing his job and being subject to court action. At workplace level, they want a rigorous set of procedures including a person assigned to listen to, record and investigate complaints, and codes of conduct backed up by training. They also argue that women 'need to learn to defend themselves more effectively by taking their own initiatives' (Didi 1995: 24). The AIDWA (1995) calls on the UN to set up a comprehensive law against sexual assault in the workplace and programmes to provide protection against sexual harassment in the workplace for all women workers.

Some argue that reactionary, religious fundamentalist forces will deal the women's movement in India a serious and perhaps lethal blow (CWDS 1995: 15). On the other hand, the contemporary Indian women's movement is seen as continuing to be 'a complex, variously placed, and fertile undertaking' (Kumar 1995: 83). The All India Democratic Women's Association (AIDWA 1995: 2) argues that 'while accepting that differences do exist, sometimes expressed sharply, the Indian women's movement has been able to work out a common approach on many of the critical challenges facing Indian women'. Despite the grim picture of increasing violence against Indian women, there is a positive interpretation of current events in India emerging and gaining consensus that holds a glimmer of hope for the future. That is that 'the common experience of vulnerability *vis-à-vis* increased violence against women, including most importantly, increased sexual harassment and exploitation at the workplace, will draw women closer together into broader actions' (AIDWA 1995: 16). Let us hope that this will be the case.

Note

1 Anagol-McGinn (1994) describes how the term Eve-teasing, with its Christian connotations, originated in India's colonial past and was likely to have been made familiar by British judges and journalists as cases appeared in court.

References

All India Democratic Women's Association (AIDWA) (1995) *A Perspective from the Indian Women's Movement. Towards Beijing.* New Delhi: All India Democratic Women's Association.

Anagol-McGinn, P. (1994) Sexual harassment in India: A case study of Eve-teasing in historical perspective. In C. Brant and Y.L. Too (eds) *Rethinking Sexual Harassment.* London: Pluto Press.

Bardhan, A.B. (1995) Women workers and trade unions. In All Indian Trade Union Congress (AITUC) *Working Women's Convention.* New Delhi: AITUC.

Centre for Women's Development Studies (CWDS) (1995) *Confronting Myriad Oppressions.* New Delhi: Centre for Women's Development Studies.

Datar, C. (ed.) (1993) *The Struggle Against Violence*. Calcutta: Stree.

Dave, D. (1994) How long can the lech get away? *The Telegraph*, Calcutta, 26 January.

Didi, S. (1995) *Escalation of Violence Against Women and Criminalization of Politics. Commission Report*, Fourteenth Congress, National Federation of Indian Women. Mohali, India: Prerna Printing Press.

Gandhi, N. and Shah, N. (1991) *The Issues at Stake: Theory and Practice in the Contemporary Women's Movement*. New Delhi: Kali for Women.

Joint Delegation of National Women's Organisations (1993) *Report on Women Against Communalism*. New Delhi: National Federation of Indian Women.

Karlekar, M. (1995) The relevance of Mohandas Karamchand Gandhi: A contemporary perspective. *Indian Journal of Gender Studies*, 2(1): 45–65.

Kumar, R. (1995) From chipko to sati: The contemporary Indian women's movement. In A. Basu (ed.) *The Challenges of Local Feminisms: Women's Movements in Global Perspective*. Boulder, CO: Westview Press.

Mathur, A.N. (1995) The improbability of full employment: A perspective from India of the emperor's new clothes. In M. Simai (ed.) *Global Employment in International Investigation into the Future of Work*. London: Zed Books Ltd.

Mazumdar, S. (1995) Women on the march: Right-wing mobilization in contemporary India. *Feminist Review*, 49, spring: 1–28.

Nadkarni, S.K. and Awate, L. (1994) *Commission Report. Religious and Fundamentalist Attacks on Women's Rights*, Fourteenth Congress, National Federation of Indian Women, Kurukshetra, Haryana.

New Internationalist (1992) We've only just begun. Feminism in the 1990s. 227, January: 18–19.

Oughton, E. (1993) Seasonality, wage labour and women's contribution to household income in western India. In J.H. Momsen and V. Kinnaird (eds) *Different Places, Different Voices. Gender and Development in Africa, Asia and Latin America*. London: Routledge.

Reddy, T. (1995) *General Secretary's Report on National Federation of Indian Women's (NFIW) Activities*. Fourteenth All-India Congress of NFIW, New Delhi.

Sarkar, L. (1995) *Women's Movement and the Legal Process*, Occasional Paper No. 24. New Delhi: Centre for Women's Development Studies.

Singh, K. (1996) *India. An Introduction*. New Delhi: Vision Books.

Stone, L. and James, C. (1995) Dowry, bride-burning, and female power in India. *Women's International Forum*, (2): 125–34.

Index

MAKING GENDER WORK
MANAGING EQUAL OPPORTUNITIES
Jenny Shaw and Diane Perrons (eds)

Making Gender Work analyses both the broad economic, legal and cultural frameworks of equal opportunities and assembles first-hand accounts from pioneers in the field. This integration of academic and practical expertise represents a major contribution to the management of equal opportunities and analysis of organizations.

For a growing number of people gender *is* their work while, for others, it is the reason why they get less (or more) pay, training and recognition *at* work. This book is a response both to the rise of jobs or careers in equal opportunities and to the conditions which make such jobs necessary. Both trends indicate that gender expertise needs to become professionalized and not remain a purely academic or analytical skill. This book indicates how those skills might be developed and the sort of broad background knowledge practitioners will need if they are to be effective change agents.

Contents
Introduction – Part 1: The socio-economic, legal and cultural context of gender work – recent changes in women's employment in Britain – The economics of equal opportunities – The role of the law in equal opportunities – Employment deregulation and equal opportunities – Towards a family-friendly employer – Organizational culture and equalities work – Part 2: Managing equal opportunities: practical issues – Women in the public and voluntary sectors – Working within local government – Implementing equal opportunities in a local authority – Equal opportunities and the voluntary sector – Trade unions and equal opportunities – The appeal and the claims of non-dominant groups – Conclusion – References – Index.

Contributors
Helen Brown, Paul Burnett, Linda Clarke, Rita Donaghy, Lisa Harker, Margaret Hodge, Sally Holtermann, Carole Pemberton, Diane Perrons, Jenny Shaw, Gillian Stamp and Ruth Valentine.

256pp   0 335 19365 X (Paperback)   0 335 19366 8 (Hardback)

COMBATING SEXUAL HARASSMENT IN THE WORKPLACE

Rohan Collier

Sexual harassment is common, hurtful to the recipient and wasteful to employers. It has to be tackled by employers and workers alike. This book offers insight from both sides as well as providing solutions. It asks:

- Why does sexual harassment occur?
- How can organizations prevent sexual harassment and deal with it?
- What is the legal standing of all parties involved?

It provides practical advice for managers, personnel officers and trade unionists on developing and implementing sexual harassment policies. In plain English this book provides a background to current legislation (including the European Union's Code of Practice) and UK practice, outlining recent developments. The author, who has many years experience in dealing with harassment issues, gives a detailed analysis of the reasons why harassment occurs, arguing that sexual harassment has more to do with power relations than with sexuality.

Contents
Introducing and defining sexual harassment – Sexism and sexual harassment – The legal challenge – Protecting the dignity of women and men at work: the EC Code of Practice – Developing sexual harassment policies – Trade unions, the Equal Opportunities Commission and advice agencies – Sexual harassment training in practice – Appendices – Bibliography – Index.

176pp   0 335 190820 (Paperback)   0 335 19083 9 (Hardback)

A SOCIOLOGY OF SEX AND SEXUALITY

Gail Hawkes

A Sociology of Sex and Sexuality offers a historical sociological analysis of ideas about expressions of sexual desire, combining both primary and secondary historical and theoretical material with original research and popular imagery in the contemporary context.

While some reference is made to the sexual ideology of Classical Antiquity and of early Christianity, the major focus of the book is on the development of ideas about sex and sexuality in the context of modernity. It questions the widespread assumption that the anxieties and fears associated with old sexual mores have been overcome in the late twentieth century context, and asks whether the discourses of Queer sexual politics have successfully fractured the binary categories of heterosexuality and homosexuality.

A Sociology of Sex and Sexuality will be of interest to students in the fields of sociology, sexual history, gender studies and cultural studies.

Contents
The specialness of sex – Sex and modernity – Enlightenment pleasures and bourgeois anxieties – The science of sex – Planning sex – Pleasurable sex – Liberalizing heterosexuality – Subverting heterosexuality – Final thoughts and questions – References – Index.

176pp   0 335 19316 1 (Paperback)   0 335 19317 X (Hardback)

RULING PASSIONS
SEXUAL VIOLENCE, REPUTATION AND THE LAW

Sue Lees

Ruling Passions explores the disciplinary processes which constrict women's lives with particular reference to sexual reputation. Sue Lees explores the way that power functions as a form of self surveillance, and operates through all kinds of institutional and social practices which serve to legitimate male violence.

Based on three research projects, involving interviews and group discussions with adolescents, the analysis of court transcripts of rape and murder trials, and the monitoring of rape trials undertaken for a Channel 4 *Dispatches* documentary, Sue Lees makes an innovative use of the method of discourse analysis to analyse how ideas and social practices function as a system of power and domination. Issues range from the criteria used to determine reputation in adolescence and credibility in rape trials to the representation of the body as a spectacle in trials and the link between marital rape and murder.

Contents
Introduction − The policing of girls in everyday life: sexual reputation, morality and the social control of girls − Sex education in conflict − Judicial rape: researching rape trials − The representation of the body in rape trials − Male rape − Marital rape appeals − Men getting away with murder: the case for reforming the law on homicide − Naggers, whores and libbers: provoking men to kill − In search of gender justice: sexual assault and the criminal justice system − Bibliography − Index.

224pp   0 335 19613 6 (Paperback)   0 335 19614 4 (Hardback)